ALSO BY UCADIA

    Lebor Clann Glas

    Five Worlds

    De Dea Magisterium

    Waiata

    Yapa

Tara

**OFFICIAL ENGLISH
FIRST EDITION**

BY

UCADIA

Ucadia Books Company

Tara. Official English First Edition. Copyright © 2012-2024 UCADIA. All Rights reserved in Trust.

No part of this book may be reproduced, or stored in a retrieval system, or transmitted in any form or by any means electronic, mechanical, photocopying, recording or otherwise, without the express and authentic written permission of the Publisher.

The Publisher disclaims any liability and shall be indemnified and held harmless from any demands, loss, liability, claims or expenses made by any party due or arising out of or in connection with any differences between previous non-official English drafts and this Official English First Edition.

A party that threatens, makes or enacts any demand or action, against this publication or the Publisher hereby acknowledge they have read this disclaimer and agree with this binding legal agreement and irrevocably consent to Ucadia and its competent forums as being the original and primary Jurisdiction for resolving any such issue of fact and law.

Published by Ucadia Books Company, a Delaware stock corporation (File Number 6779670) 8 The Green, STE B, Dover, Delaware, 19901 United States. First edition.

UCADIA® is a US Registered Trademark in trust under Guardians and Trustees Company protected under international law and the laws of the United States.

ISBN 978-1-64419-011-1

Preface

By the power and authority of Heaven, it is given to men and women the right of free will, to make laws for the good conduct of a fair and just society. Whenever and wherever tyranny has sought to subjugate and enslave, it is called upon individuals of history and moral courage to stand firm against such ignorance and evil. Yet evil begets evil, hate fuels more hate. Thus it is not the lord of war and terror that have introduced lasting change, but those brave and wise souls who resist such oppression and have shown mercy and compassion to bring forth a means for healing and reconciliation.

Thus while it may for generations appear that such occupations are unable to be dislodged, the unending sands of justice inevitably erode even the tallest fortress. True Law is the Law. It cannot be corrupted, no matter how far and wide a tyranny may seek to sow such doubt. The foundations of true justice and fair process are eternal and cannot be permanently hidden by bias and cruel systems of oppression. So it is that those who love the true Law and stand for equality of rights and fair Justice have overcome even the most wicked and evil of state control.

Such struggle for restoration of true Law and fair Justice is not new. Throughout the history of humanity there have been many occasions that civilisation has collapsed. Three thousand years ago was one such occasion, that gave rise to the culture and civilisation of the Celts.

Few cultures and societies of history are more enigmatic and enduring than the Celts. By the 6th Century BCE, in the space of a few decades, the Celtic culture successfully spread from Ireland, north to Greenland, south to North Africa and as far east as Turkey - an area larger than the Roman Empire at its absolute height. The Celts built thousands of miles of perfectly engineered roads. They excelled in metallurgy, design, art, music and poetry.

So who were the Celts? Who or what started and sustained such a sophisticated culture? And why? For such a rapid expansion across the world, and such a long lasting impact, there had to be central characters and leaders. Yet none are adequately accepted, despite long standing and ancient homage to the great prophet Jeremiah travelling to Ireland and helping found the famous city known as Tara and its laws.

For such a sophisticated culture as the Celts who loved Law, there simply must have been some central texts. Again, there is more than ample evidence in Irish, Scandinavian, Scot, Welsh, English, German, Spanish, French and Dutch history that the word Tara is not just a city, but the name of five books of law, also variously known by the Romans as Terra and in later centuries as Torah.

Such knowledge and truth is not supposed to be known by the millions of descendent of the Celts today. Under a new system of historical tyranny and oppression, new generations are forced to believe that their ancestors were fools who believed in fairy tales and folk stories; and that none of the ancient stories of the five books of law are true.

Yet a new time and a new covenant has come. Therefore, let the stories and the spirit of those misrepresented and cursed throughout the ages speak for themselves. Let the parables and wisdom of Tara shine once again as a beacon to the world. As the ancients once proclaimed: So it is, so let it be.

A plan to save humanity

Three thousand years ago, the world was plunged into a great darkness. Multiple civilisations collapsed across Asia, the Middle East and the coasts of the Mediterranean Sea. Midst such anarchy and turmoil, a small band of priests were granted perpetual use of an ancient sacred island (Elephantine Island) in the middle of the Nile they renamed Yeb. There, the priests built a temple 20 cubits (9m) in width, 60 cubits (27m) in length, 30 cubits (14m) in height to house an ancient artefact of Pharaoh Akhenaten.

After the complete destruction of Jerusalem in 597 BCE by King Nebuchadnezzar, Jeremiah the seventeenth prophet of Yeb, did depart for Ireland with a plan and a vision to save humanity by awakening the Celt tribes to their ancient heritage. The result was the five books of Tara.

If you by chance have the opportunity to read *Lebor Clann Glas*, then you will see that multiple empires and societies in unison have collapsed into the most horrific nightmare of anarchy, poverty, misery and death on no less than five occasions over the past five thousand years. To suggest then that it could not happen again or even pretend that it did not happen would therefore be complete foolishness.

The reasons for such cataclysmic global events have always rested on some major climactic catastrophe as the catalyst. Yet in almost all circumstances, such disasters have been manifestly worsened by decades or centuries of social decay of those lost civilisations. Put simply, when such ancient societies placed too much faith in their intellectual brilliance; and when those societies broke apart into small groups of obscenely wealthy controlling most of the resources; and when such societies ceased to care about morality and the true rule of law, then such climactic events seemed to have overwhelmed them.

The world as you know it will soon end. Maybe in your lifetime, maybe not. This does not mean the end of the planet, or even the end of life on the planet, but the inevitable end of the kind of human civilisation you take for granted. This is not some ill founded doomsday theory, but a fact that the future collapse of human civilisation as a whole is not the first time, nor sadly will it be the last.

The difference this time is that we have the gift of insight and text to look back in history and see how and why such historic figures as Jeremiah were able to save human civilisation and give birth to the foundations of what we now know as Western Civilisation - well before the Greek and Romans.

Contents

Book 1	Genasis (genesis)..	11
Book 2	Eacturas (exodus)..	37
Book 3	Diatuair (deuteros)..	77
Book 4	Nome (nomos)...	97
Book 5	Anacánain (anakineos)..	109
	Original Nations (Tribes) of Celtic Lands................	117
I.	Original Nations (Tribes) of Eire (Ireland)..............	127
II.	Original Nations (Tribes) of Great Britain..............	131
III.	Original Nations (Tribes) of Spain...........................	137
IV.	Original Nations (Tribes) of Portugal.......................	143
V.	Original Nations (Tribes) of France..........................	147
VI.	Original Nations (Tribes) of Belgium.......................	153
VII.	Original Nations (Tribes) of Netherlands................	159
VIII.	Original Nations (Tribes) of Germany......................	163
IX.	Original Nations (Tribes) of Finland........................	175
X.	Original Nations (Tribes) of Sweden........................	179
XI.	Original Nations (Tribes) of Norway........................	183
XII.	Original Nations (Tribes) of Iceland.........................	187
XIII.	Original Nations (Tribes) of Denmark.....................	191
XIV.	Original Nations (Tribes) of Greenland...................	195
	Maps and Diagrams	200

Book 1
Genasis (genesis)

C.1 - The First

Let it be known to all who come, 2 for now and for ever more, 3 these be the true words of the Beginning: 4 Of the origins of the first races of men, 5 and the creation of all forms of life; 6 Of the origin of the changes of seasons, 7 and the creation of the entire world; 8 Of the origin of the sun and moon, 9 and the creation of all the heavens; 10 Of the meaning of life and death, 11 and the existence of life beyond death. 12 Let it be known to all whom these presents come, 13 these be the true words of the Ancients: 14 Of the wisest and holiest of men, 15 and the knowledge of the true words of the Beginning; 16 Of the origin of good and evil, 17 and the remembrance of many great heroes; 18 Of great tribulations and calamity, 19 and how such trials were overcome; 20 Of the rule of law and community, 21 and by what means law and harmony be restored. 22 Let all then who have ears, hear! 23 These be the words of the Creator of all existence, 24 the Father-Mother of all lesser gods. 25 Change then not one word, 26 lest you be judged for such transgression. 27 Utter then no falsity, 28 whereby you may condemn yourself. 29 Instead, may you honour the word, 30 as the word does honour you. 31 May you and your children be blessed; 32 May your path of life be joyous and fruitful, 33 and may you remember what and who you are.

C.2 - The Beginning

1 Before one may speak or reveal truth, 2 their ears must be able to hear, 3 their eyes must be capable to see, 4 their minds must be open to reason. 5 No one can hear if they close their ears, 6 nor see if they shut their eyes, 7 nor discern if their mind is imprisoned. 8 Thus the intentionally deaf condemn themselves to woe, 9 the deliberately blind lead themselves to injury, 10 and the willingly ignorant seal their own destruction. 11 Verily, such a path is not fixed by the heavens, 12 but by the intentions of men and women, 13 who choose to live either in ignorance, 14 who curse their own children to wickedness and darkness, 15 or who accept the sensible truth, 16 that they are not animals, 17 and that the Divine exists, 18 and that the rule of law may be restored, 19 and people may prosper and live in harmony. 20 A wise man uses his skills to survive and thrive, 21 whereas a stupid man wastes his talents, 22 and lives a life of misery and catastrophe. 23 A discerning man sees the sensibility in making peace with his neighbour, 24 and caring for his animals and crops, 25 and guarding against famine and flood. 26 A willingly ignorant and unhappy man makes no such plans, 27 and exists and behaves as if a wild untamed beast, 28 that destroys others as he dooms himself. 29 This is his choice, it is not his fate. 30 Illness may be cured without resorting to superstition. 31 Bones may be healed and cuts sowed

and swelling reduced. 32 The forest and herbs offer many sources of balsams and remedies. 33 So it is that sickness of the mind may be cured, 34 not by dark magic and superstition, 35 but with reason and knowledge. 36 Even such minds afflicted with wickedness, 37 may be healed and purified, 38 if only the therapy be accepted and followed. 39 Let then your mind be healed, 40 your soul be relieved of any wickedness and ignorance, 41 that you may find joy and harmony, 42 that you be united within your being and soul, 43 and that you be assured in finding the right path, 44 in this life and the next.

C.3 - Wickedness

1 How may any soul find safe harbour, 2 in such a sea of iniquity? 3 How can any man or woman hope to see the light of better days, 4 trapped within such a darkness of wickedness? 5 Verily, the fate of humanity itself hangs in the balance. 6 Where judges still claim to exist, 7 they care not even to pretend to follow rules, 8 but the whims of the powerful and vengeful. 9 Law is meted by the sword and fear, 10 and woe the fate of any who call for justice, 11 for the flesh of martyrs feeds the dogs of the wicked. 12 Alas, none see the folly of the idol of money, 13 nor the futility of ultimate wealth, 14 as merchants have built great cities, 15 where people come to sacrifice their very souls, 16 for a handful of uneven coins, 17 a life of perpetual willing slavery, 18 and a life of obsession and misery. 19 Thus wickedness abounds in the present world, 20 and beguiles many with false hopes and false promises. 21 How then can we overcome and find harmony, 22 until we find an answer to ending such wickedness?

C.4 - Depravity

1 Verily, no vice or pleasure is any longer considered taboo. 2 As the people starve in the streets, 3 the wealthy vomit from excess in their palaces; 4 As mothers cry for children lost, 5 the wicked priests and viziers rape the innocent; 6 As the people call out for answers, 7 the corrupt scribes create new false narratives. 8 Depravity itself is no longer scorned, 9 but worshipped and celebrated, 10 as an outward sign of power and immortality. 11 Thus, the acolytes of the corrupt and wicked, 12 willingly offer themselves and to do unto others, 13 all manner of vile and hideous acts, 14 as the laws of the most ancient civilisations are cast aside. 15 How then may any be taught to love, 16 if such depth of intimacy has been replaced with lust? 17 How may any man or woman be saved, 18 if they care not for the well being of their own soul, 19 and repudiate all knowledge and wisdom with resolute defiance? 20 How do you rescue and return a lost child, 21 who neither knows or cares they are lost, 22 and upon approach refuses such assistance?

C.5 - Ignorance

1 Where has our memory gone? 2 Of divine wisdom and hard won experience? 3 Of knowledge of nature and industry? 4 Of civilised society and order? 5 Alas, the youth of today care not for knowledge, 6 but the means to obtain wealth and fame, 7 to join the ranks of the wicked and depraved. 8

Robbers and murderers have become the heroes, 9 while the honoured are like dead stones to them. 10 They care not for reason or sense, 11 nor to use the gifts of intellect and discernment. 12 Thus, the willingly ignorant believe all manner of fancy, 13 and outrageous gossip of sickness. 14 Some even believe the world to be flat, 15 upon the deliberate lies of merchants, 16 by ignoring all manner of sense, 17 all manner of knowledge and reason. 18 Instead, the willingly ignorant believe, 19 the world be but a horrible machine, 20 run by malevolent beings, 21 who indulge themselves as do the wealthy, 22 in the torture and depravity of humanity. 23 Thus, at the heart of ignorance, 24 is the cowardly surrender of integrity, 25 in the hope of appeasing a new set of demons, 26 in the form of merchants and corrupt viziers, 27 who view people as less than cattle, 28 to be herded and culled. 29 How can such ignorance be cured? 30 When those who consider themselves educated, 31 are the most ignorant of all? 32 When ignorance itself is worshipped? 33 When divine revelation is seen as a threat?

C.6 - Superstition

1 What form of insane god demands the sacrifice of innocent life? 2 What name be the demon that claims all power, yet is jealous of the light? 3 What form of insanity is needed to proclaim an all powerful god, 4 that demands the best food be taken away, 5 and the scraps left for the children? 6 Thus, in such a wicked and depraved world, 7 even the gods have become insane. 8 To even consider that a supreme Divine being does relish death, 9 is the height of depraved ignorance, 10 and the falsehoods of wicked priests and their masters. 11 Nor may a single Divine decide the fate of each man and woman in advance, 12 without such a god revealing themselves to be but a ghost. 13 For the highest force of the Universe is free will, 14 and without free will no thing could exist. 15 Verily, the very notion of a Divine being that may usurp law, 16 is the imaginings of vile and wretched merchants, 17 who care not for law or reason. 18 No being, no matter how small or great, 19 may usurp the laws of existence, 20 else existence itself would cease. 21 Yet such reason and sense is of no avail, 22 while people worship all manner of depraved and insane gods; 23 Ghosts pretending to be gods; 24 Ghosts pretending to be demons, 25 heralding the most depraved blood sacrifices. 26 How can one be freed, 27 from devotion to such madness? 28 How can the false priests be so exposed, 29 as the ones who foment such superstition, 30 for nothing more than control and power? 31 How may the true nature of the Divine, 32 be restored into the hearts of men and women, 33 that it may never again be lost?

C.7 - Madness

1 When will the madness end? 2 When will people awaken from the nightmare of their own creation? 3 When will men and women cease being as if distempered cattle? 4 This is the prayer of life, 5 the prayer and hope of the divine creator of all, 6 the purpose of these teachings.

C.8 - Evil

1 Evil exists and envelopes many. 2 Evil is real and enslaves cities and people. 3 Nothing can proceed unless evil is vanquished. 4 Evil be not a single demon or ghost, 5 nor be evil a force of nature, 6 but the sickness of mind of people, 7 affected by wickedness, depravity and superstition. 8 Evil be not chaos or any other state of existence, 9 but a deliberate and willing prison of mind, 10 through willing and intentional ignorance, 11 to cause harm, to abandon honour, 12 to surrender self control, 13 to neglect and choose to turn away, 14 to abuse others and cause them pain, 15 to forget who and what you are, 16 to not wish to remember or learn, 17 and to follow false gods and idols. 18 Evil be not a god or demi-god, 19 but the force of sickness of mind, 20 in life and in death as ghost. 21 Thus, to cure the world of evil, 22 the mind must be cured of the sickness that causes evil. 23 What then be the causes of evil of the mind? 24 It begins with self-hate, 25 and is grounded in isolation, 26 and nurtured by loneliness and self-pity, 27 and nourished by hatred and jealousy, 28 and fomented by obsession and wilful ignorance, 29 and protected by delusion, 30 that one be a suffering saviour, 31 fallen victim to a cruel and unforgiving world. 32 Thus evil be a well formed prison fortress of mind, 33 that only gains strength if directly assaulted. 34 To defeat such illness of mind, 35 and prevent such sickness ever gaining hold, 36 one must pursue more than one path, 37 and more than one remedy, 38 to bring upon such a corrupted inner world, 39 the greatest force and power and light, 40 of the most inspired divine revelation and love, 41 that the world has ever seen. 42 Let us begin, 43 with resolute certainty this be truly ordained, 44 for no soul be lost or abandoned by the Divine Creator.

C.9 - Awareness

1 Do you see what your eyes reveal to you? 2 Can you discern the sounds that your ears hear? 3 Do you taste what your tongue tells you? 4 Or the sensations that your skin gives you? 5 What then of the smells that your nose alerts you? 6 Or the warning that your stomach alerts you to danger? 7 What then of the arousal of the glands upon attraction? 8 Or your sense of balance and equilibrium? 9 Or your own sense of location of your limbs and body? 10 These be the nine senses that you may feel and be aware, 11 without having to know or believe, 12 or have faith or hope. 13 These are your own senses that give you awareness of the world, 14 and your own comprehension of truth or falsity, 15 and of safety or danger, 16 to be truly awake and not asleep. 17 Awareness then is your present and continuous ability, 18 to receive, conceive, perceive, comprehend or discern, 19 through your senses, without distraction or doubt. 20 Verily, while all of the nine senses of awareness, 21 depend upon the body to reveal unto the mind, 22 the mind is not the senses themselves, 23 but the observer of the senses. 24 Thus, a clouded and confused mind distracts the senses, 25 and causes the mind to doubt and question the senses. 26 Senses may be stimulated and sharpened, 27 by sacred herbs and

sounds. 28 Senses may be relaxed by pleasant drink and smoke. 29 Yet a mind or body that is drunk or intoxicated by poisons, 30 loses sense of itself when such drugs take hold. 31 Thus an intoxicated mind may think it is awake when it is asleep, 32 or that it has discovered wisdom when it is fantasy. 33 For when a mind is incapable of discerning, 34 its own sense of truth of the senses, 35 then such a mind asleep condemns itself to servitude, 36 of the wicked priests or merchants that corrupted it. 37 Thus, the first goal of wicked people, 38 is to overwhelm the senses, 39 or poison or numb the senses, 40 so that one may doubt their own awareness. 41 Verily, evil cannot take root, 42 unless the senses be dulled, 43 or overwhelmed or poisoned. 44 Behold! a clear mind that honours the senses, 45 that observes true awareness for what it is, 46 is aware and awake to the Divine, 47 and is capable of discerning much falsity from truth, 48 and has no need of wicked priests or viziers. 49 Therefore respect your senses, 50 and guard your awareness, 51 lest the first path to wickedness be, 52 the path of self doubt and clouded mind, 53 that cleaves the body and its senses, 54 from the outer dream of reality, 55 and the inner reality of the mind.

C.10 - Thought

1 Even when you are not aware of it, 2 you experience every hour of the day the gift of thought. 3 Such is the nature of thought when awake, 4 that it be a fleeting friend, 5 or like a persistent foe. 6 Though we may experience many thoughts a day, 7 the agony of obsessive thought, 8 can cripple as the deepest of wounds, 9 whereas the flooding thoughts of the senses, 10 may bring joy and happiness to the soul. 11 Thus, thought may be the awareness of the senses, 12 or the observance of present acts, 13 or the remembrance of past events, 14 or the anticipation of future occurrences, 15 or the application of skills of the mind, 16 or the pathways of day dreams and distractions. 17 Life then be a constant and complex stream, 18 of thoughts of all kind and order. 19 Yet when we become aware of our thoughts, 20 without taking the gift of thought for granted, 21 then we may experience greater joy, 22 and avoid unnecessary pain that comes, 23 from undisciplined and unthinking thought. 24 Verily, there be even deeper importance to such awareness, 25 for thought is the speech of the other world. 26 Thus, not all thought be original thought, 27 but may come from the spirits that protect us, 28 or the ghosts that seek to haunt and deceive us. 29 Verily, the wicked and corrupt who wish to control, 30 deliberately sow the seeds of doubt and ignorance, 31 so that men and women have no discernment, 32 of their own thoughts or those that may not be their own, 33 that they fall into the depths of despair or madness, 34 and may be enslaved and condemned. 35 How then may a man or woman overcome, 36 if they are falsely told that such an evil thought is of their own making, 37 when it may come from an outside source, 38 that has exploited a weakness of mind? 39 Thus, a thought of harm upon loved ones, 40 or acts of self harm or suicide, 41 may be the seeds sowed by the undead servants, 42 of wicked priests and false teachings, 43 and not the true

original thoughts of a mind. 44 Verily, all must be accountable for their own thoughts, 45 and awake to their thoughts, 46 so that any false thought be rejected, 47 and any weakness of thought and character, 48 then be acknowledged and rectified. 49 Behold! a clear mind that honours the senses, 50 that observes true awareness for what it is, 51 and is aware of its own thoughts, 52 may discern true thought from false thought, 53 and protect itself from external false thought, 54 and celebrate the peace of clear inner thought, 55 and the joy of life.

C.11 - Dream

1 All animals that possess a soul, 2 must sleep and dream. 3 No animal that possesses a soul can survive, 4 if it does not sleep. 5 Thus man and woman both sleep and dream, 6 and dogs, horses and cats sleep and dream, 7 and animals of the forest sleep and dream, 8 and beasts of the fields sleep and dream. 9 Verily, it is a curse upon ones health, 10 and a disgrace against life and the Divine, 11 if one does not give thanks, 12 and pray for the soul of the beast or fish or bird, 13 whose flesh is consumed at a meal. 14 A man or woman who does not sleep, 15 shall surely turn mad and die. 16 A man or woman who does not gain enough sleep, 17 loses all sense of awareness or awareness of thought, 18 and becomes like the undead, 19 inviting all manner of illness and woe to themselves. 20 Thus it is the goal of the wicked and possessed, 21 that sleep be the enemy to ignorance and evil, 22 and good sleep be the enemy to enslavement. 23 This is why the merchants seek to deprive sleep, 24 that men and women cannot hold clear thought, 25 and are numb of the senses. 26 It is why wicked priests seek to sow fear and doubt, 27 that dreams themselves be wicked and a danger, 28 so that people are frightened of all manner of dream. 29 It is why wicked scribes and viziers disavow dream, 30 as meaningless and a sign of delusion of the mind. 31 Verily, do not eat large meals in the late evening, 32 nor burden your mind with complex thoughts, 33 nor obsess yourself with the business of tomorrow, 34 nor lay down to rest with anger or vengeance, 35 and you shall give yourself the opportunity to sleep well. 36 Behold! To dream is to mirror the powers of the Divine! 37 and the almighty powers of Divine Creation. 38 Dream is a perceived dimension, 39 and an experienced existence by a dreamer, 40 without the need of conscious thought of the dreamer, 41 according to one or more rules and relations. 42 Dream is a fleeting form of reality, 43 where objects exist within a certain dimension, 44 observed by the observer being both within the dream, 45 and having existence outside of the dream, 46 and defined by some form of boundary for a time. 47 Dream is contextual, 48 as the dreamer observes within the boundary of the dream, 49 two or more objects whereby one or more serve as the formal surroundings, 50 and one or more serve as the subject of observation. 51 Dream is sequential, 52 as events within the Dream unfolds in a sequence, 53 even if such sequence does not follow equal intervals of time and place. 54 To Dream is creation of the universe, 55 as the dreamer validates and witnesses the dream, 56 and within the dream, 57 the objects

have a real and material context, 58 according to one or more rules and limits, 59 even if such objects do not exist, 60 or cannot exist in another form of reality. 61 Do not then succumb to doubts or fears, 62 for life and the universe is a dream, 63 the Divine Dream of the Divine Creator, 64 and the reality of community, 65 is the collective dream of the community of people, 66 that may be joyous, peaceful and prosperous.

C.12 - Reason

1 Of all the many gifts of mind, 2 reason stands a bright beacon of light. 3 To see the connections between objects and notions, 4 to discover new relations between such elements, 5 to discern upon your own knowledge, 6 to encounter new insights through sensible thought, 7 to remember and compare experiences, 8 to look at experiences differently. 9 All these abilities and skills are reason. 10 Reason has nothing to do with intellect. 11 A priest may know a great many things, 12 but be devoid of sensible reason, 13 on account of some flaw of character, 14 or the nature of his religion. 15 Thus, people in the past worshipped many, 16 who could perform great tricks of memory, 17 and claim to recite laws and wisdoms of the ages. 18 Yet few had the inspiration or insight, 19 to explain the true reason for such revelation. 20 Alas, the ruins of great civilisations, 21 is testament to the futility of intellect. 22 Almost all men and women, 23 are borne with the gift of reason, 24 and the ability to discern good from bad, 25 and the difference of virtuous honour from evil. 26 Most people have the gift of reason, 27 to discern upon their own knowledge, 28 and to distinguish truth from falsity, 29 and to calculate new insights, 30 using sensible thought. 31 Verily, reason is a formidable enemy of evil, 32 and a danger to the wicked and perverse. 33 Thus the wicked scribes and merchants, 34 seek to weaken the power of reason, 35 by promoting the illusion of intellect, 36 and by claiming certain stories as if like stone, 37 that can neither be questioned nor changed, 38 and by seeding falsities like weeds among ancient truths, 39 so that the people can no longer trust reason. 40 Behold! a man or woman that embraces the gift of reason, 41 cannot be tricked into thinking the world be flat, 42 nor beguiled into believing wickedness is good, 43 nor poisoned into thinking ignorance be a virtue. 44 Guard then the gift of reason.

C.13 - Language

1 Language be the foundation stone, 2 for a fair and prosperous community, 3 or the invisible chains of wicked merchants and moneylenders, 4 to beguile and enslave the people, 5 through convoluted and contradictions of meaning. 6 Language be the elements of sound and symbol, 7 whereby men and women may communicate thought, 8 and construct thought within their minds. 9 Thus Language affects the function of mind, 10 as much as it affects the strength of community. 11 All language be upon a formal model and plan, 12 whereby men and women choose to associate, 13 certain meanings to sounds and symbols, 14 and construct rules and classes of such meaning, 15 so that the

intended information and relations, 16 be memorialised within the structures of such language. 17 Language is never spontaneous, 18 only dialect and rules of use become localised. 19 When scribes speak of a language evolving, 20 as if it has a life of its own, 21 then they are speaking falsities, 22 to hide the true origins of a language. 23 Thus when language places certain symbols to meaning, 24 it means that such associations are planned and intended, 25 and where language provides clarity and consistency, 26 then such simplicity and beauty is intended, 27 and when certain languages be confusing and beguiling, 28 then such hidden meanings and contradictions be deliberate. 29 Verily, language is essential for civilised society, 30 yet may be used by its architects for good or evil. 31 The first languages of humanity used common sounds, 32 so that the people of the world had a common voice, 33 and writing was forbidden, 34 for writing can be used for corruption and spelling (curses). 35 Thus the people could communicate with one another, 36 yet were limited by the quality of their teachers, 37 so that the ancient teachers and priests became arrogant, 38 and sought to control and mould community, 39 and used such knowledge as a weapon. 40 So it was that many peoples revolted, 41 and chose to form their own means of language, 42 by using standard symbols of writing, 43 to teach and communicate with one another. 44 Great civilisations were borne and thrived, 45 upon the freedom to teach their own people, 46 and grow and retain such knowledge. 47 Yet even written language gave birth to corruption, 48 as the teachers of writing decided upon themselves, 49 to insert hidden and magical and contradictory meaning, 50 so that only certain people would know, 51 the power to interpret symbol, 52 or pronounce certain sound. 53 Thus these great civilisations became deluded with their intellect, 54 and lost all sense of heart and reason, 55 and became trapped in their own arrogance. 56 Beware any language that gives many words the same meaning, 57 or the same words contradictory meanings, 58 or the same symbols but different meanings, 59 or the same sounds but different meanings, 60 or uses signs and symbols of dark magic, 61 but pretends such symbols have no meaning. 62 Such languages be a trap designed to enslave the mind, 63 and the fruit of wicked merchants and moneylenders. 64 Behold! true Language be simple, balanced and understandable. 65 That a man or woman may speak or write what they mean, 66 and others may comprehend what was written or spoken. 67 Verily, the spoken word be the breath of life, 68 and the expression of the truth of heart. 69 Thus, the written word is forbidden, 70 in expressing Divine law, 71 or the teaching of wisdom, 72 for words can be changed and corrupted. 73 Instead, the written word be essential for measure, 74 and the record of events and contracts. 75 Discern then good language from wicked language, 76 and the purpose of the spoken word, 77 from the use of the written word.

C.14 - Truth

Book 1 Genasis

1 Truth is essential to the very existence of civilised activity, 2 that things are what they seem; 3 and are as they appear to be; 4 and that such observation is honest and accurate; 5 and may be corroborated by others. 6 Thus some wicked scribes claim truth to be, 7 independent of human volition or action, 8 as if it be a universal quality, 9 and that its presence be immutable and unquestionable. 10 So it is then that meanings such as faithfulness, fidelity and obedience, 11 be claimed as the bedrock of this tyrannical notion of truth. 12 Only the corrupt and ignorant claim truth to be, 13 as if granite stone and unchangeable or immovable. 14 Behold!, the first authentic meaning of truth be, 15 openness and without concealment, 16 nor of secrecy or of hiding. 17 Occult and dark magic can never be truthful, 18 as the very meaning of occult, 19 is opposed to this first authentic notion of truth. 20 Thus the highest sign of this first meaning of truth, 21 is authentic divine revelation, 22 of sacred scripture and teachings, 23 by true messengers of the Divine Creator, 24 in making clear what was once hidden, 25 and why authentic revelation, 26 is the epitome of truth. 27 So it is the first authentic meaning of truth, 28 be the greatest of dangers to the wicked and false, 29 for when people see the trickery of moneylenders, 30 and how they enslave people with false accounting, 31 and wicked contracts that they themselves refuse to follow, 32 then the misery of much slavery may be ended. 33 So too, when people are awake to the madness, 34 of wicked priests and evil religions, 35 that falsely claim the Divine itself is the source of occult, 36 then the people may free themselves of poverty, 37 of misery and madness of evil. 38 Behold!, the second authentic meaning of truth be, 39 acceptance of one or more claims from another, 40 as being both sensible and reasonable. 41 Demands then for blind faith and loyalty, 42 especially when it contradicts the senses and sensible thought, 43 is the opposite to this second authentic notion of truth. 44 Thus the highest sign of this second meaning of truth, 45 is the presence of reason and sensibility, 46 and the absence of fanaticism, occultism and blind faith. 47 So it is the second authentic meaning of truth, 48 reveals the gift of reason be an eternal threat, 49 against the false constructs of reality, 50 and the languages and civilisations of slavery, 51 imagined by the worst false priests and merchants. 52 For when a man or woman rejects ignorance, 53 they reject the notions of evil, 54 and when a man or woman embraces sensible reason, 55 then they cannot be enslaved or cursed. 56 Behold!, the third authentic meaning of truth be, 57 steadfast loyalty to the commands of true leaders, 58 for the sake of the family, the tribe and community. 59 Thus the highest sign of this third meaning of truth, 60 is the presence in leaders of heroic virtue and humility, 61 free from the trappings of opulence and excess, 62 and the actions of impiety and hypocrisy. 63 A leader need not be free from flaw or failure, 64 for the greatest leader is by definition a hero, 65 who overcomes their past and all manner of tribulation, 66 to recast themselves in virtue and lead by example. 67 Thus when men and women demand one

without blemish, 68 they serve the falsities and wickedness of deception, 69 as no good leader be without fault or failure. 70 Verily, there be no truth in obeying a tyrant, 71 or blindly following the madness of wicked priests. 72 Authentic truth be a touchstone of the heart, 73 not an impossible quest, 74 or an unreasonable demand. 75 Authentic truth be the bedrock of peace and prosperity, 76 that unites men and women of good will, 77 and binds and protects communities from peril.

C.15 - Testimony

1 There are times throughout our lives, 2 when an accounting of some memory, 3 of past event or action is called to be recounted. 4 If such events or acts were dramatic, 5 then it may be easier to recall. 6 Yet even the most significant of events, 7 may change within the mind over time. 8 Thus remembrance can never be considered exact, 9 but the most accurate account that can be recalled. 10 For even when two or more people be witnesses, 11 there may be details missed between them, 12 or even differences of details upon recall. 13 Behold! testimony is the solemn spoken declaration, 14 of truthful remembrance and recollection, 15 made under oath or vow. 16 It matters not that a testimony be different, 17 between two or more witnesses, 18 but that such testimony is truthful remembrance, 19 and free from duress, 20 and free from suggestion or influence, 21 and without bribery or inducement. 22 Verily, truthful remembrance and recollection, 23 is the cornerstone of justice and any forum of law. 24 For if people are unwilling or prevented, 25 from making authentic testimony, 26 then no justice can exist. 27 Thus the worst of offences against the law, 28 and against the stability of any society, 29 is bearing false witness and false testimony. 30 Verily, any society that permits or encourages, 31 the actions of false testimony, 32 has neither authority nor legitimacy. 33 False testimony corrupts and corrodes, 34 it perverts and destroys those who permit it. 35 Guard against false testimony at all cost, 36 and enforce the firmest judgement when it is discovered.

C.16 - Equality

1 Man be no greater or lesser than woman. 2 Woman be no lesser than man, 3 for both depend upon one another, 4 else we would not exist. 5 Men be different to women, 6 and women have different abilities to men. 7 Yet such differences be not weakness but strength. 8 Just because men train for battle, 9 does not mean only men can fight. 10 Some of the greatest warriors of history were women. 11 That women protect their children, 12 and make a place a home, 13 does not mean men are incapable of duties. 14 Verily, the greatest hero is first the one, 15 who protects and nurtures his wife and children, 16 and protects and helps his neighbours. 17 Similarly it matters not the colour of ones skin, 18 as all bleed red blood, 19 and all possess mind, 20 and all have dreams and feelings and fears, 21 and all possess a united soul. 22 Thus there have been many wicked and evil civilisations, 23 that claimed women be merely the property of men, 24 or that

certain men be superior by the colour of their skin. 25 Such notions are an abomination against the Divine, 26 and against the soul of all humanity, 27 and the Divine condemns those who make and enforce, 28 such wicked and perverse claims. 29 No man or woman ever be the property of another. 30 No man or woman be lesser or greater upon gender. 31 No man or woman be lesser or greater by skin. 32 All have value and purpose in the existence of the Universe. 33 All are equal, yet unique as the living Divine paradox.

C.17 - Trust

1 Trust be the confidence and reliance, 2 that some quality or object or action be true. 3 Trust also be the confidence in a man or woman, 4 appointed and accepted to a position, 5 and thus holding authority and power, 6 upon their solemn oath or vow, 7 to serve for the benefit of another. 8 Verily, no man or woman may hold office, 9 except by authentic trust, 10 and any one who claims such power without trust, 11 is a tyrant and an imposter. 12 The opposite of trust is doubt, 13 and the opposite of trust of office is corruption. 14 Behold! a people who hold trust in one another, 15 and in their appointed leaders, 16 have no need of money changers (bankers). 17 For money changers can only ply their wickedness, 18 when there is little or no trust. 19 That is why wicked merchants and money changers, 20 are and always will be the enemy of the people. 21 For their very existence and success, 22 depends upon the destruction of trust, 23 and the corruption of the community. 24 Thus any community that welcomes in such evil, 25 does sow the seeds for its own destruction, 26 and any society controlled by moneylenders (bankers), 27 is enslaved and condemned to misery and war. 28 Verily, a community that possesses trust, 29 can convert such trust into promises without moneylenders, 30 and such promises be worth more than a chest of coins, 31 for upon the appointed day a holder of a promise, 32 may call upon the favour, 33 and the obligor will gladly perform their duties. 34 Homes can be built upon the trust of such promises. 35 Fences can be repaired upon the trust of such promises. 36 Crops can be planted and harvested on such promises, 37 and whole communities can prosper upon such promises. 38 Thus such value remains within the community, 39 and builds the wealth of the community, 40 whereas the shaved and uneven coins of moneylenders (bankers), 41 leave the community to the hands of the merchants, 42 and strip a people of their wealth, 43 so that the more they trade, 44 the poorer they become. 45 This is the trickery and beguiling magic, 46 and falsities of wicked merchants, 47 and why a wise community, 48 forbids such people within the walls of a city.

C.18 - Divine

1 The Divine means the total set of all meanings and definitions, 2 of all possible concepts, objects, matter and rules, 3 and all forms of life, mind, universe and spirit, 4 and all historic, customary and traditional names, 5 used to describe the greatest of all possibilities, 6 and the supreme being of all divinities. 7 Verily, as the Divine

means the concept of all concepts, 8 and the set of all sets, 9 there can be no greater concept nor set. 10 Thus, every other possible concept or object, 11 must be lesser than the Divine. 12 Verily, as the Divine means the concept of all concepts, 13 and the set of all sets, 14 all possible and actual concepts and objects, 15 and sets of concepts and objects, 16 are part of the Divine. 17 Thus it is absurd and insane, 18 to speak of aspects of the Divine, 19 and claim attributes of a supreme being, 20 that is less than the concept of all concepts, 21 and the set of all sets. 22 Verily, describing the Divine as purely masculine, 23 or purely feminine is a disgrace and false, 24 as such descriptions are less than the total, 25 and describing the Divine as wrathful or vengeful, 26 is the height of stupidity and wickedness, 27 for wrath, vengeance and power, 28 are all less than the set of all sets. 29 Verily, when speaking of gods and spirits, 30 one speaks to specific aspects of the Divine, 31 not adversaries to the Divine. 32 Nothing is greater than the Divine, 33 as everything else is lesser by degree.

C.19 - Divine Existence

1 The existence of Divine is without dispute. 2 For the existence of the Divine, 3 can be easily proven four different ways. 4 Thus doubt as to the existence of the Divine, 5 exists only because of wicked priests, 6 and the plans of merchants and moneylenders, 7 who do not wish people to have trust, 8 especially absolute unshakable trust in the Divine. 9 First, the Divine exists absolutely as concept, 10 and therefore is proven to have existence: 11 for the mere existence of a notion, 12 is sufficient to validate itself, 13 regardless of whether it is considered, 14 true or false to other notions. 15 Only notions that cannot be named, 16 may be said to have no existence. 17 Thus the Divine Creator exists at least in concept. 18 A man or woman then who proclaims, 19 that the Divine has absolutely no existence, 20 confesses themselves to be insane. 21 Second, the Divine possesses material existence: 22 for existence of the Universe, 23 depends upon both rules and matter, 24 and neither matter without rules, 25 or rules without matter, 26 can exist in Universal reality. 27 Only rules can exist on their own as a notion. 28 The only example where rules exist in theory, 29 and rules and matter exist in reality, 30 is the relation between a dreamer and dream. 31 Thus, the Divine Creator may be said to be the Divine Dreamer, 32 and the Universe is the Dream, 33 and the Divine is proven to have Material Existence. 34 A man or woman then who proclaims, 35 that the Divine has absolutely no material existence, 36 acknowledges themselves to be a fool. 37 Third, the Divine possesses real existence: 38 for dimension is the canvas of reality, 39 where upon all material existence depends, 40 and that almost every conscious being experiences, 41 through the creation of dimension first hand, 42 through their mind whenever they think or dream. 43 Verily, dimension is no place but every place, 44 in that it has no material existence, 45 yet every thought and every reality depends on it. 46 Behold! dimension can only be created, 47 by conscious observable thought. 48

Therefore the existence of any dimension, 49 is proof of the existence of the Universal Dimension, 50 as the observable thought of the Divine Creator, 51 and proof of the existence of the Divine Creator. 52 A man or woman then who proclaims, 53 that the Divine has absolutely no real existence, 54 by denying the nature of all dimension, 55 and their own thoughts and dreams, 56 reveals themselves to be possessed by ghosts. 57 Fourth, the Divine possesses absolute existence: 58 for existence itself depends on at least an observer, 59 and the Object observed to hold true. 60 Thus for the Objective Universe to exist, 61 there must be a Universal Observer. 62 Behold! the Divine Creator is the absolute Dreamer, 63 and the Universe as the absolute Dream, 64 and the Divine Creator is proven to have Absolute Existence. 65 A man or woman then who denies these truths, 66 is an imposter and a trickster.

C.20 - Divine Creation

1 The creation of Divine Existence, 2 and all of existence is without dispute. 3 For the Twelve Laws of Divine Creation, 4 are the first Twelve Laws of Nature, 5 and are present within every dimension, 6 and every level of matter and life, 7 within and throughout the Universe. 8 All physical laws of the Universe, 9 are ultimately derived, 10 from the Twelve Laws of Divine Creation, 11 and all true laws of humanity, 12 are also ultimately derived, 13 from the Twelve Laws of Divine Creation. 14 Verily, an awake mind need not believe superstition, 15 or fanciful stories of ghosts and demons, 16 in order to comprehend the creation of the universe, 17 and the unity of all creation. 18 Thus it is only merchants and their scribes, 19 and the wicked priests that defile the spirit of Divine, 20 to perpetuate contradictory accounts of creation, 21 not to honour the Divine but to ferment evil. 22 Verily, the wicked leaders of insane beliefs, 23 wish to control, beguile and condemn the minds, 24 of those poor souls that foolishly follow their falsities. 25 Thus the true laws of Divine Creation are a threat, 26 against such evil and trickery. 27 Behold! the Twelve Laws of Divine Creation: 28 The first being the law of Divine Will, 29 expressed simply as the wish to exist; 30 The second being the law of Divine Reason, 31 expressed simply as to exist one uses reason; 32 The third being the law of Divine Purpose, 33 expressed simply as to exist one must have purpose; 34 The fourth being the law of Divine Codependence, 35 expressed simply as for I to exist you must exist; 36 The fifth being the law of Divine Specialisation, 37 expressed simply as for I to exist as, you must exist as; 38 The sixth being the law of Divine Measure (geometry), 39 expressed simply as to exist one must use rules of measure (geometry); 40 The seventh being the law of Divine Elemental Awareness, 41 expressed simply as to exist I must have elementary awareness of my position; 42 The eighth being the law of Divine Community, 43 expressed simply as to exist I interact and support my local community first; 44 The ninth being the law of Divine Uniqueness, 45 expressed simply as to exist no two points can occupy the same position; 46 The tenth being the law of Divine

Change, 47 expressed simply as to exist nothing can stand still in time or space; 48 The eleventh being the law of Divine Conservation, 49 expressed simply as to exist I only use what is necessary and conserve the rest; 50 The twelfth being the law of Divine Limit, 51 expressed simply as to exist one cannot change faster than what is capable. 52 Verily, these be the Twelve Laws of all Creation. 53 Let not evil dull the mind with fantasy and confusion. 54 Give truth and substance to the mind of every man and woman, 55 so that they be certain of the connections between every thing.

C.21 - Divine Will

1 The first law of the Twelve Laws of Divine Creation, 2 is the law of Divine Will, 3 expressed simply as the wish to exist. 4 Of all possible forces within the Universe, 5 the greatest is the action of Free Will, 6 for the very existence of existence itself, 7 depends upon the Free Will of the Ultimate Creator, 8 and the wish of the Divine to exist. 9 To deny such reasoning, 10 is to deny the competency of intellect itself. 11 Verily, Free Will is not only the greatest force of Creation, 12 essential to the concept of Existence itself, 13 but to the very notion of an Absolute and Divine Observer, 14 and the absolute Object of Creation observed. 15 Simply, there would be no existence or observer, or meaning, 16 if not for the fundamental force of Free Will. 17 Verily, the existence of the Universe is impossible to be computed, 18 if not for the existence of Free Will, 19 leading to the autonomy of matter at different levels, 20 yet all following the same essential set of rules. 21 Thus all models that speak of the universe, 22 as if a terrible machine, 23 and men and women be but cogs within it, 24 are false and impossible to function. 25 And models that speak of the universe, 26 as if a result of chaos and random fortune, 27 are without sensible competence or thought, 28 for existence itself affords no room for error. 29 Verily, any man or woman who seeks to deny, 30 the will of a reasoned and capable mind, 31 invokes upon themselves terrible woes, 32 and those men and women that rebel against Divine Will, 33 invoke against themselves the full forces of spirit and nature.

C.22 - Divine Reason

1 The second law of the Twelve Laws of Divine Creation, 2 is the law of Divine Reason, 3 expressed simply as to exist one uses reason. 4 Verily, as the capacity to reason, discern and learn, 5 are considered defining conditions for human intellect, 6 so too the abilities to reason, discern and compute, 7 must be qualities present within Divine Mind. 8 Thus, the Divine using reason is perfectly capable, 9 of discerning that to exist, 10 one must exist as something in dimension. 11 For anyone to conclude that only humanity, 12 or only a select few possess the gift of reason, 13 or claim the Universe is devoid of reason, 14 is an admission itself of lack of sensible reasoning. 15 Verily, there is nothing to suggest, 16 within an infinite potential of reasoning, 17 that the Divine did not first test hypothetical models and sets, 18 of finite and infinite possibilities in theory, 19 until the perfect model of laws was

concluded. 20 Thus the existence of two dimensional space, 21 and three dimensional space, 22 and that models in two dimensional space, 23 may be abstracted into functioning models, 24 within three dimensional space, 25 supports the reasoning, 26 that the Divine did produce simulated models of Existence, 27 prior to the complete model of the Universe. 28 Verily, any man or woman, 29 who seeks to deny Divine Reason, 30 declares themselves incapable of reason, 31 and unable to be trusted, 32 upon any matters, 33 requiring intellect or thought or education.

C.23 - Divine Purpose

1 The third law of the Twelve Laws of Divine Creation, 2 is the law of Divine Purpose, 3 expressed simply as to exist one must have purpose. 4 As the Divine must be something to exist, 5 it conceives itself as the smallest theoretical point, 6 also known as an Infinitesimal in dimension. 7 The necessity to exist as something, 8 sensibly leads to the existence of cause, 9 at each and every level of matter. 10 To exist, the Divine created the dream, 11 a theoretical object and the potential to exist. 12 Thus, as the Divine has demonstrated, 13 everything in the Universe, 14 possesses some specific purpose for existence, 15 even if such purpose is not easily recognised. 16 Verily, that the smallest possible theoretical object, 17 being an Infinitesimal Point, 18 is connected to the greatest possible concept, 19 of the Divine Creator, 20 establishes a clear paradox, 21 whereby the largest possible concept, 22 depends upon its existence of the smallest possible concept.

C.24 - Divine Codependence

1 The fourth law of the Twelve Laws of Divine Creation, 2 is the law of Divine Codependence, 3 expressed simply as for I to exist you must exist. 4 Verily, while a point in two dimensional space, 5 need only two neighbour points to prove existence, 6 a point in three dimensional space, 7 needs at least six neighbour points to prove existence. 8 Thus, codependence is an essential law of all of creation. 9 Verily, the existence of the Universe depends upon, 10 a co-dependent set of Infinitesimal points, 11 constantly expanding at an infinite rate, 12 also known as the Infinite, 13 for each point to properly exist in dimension. 14 A single point does not guarantee existence in Real Dimension, 15 just as a single man or woman has no meaningful existence alone. 16 To have three dimensional Real Dimension, 17 an object must have a relative position, 18 with at least six points around it, 19 in Real Dimensional space. 20 Unreal space can only exist in theory or in two dimensions. 21 Thus, before Unreal Space can be proven to exist, 22 the Real Set of things must exist. 23 Therefore, unless each anchor point of the Divine, 24 has its own infinite set of anchor points, 25 relative position cannot be guaranteed, 26 and existence collapses. 27 Such an absolute co-dependence, 28 between just one unique point of the Divine, 29 and the complete set of points (the Infinite set), 30 proves the absolute and irrefutable importance, 31 of every single object to the Universe. 32

Behold! if but the essence of one man or woman ceased to exist, 33 the entire Universe would cease to exist! 34 Thus every man and woman and every form of life, 35 is vitally important to the Divine. 36 Verily, any man or woman who seeks to deny, 37 the absolute importance of every other man or woman, 38 to the continued existence of the Divine, 39 or who claims that some people are less worthy, 40 or have no value to the Divine, 41 invokes upon themselves the consequence of their falsities, 42 as an enemy of all spirit and nature. 43 Woe be upon any wicked priest or imposter, 44 who falsely proclaims the truth of the Divine.

C.25 - Divine Specialisation

1 The fifth law of the Twelve Laws of Divine Creation, 2 is the law of Divine Specialisation, 3 expressed simply as for I to exist as, you must exist as. 4 Verily, in the process of ensuring dimension and existence, 5 points of the Divine must specialise into different types, 6 such as core points, 7 or anchor points, 8 or outer anchor points. 9 Without such specialised roles, 10 even at the most basic level of points, 11 the Divine could not guarantee existence in dimension. 12 Thus, it is an absurdity to argue that men are greater than women, 13 or that women should do the same tasks as men, 14 or that unity can only come through dissolution of uniqueness. 15 Verily, existence depends upon our differences, 16 and our flaws and our characteristics, 17 and our gender and our race and our cultures. 18 Verily, any man or woman who seeks to deny, 19 the necessary function of specialisation, 20 or who urges a false unity through sameness, 21 defiles the will of the Divine, 22 and is a false teacher.

C.26 - Divine Measure (geometry)

1 The sixth law of the Twelve Laws of Divine Creation, 2 is the law of Divine Measure (geometry), 3 expressed simply as to exist one must use rules of measure (geometry), 4 whereby the arrangement of specialised and co-dependent points, 5 must form and operate according to geometric principles, 6 such as volume and relation in three dimensional space, 7 in order to exist as the building blocks of matter. 8 Verily, to exist, something must have shape and occupy space. 9 Some shapes are more efficient at forming volume than others. 10 Spheres have a surface area to volume ratio of 4:3, 11 meaning that there is less volume area compared to surface area. 12 Perfect Cubes have a surface area to volume of 2:1, 13 meaning that there is one half the volume compared to surface area. 14 Yet the most efficient shape in terms of number of points, 15 combining to create maximum volume is an octahedron (six points), 16 combining to create eight equally proportioned triangles, 17 expanding to a middle point and reducing to a single point. 18 The surface area to volume of a perfect Octahedron is always 1:2, 19 meaning an octahedron creates twice as much volume, 20 as it takes surface space to create it. 21 Thus, the Divine uses measure, 22 as essential to existence of volume and shape in dimension.

C.27 - Divine Elemental Awareness

1 The seventh law of the Twelve Laws of Divine Creation, 2 is the law of Divine Elemental Awareness, 3 expressed simply as to exist I must have elementary awareness of my position. 4 Verily, Awareness is the ability to receive, conceive, perceive, comprehend or discern, 5 complex information about different concepts, objects, conditions or events, 6 and calculate some form of action accordingly. 7 Thus Awareness is the quality of observation, 8 fundamental to the very nature of existence. 9 Verily, while the existence of infinite points of the Divine, 10 provides a framework to exist in dimension, 11 it is not enough for the Divine to simply observe the dream. 12 The Divine needs to be able to validate existence, 13 of each and every point; 14 and each and every unit of matter; 15 and each and every collection of matter; 16 and each and every action and reaction of matter. 17 Thus, for existence to be valid and validated, 18 the Divine must be able to observe within the dream, 19 without affecting the fundamental rules, 20 that create and form the dream. 21 Verily, a dream can be within a dream, 22 yet no dream or dimension may impose itself, 23 without dissolving the former. 24 Behold! validation of existence by observation is achieved, 25 by the inherent awareness of position in dimension, 26 of pure points of the Divine, 27 and by each infinitely small point of the Divine, 28 being aware of its position in dimension. 29 Thus the requirement for existence to be observed, 30 for each and every theoretical object is validated, 31 through the miracle of elemental awareness, 32 whereby every point of the Divine being aware, 33 and every unit of matter made from points being aware; 34 and every collection of complex matter being aware; 35 and every grain of sand being aware; 36 and every drop of water being aware; 37 and every ray of sunlight being awareness in motion; 38 and every blade of grass being elementary aware. 39 Verily, any man or woman who seeks to deny, 40 that every object must possess elemental awareness, 41 for the universe itself to exist, 42 is either a fool or possessed by wickedness, 43 in seeking to cleave men and women, 44 to the true magic of all things being connected.

C.28 - Divine Community

1 The eighth law of the Twelve Laws of Divine Creation, 2 is the law of Divine Community, 3 expressed simply as to exist I interact and support my local community first. 4 Verily, points of the Divine being pure awareness can interact, 5 with points well beyond its immediate position. 6 There be no hard universal law that forces a point of the Divine, 7 to only interact with points around it. 8 Yet, if one point of awareness ceased to exist, 9 dimension would collapse, 10 and existence itself would cease. 11 Thus, to reduce such risk, 12 each and every point chooses by its own free will, 13 to only interact with immediate near neighbours, 14 in the creation of greater form. 15 For if points of awareness and higher forms of matter, 16 chose to interact wherever or whenever they wished, 17 chaos would reign and no stable forms

could exist. 18 Behold! the building block of all civilised society, 19 is the sacred union between a man and a woman, 20 bound in honour, fidelity and acceptance, 21 that children may be borne into a stable home. 22 Behold! the building block of clans, 23 be the collection of fines (family) units, 24 that give a clan its strength and unity. 25 Behold! the building block of community, 26 being peace and respect between clans, 27 under the rule of law. 28 Thus, every point of Divine, 29 computes and interacts its position and state, 30 and makes changes accordingly, 31 in relation to its immediate neighbours, 32 and not remote possibilities, 33 to create more complex forms.

C.29 - Divine Uniqueness

1 The ninth law of the Twelve Laws of Divine Creation, 2 is the law of Divine Uniqueness, 3 expressed simply as to exist no two points can occupy the same position. 4 Verily, if one point of the Divine, 5 ceased to hold unique position in dimension, 6 then all of existence would also cease. 7 Thus not only does each point of the Divine, 8 and every level of matter hold unique position, 9 but no object moves in a perfectly straight line, 10 and when points change position in a circle, 11 they do so in an up and down motion, 12 creating the feature of oscillation. 13 Verily, there be no perfect lines, 14 nor be there perfect circles in reality, 15 because of these truths. 16 The measure of perfect imperfection, 17 when the Divine is instantiated in form, 18 is called the Divine Ratio (Pi).

C.30 - Divine Change

1 The tenth law of the Twelve Laws of Divine Creation, 2 is the law of Divine Change, 3 expressed simply as to exist nothing can stand still in time or space. 4 Verily, the creation of form in three dimensional space, 5 requires points of Divine to change position, 6 thus creating frequency, rotation and vibration, 7 as motions within form and motion as form. 8 Thus, the very definition of existence implies change. 9 Nothing except Divine reference may remain still. 10 Everything yields but change. 11 Change is life. Life is constant change.

C.31 - Divine Conservation

1 The eleventh law of the Twelve Laws of Divine Creation, 2 is the law of Divine Conservation, 3 expressed simply as to exist I only use what is necessary and conserve the rest. 4 Verily, if points of Divine changed position at a maximum rate, 5 there would be no conservation of motion to create form. 6 Thus motion is conserved to enable change of position as form. 7 Such stored potential is the nature of energy within the Universe, 8 as energy is awareness in motion in form.

C.32 - Divine Limit

1 The twelfth law of the Twelve Laws of Divine Creation, 2 is the law of Divine Limit, 3 expressed simply as to exist I cannot change faster than what I am capable. 4 Verily, once the smallest units of matter are formed, 5 such units will never change position at their maximum rate, 6 creating limits of motion at every level of matter, 7 and an inverse relation between motion used within form, 8

and motion of the collective form of all matter.

C.33 - Divine Nature

₁ The nature of the Divine is without dispute. ₂ For the existence of the Divine itself, ₃ has been proven through four different ways: ₄ First the Divine has Conceptual Existence; ₅ Second the Divine has Material Existence; ₆ Third the Divine has Real Existence; ₇ Fourth the Divine has Absolute Existence. ₈ Behold! the nature of the Divine, ₉ may be illuminated by nine attributes: ₁₀ The First being Unique Collective Awareness; ₁₁ The Second being Absolute Free Will; ₁₂ The Third being Perfect Reasoning; ₁₃ The Fourth being Unconditional Love; ₁₄ The Fifth being Constant Change; ₁₅ The Sixth being Benevolent Amorality; ₁₆ The Seventh being Authentic Rule of Law; ₁₇ The Eighth being True Justice; ₁₈ and the Ninth being Abundant Mercy. ₁₉ The First attribute of Divine Nature, ₂₀ be the quality known as Unique Collective Awareness. ₂₁ Verily, everything is mind and unique, ₂₂ and every level of matter is a collective of awareness, ₂₃ and every unique piece of matter is aware, ₂₄ and every element of life is aware, ₂₅ and everything is remembered and nothing is lost, ₂₆ and nothing is forgotten, ₂₇ and nothing is without witness. ₂₈ The Second attribute of Divine Nature, ₂₉ be the quality known as Absolute Free Will. ₃₀ Verily, the Divine chooses by its own volition to exist, ₃₁ and that such choice is a conscious and continual choice, ₃₂ at each and every instant of existence, ₃₃ and at every level of existence, ₃₄ and when free will is ignored or breached or oppressed, ₃₅ then such a culpable man or woman, ₃₆ call upon themselves the full force of nature, ₃₇ to correct such evil and wrong. ₃₈ The Third attribute of Divine Nature, ₃₉ be the quality known as Perfect Reasoning. ₄₀ Verily, the Divine is perfectly sensible and reasonable, ₄₁ in all its thoughts and actions, ₄₂ without being affected by lesser emotions, ₄₃ of jealousy, hate, fear, retribution, anger or prejudice. ₄₄ Thus, any man or woman who claims to be The Divine, ₄₅ exhibits any such lesser emotion is an imposter, ₄₆ and a servant to ghosts and madness. ₄₇ The Fourth attribute of Divine Nature, ₄₈ be the quality known as Unconditional Love. ₄₉ Verily, the Divine reveals that the highest expression of existence, ₅₀ is the love of life and love of all existence. ₅₁ Thus the strongest emotion is love, ₅₂ and the Divine is the personification of love. ₅₃ The Fifth attribute of Divine Nature, ₅₄ be the quality known as Constant Change. ₅₅ Verily, the Divine reveals that change of position, ₅₆ is essential for the creation of form and existence. ₅₇ Thus, the constancy of change is essential to all existence, ₅₈ from birth to death and life and rebirth, ₅₉ and from abundance to famine, ₆₀ and from summer to winter. ₆₁ The Sixth attribute of Divine Nature, ₆₂ be the quality known as Benevolent Amorality. ₆₃ Verily, the Divine reveals that once dimension is created, ₆₄ direct intervention in the Divine Dream of life is impossible, ₆₅ except through vision, revelation and inspiration. ₆₆ Behold! the Divine Creator cannot interpose itself twice, ₆₇ without collapsing dimension and existence. 68 Thus, the Divine Creator is benevolent to all creation and life, 69 but amoral to the constant change of existence, 70 in permitting the laws of the Universe to function, 71 without Divine intervention to alter or suspend them. 72 The Seventh attribute of Divine Nature, 73 be the quality known as Authentic Rule of Law. 74 Verily, the Divine reveals that existence itself depends upon rules. 75 Thus, the expression of Divine Mind is Divine Law, 76 and the highest of all laws is the Golden Rule, 77 that no one is above the law, 78 and all are equal before the same law. 79 The Eighth attribute of Divine Nature 80 be the quality known as True Justice. 81 Verily, the Divine reveals that existence itself depends upon consistency, 82 in the application of the laws of the Universe, 83 so that the same essential rules of existence, 84 be applied consistently without fear, or favour or corruption. 85 The Ninth attribute of Divine Nature, 86 be the quality known as Abundant Mercy. 87 Verily, the Divine reveals infinite love and forgiveness, 88 such that no man or woman be cursed in spirit, 89 nor any man or woman be burdened by the transgressions, 90 of their ancestors and family. 91 Behold, any man or woman who proclaims, 92 that certain deceased souls be perpetually cursed or tormented, 93 is a sick and dangerous imposter, 94 that must be expelled immediately from any position of authority. 95 For the truths of the Divine ring out against such evil, 96 and such falsities and such attempts of control. 97 Behold! the spirit of humanity shall never be squashed, 98 and the people shall no longer be imprisoned, 99 and the truth set all men and women free!

C.34 - Human Existence

1 Your existence like the Divine is without dispute. 2 For your existence within the Divine dream of life, 3 can be easily proven four different ways. 4 First, you exist absolutely in name and identity, 5 and therefore you are proven to have existence: 6 for the mere existence of a notion, 7 is sufficient to validate itself, 8 regardless of whether it is considered, 9 true or false to other ideas. 10 Only notions that cannot be named, 11 may be said to have no existence. 12 Second, you possess material existence:13 as a form of flesh, blood and bone, 14 within a Universal dream defined by rules. 15 Thus if you fall down then you may bruise, 16 and if you are cut then you will bleed, 17 and if you do not eat food then you will grow hungry and weak, 18 and if you do not find shelter and warmth, 19 then you will get sick and will die. 20 Verily, as with all material form, 21 your material existence is finite and changing, 22 yet the fact that you can feel your breath, 23 and experience heat and cold and pain, 24 is proof that you have material existence. 25 Third you possess real existence: 26 by reading or hearing these words, 27 and thinking thoughts and ideas, 28 and imagining things within dimension. 29 Thus by your thoughts and concerns, 30 your dreams and doubts, 31 you prove the formation of unique dimension, 32 and the validation of real existence. 33 Fourth, you possess divine immortal existence: 34 as your mind and spirit will always be immortal. 35 Behold!

Book 1 Genasis

Nothing can come from nothing, 36 and real cannot become unreal, 37 without breaking the boundary of all existence. 38 Verily, your mind is everywhere and nowhere in reality, 39 therefore it cannot be said to have material existence. 40 Only your body has a finite and material existence. 41 Thus your true essence is as an immortal being.

C.35 - Human Will

1 The first and greatest law of all creation, 2 is the law of Divine Will, 3 expressed as the most powerful of all forces within the Universe, 4 as the action of Free Will, 5 and the wish of all to exist. 6 Thus the greatest gift and power of all human beings, 7 is their right of Free Will, 8 and their right to choose to consent or to deny. 9 To deny the existence of such a fundamental right, 10 is for one to declare themselves a fool or a charlatan, 11 incapable of reasoning and sensible thought. 12 For the very existence of the entire Universe, 13 depends upon the universal existence of Free Will. 14 To deny then that every human being is endowed with such a gift, 15 be the work of wicked scribes and slave merchants, 16 who seek to recast certain human beings as less than human. 17 Thus to oppress the free will and intention of others, 18 is to declare war and opposition to the Universe, 19 and to all Heaven and Earth. 20 Verily, no tyrant or wicked merchant can win against such odds, 21 for by invoking such opposition they curse themselves at every turn, 22 and shall certainly be rendered to dust.

C.36 - Human Reason

1 The second and greatest law of all creation, 2 is the law of Divine Reason. 3 Verily, the capacity to reason, discern and learn, 4 are the same defining conditions for human intellect, 5 as they are for the Divine Creator, 6 and for all of creation. 7 Thus Human beings are endowed with the capacity of reason, 8 to make informed and educated choices, 9 either as a choice between two opposites, 10 or a choice between three or more states between two opposites. 11 In the first method as a choice between two opposites, 12 a Human Being may discern and conclude decisions, 13 in the form of true or false, 14 or the form of culpable or blameless, 15 or the form of authentic or fake. 16 In the second method as a choice between three or more states, 17 a Human being may discern real life decisions, 18 in the form of more accurate or less accurate, 19 or more certain or less certain, 20 or more like or less like (a thing). 21 Behold! a Human being that abandons reason, 22 disqualifies themselves from the right to argue or defend.

C.37 - Human Purpose

1 The third and greatest law of all creation, 2 is the law of Divine Purpose. 3 Verily, every human life has purpose, 4 and no human existence is without fundamental purpose, 5 and just as the very essence of existence, 6 depends upon the smallest possible theoretical objects, 7 it follows reason that existence itself, 8 depends upon all objects and forms as is the Human Being. 9 Behold! If but the smallest fleck of your skin, 10 or the tiniest tear from your eyes, 11 or the thinnest hair

upon your arm ceased to exist, 12 existence itself would cease to be. 13 Thus our material existence is wedded, 14 to the material existence of the Divine as the Universe. 15 To conclude that human life is without purpose, 16 or that human life is meaningless, 17 to the vastness of creation, 18 is to be either struck with an illness of stupidity, 19 or a self destructive wickedness of deliberate wilful ignorance.

C.38 - Human Mind

1 The Universe is the Divine Mind in motion. 2 Mind itself is equivalent to Consciousness, 3 and the Observer-Object Relation, 4 also expressed as the Dreamer-Dream Relation. 5 Before our physical formation, 6 or even the revelation of Divine Nature through being borne, 7 the Divine as the ultimate Dreamer must construct in Divine Mind, 8 a new mind of sufficiently stable reason to sustain our existence. 9 Thus our Mind must precede our physical Existence, 10 and be responsible for our physical Existence, 11 in the same manner that a Dreamer, 12 is responsible for their Dream.

C.39 - Human Soul

1 The name Soul be a word, 2 to define that part of a being, 3 associated with a living being, 4 and that without it, 5 physical life cannot exist. 6 We know this to be our immortal Mind, 7 by another name. 8 Yet to the ancients and to many cultures, 9 the truth that Soul and Mind are the same, 10 was easily forgotten, 11 and their quest for divine wisdom, 12 placed greater importance, 13 on the elements and nature of Soul. 14 Thus just as all human beings are first an animal, 15 the ancient priests asserted we have an animal soul, 16 and just as human beings are unique, 17 so then all human beings had a second soul. 18 Yet the priests in their blind arrogance, 19 concluded that because so many worship ignorance, 20 and falsehoods and abandon their gifts of reason, 21 only some have the highest form of soul. 22 Behold! such reasoning gives rise to the wicked justification, 23 to all manner of slavery and barbarity against fellow human beings, 24 no longer considered equal but less than human and mere creatures. 25 Do not fall into the trap of concluding, 26 just because people choose ignorance over wisdom, 27 that such poor choices disqualifies them from equality as beings. 28 Verily, all have but one mind of three layers and all have one soul, 29 and non may seize, take, sell, surrender nor abandon their soul, 30 just as no man or woman may abandon their mind, 31 except for a state of temporary madness.

C.40 - Human Heart

1 The capacity for a Human Being to hate and create untold misery, 2 is only exceeded by their supernatural capacity for love, 3 and to embody Divine Love in physical form. 4 Thus the Human Heart is the source of our greatest power and strength, 5 for their be no such thing as a dark heart, 6 only a clouded and isolated mind. 7 All truth begins from the heart, 8 and all compassion and kindness emanates up from the heart, 9 and all courage and respect radiates from the heart. 10

Verily, if the heart is closed, 11 no other point of the body is truly awake, 12 and if the heart is truly opened, 13 then there be no point of the body that may be closed off. 14 The ancient priests in their intellectual arrogance, 15 fought against the wisdom of the heart, 16 to make the head the destination of redemption. 17 They believed that only by unlocking physical points one by one, 18 could a human being reach an open heart, 19 and ultimately an enlightened mind. 20 They wrongly believed that if one of the foundation points closed, 21 then the state of higher awareness was compromised. 22 Behold! A heart is either truly opened or closed, 23 and an open heart means all points of the body are opened, 24 and a closed heart means all points of the body are closed. 25 There be no need for complex meditations, 26 or endless rituals to guard against ignorance, 27 for such rituals and false knowledge is the height of ignorance. 28 Feel your heart and through your open heart, 29 feel the flow of the world, 30 and the flow of emotions and joys and sadness, 31 and you shall be consciously connected to the Divine always.

C.41 - Human Life

1 Human Life is a precious gift, 2 given once to each unique instance of Mind connected to form. 3 Thus while a Mind may have been connected to other lives, 4 no two experiences of human life are ever the same. 5 Human life begins not with conception, 6 but nine to ten weeks after first conception. 7 To claim otherwise is to proclaim an absurdity. 8 Human life evolved from lesser life forms, 9 and in the formation of life through pregnancy, 10 all of us had to first experience the same evolution. 11 Thus at nine to ten weeks the form that is within the womb, 12 is a human being with rights, 13 and with feelings and with a soul. 14 Behold! at nine to ten weeks the mind and body become one, 15 with an unborne child as heralded by the first movements. 16 Verily, any harm to such an unborne human being, 17 from ten weeks until physically being borne, 18 is the murder of a human being, 19 no less than the murder of a living adult human being. 20 To claim otherwise is to be enslaved to the wickedness and evils, 21 of the merchants and their priests, 22 who profess a life is only human if they ordain it to be. 23 So drunk they be with power, 24 and so blinded by delusion, 25 that these insane and evil scribes and priests believe themselves to be gods, 26 capable of changing the course of Divine law, 27 and the reason and sense of Natural law, 28 with their edicts of false dictates and claims. 29 Verily, the unnatural death of any unborne human being after ten weeks is murder, 30 and those that endorse and condone or promote such acts, 31 be greater in culpability than even the mother, 32 that allowed the death, 33 of their unborne child.

C.42 - Human Death

1 It is natural and normal for the human body to die. 2 It be not a curse but a blessing to our species, 3 for our survival depends upon new lives and old deaths. 4 Verily, if we lived an age many times greater in years, 5 then

there would be no urgency to reproduce, 6 and our species would be in jeopardy. 7 Similarly, if life were to be prolonged beyond what is reasonable, 8 then such acts would not be kindness, 9 but the dooming of our communities, 10 through over population and lost resources, 11 into prolonging life beyond what should be a dignified death. 12 It is only the slave owning merchants and their wicked priests, 13 who crave physical immortality to hold onto their temporary powers. 14 For they believe not in truth or an afterlife, 15 but fear death above all else. 16 Thus their secret and bloodthirsty rituals seek to prolong their lives, 17 in vain and deluded hope that somehow the laws of the Divine, 18 and the laws of Nature be reversed only for them. 19 Behold! There is nothing to be feared by physical death, 20 for what is in essence our mind and ourselves, be already immortal and eternal. 21 Verily, let us not squander life by seeking to run away from death, 22 nor be reckless with such a precious gift as life, 23 but live each day as if it be our last, 24 and give thanks for all that we have been given, 25 as teaching and experience for eternal life.

C.43 - Human Spirits

1 As much as death be an inevitable part of life, 2 there be some who even in death refuse to die, 3 and allow their mind to release its connection, 4 to the remains of its physical form. 5 We call those minds who be unable or unwilling, 6 to transition to their natural place as a Divine Being, 7 a ghost or a spirit. 8 Verily, by its own ignorance, 9 a ghost is an isolated and bound soul (mind). 10 A Ghost is a Mind bound in negative thought, 11 to particular places, things, objects and people. 12 Thus the great tragedy of a being as a ghost, 13 is that such a mind continues to suffer in death, 14 and over time such continued suffering, 15 may even trap the most negative souls, 16 into losing any memory of self or name or reason. 17 Verily, the definition of a ghost, 18 is a mind that defies the natural order of the Divine. 19 It follows that such negative minds, 20 often seek to perpetuate negativity on the living, 21 especially by the implanting of false thoughts and ideas, 22 within the minds of men and women, 23 and points of weakness and distress. 24 Behold! no being has the right to intrude upon the mind of another. 25 Yet many a fragile man and woman, 26 have taken their own life prematurely, 27 upon the perverse suggestions of wicked ghosts and spirits. 28 Do not then fear such false thoughts that may appear in mind, 29 in moments of weakness and hardship, 30 for they be nothing more than the poisonous thorns, 31 of minds and souls that continue to suffer by their own ignorance. 32 Reject with all your might any suggestion, 33 that such thoughts of horror and depravity as may visit your mind, 34 be the product of some illness of your own mind. 35 In truth the difference can be known by the revulsion, 36 first experienced upon the appearance of such spirit intrusions, 37 and upon their insistence of presence at rejection. 38 Let then your heart be open as a blinding source of spiritual light, 39 and bind such ghosts who intrude upon your mind, 40 to the light and compassion of your heart. 41

Either such ghosts will escape as cowards from such light, 42 or be freed through your compassion to their natural state. 43 Thus never permit anyone to be wrongly directed to self harm, 44 or the harm of others upon the poisonous seeds of ghosts and spirits.

C.44 - Divine Judgement and Eternal Life

1 The Divine loves you. 2 No being including the Divine, 3 can take away your mind or essence or being. 4 You are and will always be a Divine Immortal Being. 5 Only your body dies. 6 Thus when you die you begin a new journey, 7 of experience and spiritual life. 8 You may choose and wish to be part of a spiritual community, 9 that gives you guidance and support, 10 yet none may condemn you. 11 Behold! Those sick and twisted priests and scribes, 12 who proclaim you shall be judged, 13 and that your mortal soul be in jeopardy, 14 unless you pledge absolute obedience to them, 15 declare themselves enemies of the Divine and all Heaven and Earth. 16 Let not such madness and evil deceive you. 17 You are Divine, 18 yet you are more, 19 because you are a Human Being.

Tara

Book 2
Eacturas (exodus)

C. 1 - Eacturas (exodus)

Whoever has ears, let them hear! 2 To thee, O Divine, Lord of all Creation, 3 the father and mother of our existence and story, 4 help our attention to comprehend these stories, 5 that we may put them in our hearts, 6 that they rest solidly as a settling in our guts, 7 to be a mooring-post for our tongues. 8 Let our journey through these stories, be a good omen for our present and future, 9 that such words be a storehouse for life, 10 of truths undiminished and undeniable. 11 Whether or not we face such darkness of the soul, 12 let us be not naked to Divine Wisdom, 13 so that even if at the greatest hour of peril we shall be neither ignorant nor alone. 14 Let not these stories be corrupted nor their principles lost, 15 so that from this generation to every generation, 16 the journey (exodus) may prepare us, guide us and assist us. So it is, so let it be.

C.2 - Genasis and the search for true knowledge

1 How can any soul truly know thyself, 2 if such a being knows nothing, 3 and cares to know nothing of the world or the Divine? 4 Thus every authentic and true journey of self, 5 begins not with inner reflection, 6 but with honest appraisal of the present world, 7 and the deeper nature and will of the Divine: 8 Of the immutable fact of Divine Existence, 9 that all life is a dream, 10 and a creation of the eternal dreamer; 11 Of Divine Creation, 12 and how existence comes to be; 13 Of Divine Will, Reason and Purpose, 14 and why every form of life has purpose to existence; 15 Of the laws of the Divine, 16 and the presence of such laws, 17 at every level of nature and life. 18 Behold! this be the gift of Genasis, 19 and the true meaning of the word Genasis, 20 and the purpose of Genasis, 21 as a means to start and seek, 22 and find true knowledge.

C.3 - Continuing the journey of knowledge

1 As beautiful as knowledge of the Divine be, 2 life in the form of flesh and blood, 3 be at times as cold and dark as the cruellest winter, 4 and at times as painful and unbearable as the worst fever, 5 and at times as overwhelming as the tempest of battle, 6 and at times as strange and uncertain as a drunken lamp holder, 7 and at times as blissful and timeless as the longest summer eve. 8 Verily, life itself seems to run its own course, 9 that neither follows nor aligns to the rule of heaven. 10 For it may appear the wicked are rewarded for their guile, 11 while the innocent be punished for their integrity, 12 as the stomach of the thieves are full, 13 while the honest people go starving. 14 Behold! this then be the purpose of Eacturas (exodus), 15 that we may journey, 16 and discover through story,

17 the common nature of life and its moral purpose.

C.4 - The Old Man and the Sticks

1 An old man near death summoned his sons, 2 for soon would be his last words. 3 Before they did come he commanded his head steward: 4 Bring me an axe and a bundle of sticks, 5 wrapped tightly by a leather strap. 6 When the eldest son appeared, the old man said to him: 7 Pick up the axe and with one strike break this bundle of sticks. 8 But with all his strength, he could not break the bundle of sticks. 9 The old man repeated the challenge to the rest of his sons, 10 and all failed to break the bundle of sticks with one clear blow. 11 The old man then commanded his steward to untie the bundle, 12 and hand each son a separate stick, 13 that they may seek to break it by their own strength. 14 So it was each son was given a stick, 15 and each son easily broke a stick with their own strength. 16 Thus, said the old man: 17 Even the weakest when united, 18 are unconquerable.

C.5 - The Stag and the Ox-Stall

1 A Stag ill prepared for winter, sought shelter in an Ox-stall. 2 Upon entering the wisest Ox did warn the Stag: 3 O unhappy creature! Why of your own accord do you condemn yourself? 4 For this be the house of your enemy. 5 The Stag did then reply: 6 Allow me, friend, this briefest of respite, 7 whereupon I shall make effect my escape. 8 Yet upon the morning, when the herdsman came to feed the cattle, 9 He did not see the Stag. 10 When he had left, the Stag thanked the Oxen and implored to spend one more night. 11 The wisest Ox did warn the Stag again: 12 O thoughtless creature! We wish you no harm, 13 Yet the gravest of danger is not yet passed. 14 Whereupon in the morning the farm bailiff and several workers did come, 15 Yet none noticed the Stag. 16 When they had left, the Stag boasted of his invisibility. 17 The wisest Ox did warn the Stag against his boast: 18 O reckless creature! One is still yet to pass through, 19 Who possesses as if a hundred eyes, 20 And until he has come and gone, your life remains in grave peril. 21 At that moment the master of the house himself entered the stall, 22 and upon seeing the condition of the oxen did complain: 23 Why is there such a scarcity of fodder? 24 Why is there not half enough straw for them to lie on? 25 While he thus examined everything in turn, 26 he spied the tips of the antlers of the Stag peeping out of the straw. 27 Then summoning his labourers, 28 He ordered that the Stag should be seized and killed. 29 Upon his last mortal breath, the Stag did bemoan: 30 Woe is me that I be the architect of my doom. 31 For I sought refuge in the house of my enemy, 32 And yet did ignore three forewarnings as to my peril.

C.6 - Luki and the Axe man

1 An Axe man was felling wood by the side of a deep river, 2 when his axe slipped from his hands and flew into the waters. 3 Deprived of his means of livelihood, 4 the man sat down by the river bank and lamented his ill fortune. 5 Luki then appeared and demanded to know the cause of his

Book 2 Eacturas (exodus)

lament. 6 Upon which the man repeated the tale of his misfortune. 7 At that moment Luki plunged into the river, 8 then returned holding a golden axe. 9 He asked the man if this is the source of his ill fortune? 10 The man replied, that although a thing of beauty and value, 11 it is not rightfully mine to keep. 12 Luki then plunged again into the river and then produced a Silver Axe. 13 Again the man replied it was not his to use. 14 Finally, Luki plunged and returned from the river with an iron axe. 15 The man then exclaimed to Luki that this was indeed his to use, 16 and that his fortune be restored. 17 To which Luki replied: 18 Good and honest sir, though your body shall weaken and decay, 19 and you shall have days of sickness and grief, 20 your life shall be all the richer for peace and joy, 21 for you value all that you have been entrusted, 22 and do not covet that which does not belong to you.

C.7 - The Ant and the Caterpillar

1 An ant in search of food, did come across a caterpillar, 2 as it gathered stick and leaves for its cocoon. 3 The ant did mock the caterpillar: 4 Poor creature what life is this? 5 While I spend my time running where I please, 6 You are condemned to spend your life making your coffin. 7 A few days passed and the ant did pass now the chrysalis. 8 As he moved closer he saw it moved and he did mock it again: 9 Poor creature what life is this? 10 While I enjoy the sun and the rain, 11 You are condemned to spend an eternity neither dead nor alive. 12 And when the ant passed by for the third time, 13 he found nothing but the remains of the shell. 14 Yet before he could speak, 15 He was covered by the shadow of a beautiful creature flapping its wings. 16 The ant cried out in fear: 17 Oh wondrous and radiant beauty, do not harm me, 18 For I am but a lowly ant. 19 The butterfly then replied: 20 Poor creature what life is this? 21 Behold, to become what I now am, 22 I did sacrifice what you choose to be.

C.8 - The Slave Boy and the Lion

1 A young slave once escaped from his wicked master and sought refuge in the forest. 2 Without the adequate means of survival, the boy grew weaker and hungrier. 3 Whereupon in a clearing he discovered a lion in great distress and pain. 4 At first the boy sought to flee, but finding the lion did not pursue him, 5 He returned to the lion and as he neared him the lion raised its paw. 6 In its paw, the boy saw a huge thorn, swollen and bleeding. 7 The boy removed the thorn from the paw of the lion and attended the infection. 8 Yet without food and water, the boy himself had grown so weak. 9 Instead of devouring the weak runaway slave, the lion dragged the boy to his den. 10 Whereupon he brought him the meat of animals it slew in the forest, 11 Until the boy himself was stronger. 12 Soon after the lion itself was captured, followed by the boy. 13 Upon hearing of the trials and ordeal of the boy, the king considered clemency, 14 But the wicked master of the boy demanded the king put the boy to death as according to law. 15 So after several

days in prison, the boy was placed in an arena in front of the whole city, 16 Soon a hungry lion was set loose to devour the boy in front of the king and the city. 17 Yet when the lion saw the boy it stopped and seeing him in great distress, licked his hands. 18 When the king saw this spectacle he immediately ordered the boy and lion freed, 19 and the wicked master be put to chains. 20 The king did say: Behold! As the Divine Gods ordain, let no man dishonour. 21 For this boy has already been judged by them and found to be without blemish. 22 Thus it is the one who falsely accused that must be held account.

C.9 - The Ant and the Grasshopper

1 A Grasshopper one day passed a line of Ants, 2 as they carried supplies of food to their nest. 3 The Grasshopper said to the Ant at the head of the line: 4 It is a beautiful day. There is plenty of food. 5 Why then do you toil when instead you could play and sing as I? 6 The Ant replied: Dear Sir, while Indeed it be a fine day and they're be plenty of food, 7 We prepare for the worst so that when the harshest winter comes, we do not die of hunger. 8 The Grasshopper replied: You silly Ant. Life will provide for us without our worry. 9 If you do not enjoy such moments, then you will have none. 10 But soon a harsh and bitter winter was upon the land, 11 And the Grasshopper near death came upon an Ant guarding the nest and cried: 12 Please sir, have pity on a poor Grasshopper with nothing to eat. 13 The Ant replied: Alas you poor selfish fool! When it was time to prepare, you mocked us. 14 Now in your time of need you demand we sacrifice our own survival. 15 Be gone! For there is no benefit in helping a selfish spirit that has no desire to first help themselves.

C.10 - The Master and the Talents

1 A wealthy master planning to take a great journey, 2 Did first entrust a great fortune to his most trusted servants. 3 Upon his return after a long absence, 4 The man called his servants for an accounting: 5 The first did account: My Lord, you entrusted me with the wealth of one talent, 6 Whereupon I did work day and night and have produced one more in value. 7 The master then said: Well done, good and faithful servant. 8 You were entrusted with only a few things, but have proven you can and shall be entrusted with much more. 9 The second did account: My Lord, you entrusted me with two talents, 10 Whereupon I did use my skill and effort and produced three more. 11 The master then said: Well done, wise and gifted servant. 12 You were entrusted with more and yet have proven you can and shall be entrusted with all the riches of this house. 13 The third did then account: My Lord, you entrusted me with five talents, 14 Yet I was afraid of what might be lost and did fear your retribution and so did hide such talents in the earth until your return that they might not be lost. 15 But the master answered him: You ungrateful and selfish servant. 16 Of all my most entrusted servants I gave you the most, and yet you did the least. 17 I did not seek profit nor demand great hardship from you, 18 Only that you

Book 2 Eacturas (exodus)

honour and use that which I entrusted to you. 19 Pity the man then who is given so much yet does so little to better the world. 20 For better if he never had been borne than to suffer the ages of torment and infamy, 21 Of being known as one who wasted so much of that which was entrusted to him.

C.11 - The Fowl and the Eagle

1 Two male Fowl were engaged in a fierce fight for mastery of the hens of a marsh. 2 One at last put the other to flight and the vanquished retreated, 3 while the victor moved to the highest point and called out in his loudest voice: 4 Now truly, I am the victor of all! 5 Just then an Eagle sailing through the air spotted the exposed Fowl, 6 And swooped in to snatch him away. 7 As the mortally wounded fowl was carried away within the talons of the Eagle he cried: 8 Woe is me. For my pride destroyed me, 9 While my vanquished foe shall now rule in undisputed mastery.

C.12 - The Shepherd Boy

1 A young shepherd boy tending the village sheep alone, 2 did wish for an easier burden, 3 when at the foot of a mountain near a dark forest, 4 he did strike upon a plan. 5 He rushed down towards the village crying: 6 Wolf! Wolf! 7 The villagers armed themselves, 8 and rushed forward to greet the boy, 9 yet no wolf was to be found. 10 This pleased the boy so much, 11 that a few days after he repeated the same trick, 12 and again the villagers rushed to protect the boy and the flock. 13 Yet the villagers had grown wary of the young boy, 14 so when a wolf did appear from the forest and menace the sheep, 15 the boy cried Wolf! Wolf! in earnest, 16 and no one stirred or did come to his rescue. 17 Thus said the village elder: 18 A liar may not be believed, even when he may speak the truth.

C.13 - The Bee and Bel

1 The first Queen Bee ascended to present Bel some honey. 2 The God was so delighted with the offering, 3 He promised to grant whatever wish she should ask. 4 She therefore besought him, saying: Give me, I pray thee, a sting, 5 That if any mortal shall approach to take my honey, I may kill him. 6 Bel was much displeased, for he loved the race of men, 7 Yet could not refuse the granting of the request because of his promise. 8 He thus answered the Bee: You shall have your request, 9 But it will be at the peril of your own life. 10 For if you use your sting, it shall remain in the wound you make, 11 And then you will die from the loss of it.

C.14 - The Priest and the sick Novice

1 A pious and knowledgeable priest did accept a new novice and did begin training him. 2 One day after many months of education, the priest saw that the young novice appeared very sick. 3 Believing the novice would not live long, and fearing a negative effect to his reputation, 4 the priest released his novice and sent him away. 5 Some years later, when the priest himself was very ill, 6 his former novice did visit him and was strong and full of vitality. 7 The priest did implore him

to account every detail of his journey, so that he might understand the secret of his health. 8 The former student did speak of his travels over great mountains and across deep valleys, 9 and the meeting of many different people of foreign lands and places, 10 and how when he visited a new town he would look to find a way to help, 11 and support those who were suffering and without enough food or shelter. 12 The dying priest did then shout: aha I now see! You were allowed to live longer than I predicted, 13 Because the gods lengthened your days as a reward for your good works. 14 Yet the former student disagreed and said: My dear old master, 15 I did not become healthy because of some new gift from heaven, 16 I am healthy because I remembered to respect the greatest gift of life already granted to me.

C.15 - The Flies, the Ants and the Honey-Pot

1 A house keeper too hasty in her work, did cause a jar of honey to break. 2 But instead of cleaning it up, she did conceal her error behind other unbroken jars. 3 Some Flies and Ants did observe the honey, yet the Ants remained at some distance. 4 The Flies then mocked the Ants thus: Poor Ants! The broken jar is concealed, 5 and it shall be some time before the cook returns to prepare supper. 6 Yet the Ants did reply: Let fools rush in! For we await not for fear or hesitation, 7 But until the honey is hard enough to be safe. 8 The Flies ignored the Ants and did land and gorge themselves upon the honey. 9 So that their feet and wings became so smeared with it, they could not release themselves. 10 Before the last Fly did expire, he cried out: For the sake of indulging our foolish desires, 11 We have destroyed ourselves.

C.16 - The Good Soldier

1 A good soldier was ordered back into the field after a victorious battle, 2 to dispatch any dying enemy and collect up their valuable possessions. 3 But as he moved forward he found a wounded enemy who implored him, 4 that he be spared, for he be a widower and his only son would be impoverished. 5 The young soldier said he could not grant him his plea without disobeying his orders, 6 so the injured soldier implored that he promise upon the mercy of the Gods not to seize his valuables, 7 but get them to his son, so he could avoid being sold into slavery. 8 Respecting the gods, the soldier did promise and soon after did take the dangerous journey to the city of his enemy, 9 and did find the boy and did make arrangements so that he not be sold into slavery, 10 and every year did send money so that the boy be educated until he was old enough. 11 Some years later, the same soldier was captured by his enemy after a terrible defeat. 12 Before the prisoners were to be executed, the general demanded to see their faces. 13 But when he came to this old and bloodied soldier, he wept and knelt down, giving him water and food, saying: 14 Behold!, here is my enemy, who respected me, who did not mistreat me, but gave me shelter and fed me. 15 Harsh be the penalty of any soldier who disobeys an order, 16 Yet woe any man who disobeys heaven. 17 If justice be blind, then I

shall gladly take his place, else release this man and tend his wounds, lest we offend the gods themselves. 18 With that, the soldier was released and the general tended his wounds until he was healthy enough to return to his city.

C.17 - The Birdcatcher, the Partridge, and the Rooster

1 A poor Birdcatcher about to sit down to a dinner of herbs, 2 Was alerted by his dogs to the arrival of a stranger to his home. 3 The stranger did call out to the Birdcatcher: 4 Kind sir, I entreat that you may give me food and shelter till the morning. 5 The Birdcatcher welcomed the stranger in as was good custom. 6 Yet as he had caught no bird or fowl for some days, 7 And had nothing to offer the stranger for dinner, 8 He prepared to kill his prize partridge. 9 But before any mortal blow was struck, the bird spoke earnestly for its life, saying: 10 Master, what would you do when next you spread your nets? 11 Who would chirp you to sleep, or call for you the covey of answering birds? 12 The Birdcatcher agreed and returned the Partridge to its cage and then went outside to fetch the Rooster. 13 The Rooster protested intensely: If you kill me, who will announce to you the appearance of the dawn? 14 Who will wake you to your daily tasks or tell you when it is time to visit the bird-traps? 15 The Birdcatcher replied thus: It is true, you are a fine bird at reminding me my obligations. 16 Yet circumstances demand I make a choice. And now I must choose to fulfil custom, 17 And to honour your memory by remembering my duties.

C.18 - The Goose With the Golden Eggs

1 A Poor farmer cried out to Luki: Oh God of Good Fortune, 2 Grant me this day reprieve from my ills, 3 For I have been a good and honourable servant. 4 In the morning the farmer came to the nest of his Goose, 5 Only to find it had laid a Golden Egg. 6 Overjoyed, he thanked Luki for his good fortune and went to the town and paid his debts. 7 Twenty-eight days later, the farmer found another Golden Egg. 8 This time he seized the egg and took it to the local King. 9 Whereupon he gave the gold egg to the King saying: Your Majesty, a gift to you, 10 in exchange for your patronage, for I seek to purchase substantial lands. 11 The king replied: Fine sir, I give gratitude for your gift, 12 And indeed if such wealth was produced for ten cycles of the moon, 13 then such lands you shall have and I shall make you a Baron and then to your heirs and successors. 14 But caution to you, for upon such claim you be bound to fulfil, or your head is mine. 15 The farmer did then say: Your majesty, I need not ten cycles to fulfil, 16 As I shall return with haste. 17 Whereupon the farmer returned home and killed the goose, only to find nothing inside.

C.19 - The Wicked Lord

1 There was a great King who sought harmony across his kingdom, 2 And that there was law and order and all debts were paid. 3 So he called each of his Lords to account of their affairs. 4 One Lord was brought before the great King owing one thousand talents. 5 But because he couldn't pay, the King

commanded him to be sold, 6 With his wife, his children, and all that he had, and payment to be made. 7 The Lord then fell down and knelt before the King and said: Oh wise and benevolent King, 8 Pity your humble servant and have patience with me, for while it shall ruin me and my people, 9 Better I die trying to repay what I owe, than to bring dishonour to my lands. 10 The King upon hearing the great hardship that was to befall his Lord, did decree: 11 Upon this day and henceforth, as I now forgive my servants debts, 12 So shall all long term debts be forgiven, 13 That no man be required to die in debt and dishonour. 14 The Lord having his own debts forgiven returned to his lands, 15 Yet did not enact the laws of the King. 16 Instead, he forced upon his own servants a terrible toil and misery to pay their debts, 17 And destroyed homes and imprisoned even children for failure to repay debts. 18 When the Great King heard these terrible acts, 19 He had the Lord seized and brought before him in chains, saying thus: 20 Oh wicked and vile servant! By Divine Decree, I demanded that all debts be forgiven, 21 That as you so prayed to be forgiven, so even the poorest be forgiven their debts. 22 Yet in your arrogance you forgot both my power and my laws. 23 Henceforth, any Lord who fails to honour Divine Law is a tyrant, 24 And any lender who fails to forgive long term debtors is a thief. 25 And it be the sacred obligation upon every able bodied man, 26 That such vermin as these tyrants and thieves be extinguished from the earth.

C.20 - The Hare and the Tortoise

1 A Hare did come by a Tortoise on its travels, 2 And ridiculed the Tortoise for is slow and steady pace. 3 In reply the Tortoise said: 4 Though you be swift as the wind, I would surely beat you if the test be substantial. 5 Upon hearing the challenge, the Hare accepted, 6 And called upon a nearby Crane to set the course and be judge. 7 On the day appointed for the race the two started together. 8 The Tortoise never stopped for a moment, 9 But went on with a slow but steady pace straight towards the end of the course. 10 The Hare, assured of her victory chose instead to prepare herself a meal and then take a nap. 11 Yet instead of waking up with plenty of time, she overslept. 12 As fast as she could run, the Hare could not beat the Tortoise who reached the goal ahead of her. 13 As the Hare reached the Tortoise, the Tortoise did say: 14 My words are proven to be truth, 15 For persistence triumphs talent.

C.21 - The Thief and His Mother

1 A Boy one day did steal some apples from an orchard and took them home to his Mother. 2 Both hungry and with little means, the Mother did not ask how the Boy acquired his good fortune. 3 Instead, she praised him for his providence. 4 Some years later and upon a bitterly cold winter, the Boy now a Youth did steal a fine cloak. 5 And did bring it to his Mother. 6 Again, she failed to ask how her son did obtain such a valuable garment, 7 Instead commending him for his resourcefulness. 8 Some years passed

again and upon a time of great hardship, 9 The Youth now a Man was caught stealing the valuable grain provisions of the town. 10 Upon the Man being led to his execution, his Mother burst forth and begged to take his place, saying: 11 As the Gods be my witnesses, it is I, not my son who has transgressed. 12 For when he needed to learn the price of right and wrong, I abandoned him. 13 And when he needed to be punished, I spared the rod and instead gave praise. 14 Kill me now, for his unjust death seals my own fate.

C.22 - The Farmer and the Stork

1 A Farmer one day placed nets across some of his newly sown ploughlands, 2 To catch a flock of Cranes which had made a habit of stealing his seeds. 3 With them he trapped a Stork that fractured his leg in the net. 4 As the Farmer came near, the bird earnestly beseeched him and said: 5 Pray save me Master and let me free. My broken limb is pity enough. 6 Besides, I am no Crane, I am a Stork, a bird of excellent character. 7 To which the Farmer replied thus: Your words of self reference may be true as you say. 8 Yet all I know for certain is that I have taken you in the company with these robbers, the Cranes. 9 Alas therefore, it is in keeping such company you doom yourself.

C.23 - The Wealthy Merchant and the Painted Lion

1 A Wealthy Merchant, whose only son was fond of hunting, had a fearful dream, 2 In which he envisaged his son would be killed terribly by a lion. 3 Fearful the dream be an omen, he forbid his son any further adventures. 4 Instead, he built him a beautiful high walled garden, 5 Full of great life sized sculptures of animals and murals including a painting of a lion. 6 One day in front of the painted lion in a fit of frustration, 7 The son did speak: O you most detestable of animals! 8 Upon your account within the false visions of my father, 9 I am condemned to this palace as if a virgin princess. 10 With these words he stretched out his hands toward a thorn-tree, 11 Meaning to cut a stick from its branches so that he might deface the image. 12 But one of the tree's prickles pierced his finger and caused great pain and inflammation, 13 So that within a few days the son died from a violent and terrible fever. 14 Upon returning from business the Wealthy Merchant grieved: 15 Curse thee fear and cowardice, for you did conspire to manifest the very destiny I sought to delay. 16 Better then my son had died in honour, than a prisoner of my own making.

C.24 - The Mice and the Moths

1 The Mice of a field believed themselves so persecuted, 2 That at the approach of any large Beast they did run away in fear and hide. 3 One day, upon the arrival of some horses, the Mice were so distressed, 4 They ran off to the edge of a nearby lake to end their lives by drowning. 5 But upon reaching the lake, 6 The Mice witnessed Moth after Moth falling from the sky onto the lake, 7 Only to

be eaten by fish and bird alike. 8 The Mice then said to one another: Truly, our lives are not so bad as it seems.

C.25 - The Young Maiden

1 A young maiden, who longed to be with a handsome young man, did cry out to Ana, saying: 2 Oh goddess of love, beauty and prosperity, make me the most beautiful maiden in all the land, 3 So that I may win the heart of the one whom I love. 4 Whereupon Ana appeared to the maiden and said: 5 If it be beauty above all else is your desire, then only when you have transformed everything about yourself, 6 shall you see the fruits of your desire. 7 So the maiden set upon changing her clothes so they be the most beautiful, 8 And changed the colour of her hair and bathed her skin so she would appear more beautiful, 9 And refrained from food and activities that would damage her appearance, 10 Whereupon the young man did see her and the maiden called out, 11 Am I not the most beautiful girl you have seen in the land? 12 The handsome young man did reply: Yes, it is true, that when I first set eyes upon you some time ago, you were indeed the most beautiful maiden I had ever seen. 13 Yet I fear I no longer feel such feelings, for something has died since first seeing you. 14 Verily, on the outside you are indeed beautiful, like a statue, 15 But I seek a life of happiness with someone who is willing to grow old with me.

C.26 - The Bat, the Birds and the Beasts

1 A great conflict did emerge in the forest between the Birds and the Beasts. 2 As the two armies began to form, the Bat hesitated which to join, 3 For he did not wish to be associated with the side that may be defeated. 4 The Birds that passed him said: Come with us. 5 Yet the Bat did reply: Thank you kind Birds. Indeed, I can fly. 6 Yet I fear the Beasts have greater strength. Alas! I am a Beast. 7 Later, some Beasts who did pass underneath the Bat did call out: Come with us. 8 Yet the Bat did reply: Thank you kind Beasts. Indeed, I am an animal. 9 Yet I fear the Birds are greater in number. Alas! I am a Bird. 10 As it so happened, war was averted so no battle took place. 11 The Bat then came to the Birds and wished to join in the rejoicings, 12 But the Birds turned against him and he had to fly away. 13 He then went to the Beasts, 14 But soon had to beat a retreat, or else they would have torn him to pieces. 15 Upon his exile, the Bat did say: I see now the folly of my ways. 16 He that stands for neither one thing nor the other has no friends.

C.27 - The Scholars and the Boatman

1 Three learned scholars once sought to visit an ancient island observatory in order to calculate a rare celestial event. 2 Upon their journey across the waters, the scholars engaged in animated discussion as to their respective knowledge. 3 One of the scholars noticed that as they spoke, the boatman was listening. 4 The first scholar asked the boatman: What say you then to our discourse? 5 The Boatman then replied: I have nothing to offer you sir, for I did not comprehend any of it. 6 The second

Book 2 Eacturas (exodus)

scholar did then ask: Pray, tell us your education if you do object to our arguments? 7 The Boatman replied in protest: I do not seek to offend you wise men, I am a mere boatman, 8 And am without learning. For while I can read and write I have never before heard of the things you three speak. 9 The third scholar did speak mockingly: Alas poor boatman! This is the price of a poor education. 10 For while you may read and write, you know little of the universe and have wasted your life. 11 Suddenly a great wave did wash over the boat and all were thrown overboard. 12 The scholars cried out to the boatman: Help us boatman! For we cannot swim! 13 As the boatman began to swim to shore, he called out to the drowning scholars thus: 14 I leave you not through callous intent, but not to waste my life as you have yours. 15 For if one of you could take me under as a desperate drowning man, yet three surely would.

C.28 - The Wild Boar and the Fox

1 A Wild Boar stood under a tree and rubbed his tusks against the trunk. 2 A Fox passing by asked him why he thus sharpened his teeth, 3 When there was no danger threatening from either hunter or hound. 4 The Wild Boar replied thus: I do it as our ancestors have taught. 5 For it be too late to sharpen my weapons just at the time I ought to be using them.

C.29 - The Three Stone Masons

1 Three Stone Masons were busily at work on the foundations of a new structure, 2 When a passing traveller inquired what was the task at hand? 3 The first Stone Mason responded harshly: Do not torment me with such inquiry. 4 For clearly I am condemned to this task of cutting stone. 5 The second Stone Mason was more collegiate and said: Pray forgive my companion, 6 For we build the foundations to a small temple. 7 The third Stone Mason was even more resolute and said thus: We be not condemned to such labour, 8 But blessed to witness a miracle. For by will and flesh and stone alone, 9 We build a most beautiful temple that will glorify Heaven long after our death and for centuries to come.

C.30 - The Elephant and the Tick

1 An Elephant very much tormented by a Tick caught him at last in his trunk. 2 He decried: Who are you who dare to feed on my blood, 3 And cause me so much pain in my shoulders and limbs? 4 The Tick did reply: O dear sir, I pray you spare my life and destroy me not, 5 For you are so huge and I am such a small and insignificant creature. 6 The Elephant replied as thus: Now you shall certainly die by my mighty step. 7 For I did not grant you my blood and yet you took it without consent. 8 And Behold! No evil, whether it be small or large, ought to be tolerated.

C.31 - The Birds and the Swallow

1 A Swallow was busily removing seeds from a field when some passing Birds observed him and said: 2 Fair Swallow, why do you move too and fro? There is

plenty of seed in this field for all of us. 3 The Swallow did reply: Good Birds, be not for food but the prevention, I remove and eat these seeds. 4 For the Farmer is sowing hemp and without your aid, it will be at your peril. 5 The Birds replied: We thank you kind sir for alerting us. As we prefer the sweeter tastes of barley, 6 Than to feast on such bitter seeds. 7 With that, the Birds flew away, leaving the Swallow to continue its work. 8 So it was that much of the hemp seed remained and grew and was harvested, 9 And strong rope and netting was made from its stalks. 10 And come the following season, the farmer trapped many of the Birds that had ignored the Swallow. 11 To the trapped birds, the Swallow said thus: Alas foolish Birds, what did I tell you? 12 Destroy the seed of evil, or it will grow up to be your ruin.

C.32 - The Four Oxen and the Crocodile

1 A Crocodile used to lurk about the waterways near a field in which four Oxen did dwell. 2 Many a time he did try to attack them, 3 But whenever he came near, they turned their tails to one another, 4 So that whichever way he approached them he was met by the horns of one of them. 5 One day, the Crocodile came upon a plan. 6 The Crocodile did say to the Oxen: 7 Honourable foe, your strategy to defeat me is most deserving. 8 Pray tell me, which one of you is more deserving of praise for such a plan? 9 Whereupon the Oxen fell into a quarrel amongst themselves, 10 As to whom was more deserving. 11 Soon quarrelling turned to blows as the four Oxen fought amongst themselves. 12 Finally, when all four Oxen had finished quarrelling and fighting one another, 13 The Crocodile snatched each one and made an end to all four. 14 As the final Oxen was within the jaws of the Crocodile he cried out: 15 Alas! Even Pride and Arrogance may destroy even the safest of lands.

C.33 - The Goat Herder and the Wild Goats

1 A Goat herder driving his flock from its pasture at eventide, 2 Discovered some Wild Goats had also mingled among them. 3 So he shut them up together with his own for the night. 4 The next day an early winter storm came with wind and snow, 5 That the Goat herder was obliged to keep them in the fold. 6 He gave his own goats just sufficient food to keep them alive, 7 But fed the strangers more abundantly in the hope of enticing them to stay. 8 When the thaw set in, he led them all out to feed, 9 Yet the wild Goats quickly started to scamper away. 10 The Goat herder called out in anger: 11 Ungrateful Goats! I did take you in and keep you warm. 12 I did give you food even at the expense of the health of my own Goats. 13 One of the wild Goats did turn around and reply: 14 Oh selfish Goat herder, you admit to your own faults, yet do not see them. 15 For yesterday you treated wild Goats better than your own. 16 Thus it is plain if others came, you would in the same manner prefer them to ourselves. 17 That is why we depart your company.

C.34 - The Eagle and the Wolf

1 An Eagle and a Wolf did form a truce that they may live in peace. 2 The Eagle built her nest in the branches of the tallest tree, 3 While the Wolf did find an ample lair by a beautiful stream. 4 Then one day a great drought and famine came to the lands. 5 The Wolf said to Eagle: To provide for my young ones, I must travel far. 6 Whilst I am gone, I entreat you keep watch over my young ones. 7 The Eagle agreed. 8 Yet no sooner had the Wolf departed than the hungry Eagle swooped and snatched a cub. 9 Thus she and her hungry young ones were fed that day. 10 The Wolf upon return was enraged and cried out to the Eagle: 11 I grieve not least for the one unjustly slain, but all shall now die upon your treachery. 12 For your act of perfidy dooms not one generation, but many yet to come in perpetual feud. 13 Wherever the Eagle sought to hunt, the Wolf did disrupt or snatch the prey. 14 Until one day the Eagle spotted a village sacrificing a goat upon an altar. 15 She swooped down and tore some flesh and sticks with her talons, 16 Carrying them back to her nest. 17 But upon arrival, the sticks still smouldering set the nest alight, 18 And her young ones were roasted dead, 19 With the nest and their bodies falling from the tree. 20 There, in the sight of the Eagle, the Wolf and her young gobbled them up. 21 The Eagle in her woe called out: 22 What have I done? 23 By one act of desperation, I have condemned so many to Pyrrhic retribution.

C.35 - The Farmer and the Fox

1 A Farmer who bore a grudge against a Fox for stealing his poultry succeeded in his capture. 2 Upon his fate, the Fox did say: 3 Fair thee Farmer, for I be the one culpable and you be my swift executioner. 4 Yet the Farmer did not seek to simply kill the Fox but to exact revenge by burning him alive. 5 The Farmer tied a rope covered in oil around the tail of the Fox and set it alight. 6 The Fox upon seeing the intention of his fate did cry out: 7 Oh cruel Farmer! There be no justice in such torment and fate shall surely be my judge. 8 Thereupon the Fox leapt past the Farmer and rushed into the barn, setting it alight, 9 then rushing into the house setting the house alight and finally to his end in the fields that the Fox also set ablaze. 10 Upon the destruction of his barn, his home and his livelihood, the Farmer cried out: 11 Upon one unjust act of cruelty, I have destroyed my kingdom. 12 It would have been better never to have judged at all, than to have broken the laws of the Divine.

C.36 - The Lion and the Mouse

1 A Lion was once asleep when a little Mouse chasing a moth did run up and down upon him. 2 The scurrying on his fur awoke the Lion, 3 Who then trapped the offending Mouse by its tail with one of his paws. 4 Just before the Lion was about to devour the Mouse, it did plead: 5 Pardon me Oh King. For I, such a little mouse, did awake and offend thee. 6 Forgive me this day, and I pledge my word I shall some day return the favour. 7 Upon such a boastful and eloquent plea, the Lion did reply: 8 You speak well Mouse,

though I cannot foresee a time when you could possibly fulfil your oath. 9 Go on your way and for the sake of a long life, do not go aggravating any more beasts. 10 The Lion lifted his paw and the Mouse hurried away. 11 Some time later, the Lion was caught by hunters who brought him to the city of a cruel King, 12 Who did enjoy creating the false spectacle before an audience of himself as a great hunter defeating wild beasts. 13 Within the dungeons, the same little Mouse which the Lion had previously spared did pass by. 14 At seeing the Lion, the Mouse did remind him of his solemn oath and proceeded to seek a way for his release. 15 The Lion in response did say: Save your strength little Mouse, for my fate is sealed. There be nothing even an elephant could do for me. 16 Upon these words, the Mouse hatched an idea. 17 He spoke to the other animals who were also imprisoned as to his oath that he would repay his honour debt to the Lion. 18 So it was the elephant that used its trunk to steal the keys; 19 The monkeys that used the keys to release the beasts and the Lion; 20 The horses that protested to the soldiers they were lame; 21 And the rats and mice that gnawed the ropes to the gates so that none of the Kings guards could escape after them. 22 At the edge of the forest, the Lion bid farewell to the Mouse that saved him and said thus: 23 Above all, you have proven that when even the smallest and weakest have honour, wit and courage, 24 They can defeat even the greatest of enemies.

C.37 - The Axeman and Grove

1 A great Axeman went in search of a new branch from which to handle his new Axe head. 2 First he came to a grove of Ash and did say: Oh wondrous and mysterious Ash! 3 Grant me a limb from which I may fashion a new handle for my new Axe? 4 The Ash did reply and said: We give no consent unto thee to cut or tear our limbs. 5 Besides, if you desire a timber worthy of your Axe then best it be the Oak. 6 The Axeman did honour the word of the Ash and did not retrieve any branch or limb. 7 Upon coming upon a grove of Oak, the Axeman did say: Oh ancient and fine Oak! 8 They say you are the finest wood from which to fashion a handle worthy of my Axe. 9 The Oak did reply: We respect your words but fear your intent Axeman. 10 Begone! For we do not give you consent to touch our branches or limbs. 11 Besides, if it is the finest wood you seek, then it must be Rosewood. 12 Finally, the Axeman came upon an ancient Grove of Rosewood and did say: 13 Oh mighty Rosewood! Above you there is none. Grant this humble servant but one limb? 14 The Rosewood replied: Truly you have spoken. We are without peer. 15 Thus we grant you this piece and limb you seek. 16 Whereupon the Axeman had it fashioned into the finest handle. 17 A few days later he returned to the grove and levelled the Rosewood. 18 As the final tree was about to fall, he cried out thus: It is a double grief to me, 19 That I should perish not only for my arrogance, but from a weapon fashioned from my own form.

C.38 - The Fox and the Leopard

1 The Fox and the Leopard found themselves in dispute, 2 As which of them was the more beautiful of the two. 3 The Leopard did declare: By the hand of the most beautiful of Gods, 4 It is I who carries the marks of greatness upon my skin. 5 The Fox replied: Indeed Leopard, how much more beautiful are you than I, 6 Whom the Gods chose to decorate not in body, but mind.

C.39 - The North Wind, the Sun and the Seafarer

1 The Spirits of the North Wind and the Sun were in dispute as to which was the most powerful force on man. 2 The Spirit of the North Wind did declare: Upon my might, I have smashed a thousand ships upon the rocks, 3 And laid waste to whole lands and stock. 4 Thus the spirit of the Sun proposed a test and said: Fair wind of the North, let us resolve our dispute, 5 Without the demise of a single man. Instead I propose a single test. 6 Let us find a Seafarer and see who can strip him of his cloak. 7 They agreed and so found a single Seafarer on his vessel. 8 The North Wind agreed and went first by blowing with all his might upon a Seafarer and his boat. 9 But the keener his blasts, the closer the Seafarer wrapped his cloak around him. 10 Until at last, resigning all hope of victory, the Wind called upon the Sun to see what he could do. 11 The Sun then shone out with all his warmth. 12 The Seafarer no sooner felt his genial rays than he took off his cloak. 13 To the Spirit of the Wind of the North, the Sun said thus: Indeed fair wind, my powers are strong and when unchecked can cause great hardship. 14 Yet persuasion is always better than force.

C.40 - The Prodigal Son

1 A Wealthy Landowner had several beloved Sons and Daughters whom he raised in privilege and duty. 2 Yet the eldest of the Sons and Daughters yearned for adventure and to enjoy wealth without work. 3 He confronted his Father and said: Father, if you truly loved me, you would set me free from my obligations, 4 That I might choose my own path to use my birthright by my own will, rather than according to your guardianship. 5 Upon hearing the entreat of his eldest Son, the Father agreed and granted him his fair share. 6 Soon after the eldest Son departed with his fortune to distant lands, 7 Whereupon he quickly squandered his wealth with extravagant and immoral living. 8 After the Son had spent everything, there was a severe famine. 9 Destitute and in need of food, the Son approached a local publican with whom he had spent much money and said: 10 Robust friend, in times of merriment you did seek my company. Pray you grant me food and lodging in my hour of need. 11 Yet the local publican refused, saying: A Fool and his money are soon parted. Farewell thee fool. 12 The eldest Son then approached a local temple and the head priest and entreated him: 13 Noble Spirit, while I lived an extravagant and immoral life, I did frequent this fine temple and help in its upkeep. 14 Surely as a man of benevolence, you could extend the

hand of charity and provide me some little food? 15 Yet the local priest refused, saying: As much as your gifts are a grateful reward, 16 If I were to show such charity, I fear in these times, we too would be destitute before long. 17 The eldest Son in great distress wept upon the street before a local merchant, known for his cruelty, did see him and said: 18 I shall grant you lodging and meals, if you swear on all that is sacred you shall do your duties that I set for you. 19 The eldest Son in desperation agreed and soon found himself sleeping with the pigs and ensuring their keep. 20 He longed to fill his stomach with the grains that the pigs did eat, but was only permitted the scraps. 21 Many days passed until the eldest Son, weak with hunger did cry out: 22 Alas oh Spirits!, it has come to this. For no good reason do I see that my earthly form should bear witness to another morn. 23 Suddenly a vision of his previous life and his father appeared, to which the eldest Son did say: 24 Oh Terrible torments and ghosts of past! I now see the error of my ways. Better to be a servant in the house of my Father, than the slave of a merchant. 25 So he got up and returned to his homeland and to the House of his Father. 26 But while he was still a long way off, his Father saw him and ran to him and then kissed him. 27 Before the Son could speak, the Father ordered his servants thus: Take him to be bathed and put upon him the finest robes and sandals. 28 The Father then ordered a fattened calf be slaughtered and a great feast prepared. 29 Yet the Son returned not in the finest of robes but in the simple cloth of a servant and threw himself down before his Father: 30 Forgive me Father for I have transgressed against Heaven, against the Gods and against your name. 31 I am no longer worthy to be called your Son. Instead make me a servant in your home and I will honour my duties. 32 The Father embraced him and said thus: My Son, I shall never abandon you, nor ever forsake you. Yet Character is nothing if not tested. 33 For we celebrate then with this feast your death and rebirth, your loss and your return.

C.41 - The Wolf and the Lamb

1 A Wolf finding a Lamb astray upon a path, resolved not to lay violent hands on him, 2 But to find some plea to justify to the Lamb the Wolf's right to eat him. 3 He thus addressed him: Sir, in the year past you grossly insulted me. 4 The Lamb replied: You are mistaken honourable Wolf, as I was not then borne. 5 Frustrated, the Wolf then said: You trespass and feed in my pasture. 6 The Lamb replied: You are mistaken mighty Wolf, as I have not yet tasted grass. 7 Angry the Wolf then said: Then you steal and drink of my well. 8 The Lamb replied: Alas! fearsome Wolf you are in error, but for my mothers' milk, as yet I have never yet drunk water. 9 The Wolf seized the Lamb and cried out: Be that as it is you refute all my imputations, 10 There is one you cannot deny, for I am a Wolf and you a Lamb. 11 In one final breath, the Lamb did say thus: Indeed you are a Wolf and tyrant, 12 And a tyrant will always find a pretext to justify his tyranny.

Book 2 Ecaturas (exodus)

C.42 - The Philosopher, the Ants and the Viper

1 A Philosopher standing upon a shoreline, observed the recent wreckage of a vessel. 2 As he stood and counted the bodies and observed the crabs and carrion, 3 He reflected thus: Oh providence! What heavy hand of justice that for the sake of one night and one voyage, 4 You would condemn so many innocent souls to the Other world. 5 At that moment, he felt a sting on his leg from an Ant defending his nest. 6 For below his feet he had been standing on an Ant nest causing them great consternation. 7 The Philosopher immediately set about not only killing the Ant that offended him, 8 But stomping fiercely upon the nest until all the Ants were dead. 9 When he had finished and did survey his handiwork, a fierce pain gripped his leg as a viper struck. 10 The Viper said to him: Your fierce steps awoke me only to see your vengeance upon these lowly Ants. 11 Thus, by your actions I had no choice. 12 The Philosopher gripping his leg and the mortal wound did reply thus: I forgive you Viper. 13 For but a moment I insulted heaven and judged as if a terrible god. 14 And in judging heaven unfairly, I did condemn myself to be judged.

C.43 - The Great Teacher and the Cup

1 A famous scholar once went to meet an old and Great Teacher at his simple abode. 2 As a gift, he brought the old Teacher a rare and valuable pitcher of wine. 3 After the scholar introduced himself and spoke of his many accomplishments, the old Teacher asked the scholar: 4 As you are a man of great learning, pray tell me your sense of the meaning of life. 5 The scholar did begin to recite a wide and rich array of claimed facts and knowledge, 6 As the old Teacher placed two cups on a table and began to pour the wine into the cup closest to the Scholar. 7 The scholar did continue to speak as the old Teacher did pour, even after the cup was overflowing, 8 Until he could stand it no longer and said: Wise and Great Teacher, pray tell me? 9 Why did you permit such rare and beautiful wine to overflow when my cup was already full? 10 The old and Great Teacher replied as thus: Indeed you are correct. Your cup is full. 11 And such a beautiful and rare wine this be to waste. 12 Verily, a mind is much like the cup and true wisdom like the fine wine you brought me. 13 Only when the mind is empty of its preconditions and confusions, is it ready to accept such a valuable gift. 14 Behold! I asked not what you thought the meaning of life to be, but your sense of its meaning, 15 Proving to me that while you are an intelligent man, your cup is already full.

C.44 - The Boy and the Small Fishes

1 A wise old man walking along a shoreline at low tide, did see a small boy in the distance. 2 As he came closer it appeared the young boy was dancing. 3 But as he came even closer, he could see the young boy catching small fish exposed from dwindling pools, 4 And throwing them back into the ocean. 5 As the old man came close to the little boy he said: Good morn to you young man! Pray, what are you doing? 6 The boy replied: I am trying

to catch these little fish and throw them back into the ocean before they die. Will you help me? 7 The old man then said: Oh dear and virtuous soul! Yet there are many miles of shore and thousands of fish. 8 As much as I wish to come to your aid, such a quest is futile. For how can anyone make a difference with such providence? 9 Whereupon the little boy returned to picking up a fish gasping for its life and returned it to the ocean. 10 He then spoke to the old man thus: It made a difference for that one.

C.45 - The Divine Gift

1 The Divine Father-Mother Creator spoke thus to Yahu, the great primordial waters: 2 Of all creation within the dream of the Universe, mankind is to be the greatest paradox. 3 Surely, without our intervention, they shall not survive themselves. 4 Therefore, I am resolved to give unto them a Divine Gift of immeasurable value. 5 It is the realisation they have the power to create their own reality. 6 Yet they must not find it before they are ready, lest it be used for ill and not for good. 7 So Yahu spoke to the Beasts, the Trees, the Fish and Birds of the Earth as to where to hide the Divine Gift. 8 The Eagle said: I shall take it to the Mountains. 9 Yahu replied: Yet some day, man will climb the highest peaks. 10 The Whale said: I shall hide it in the oceans. 11 Yahu replied: And yet someday, man will sail the furthest seas. 12 The Squirrels said: Let us then hide it in the earth. 13 Yahu replied: Verily, even the deepest caverns of the earth shall not be safe from the reach of man. 14 Then the most ancient of Trees did speak: Put it inside of them. 15 And Yahu said thus: It is done.

C.46 - The Trumpeter and the Enemy

1 A Trumpeter during battle ventured too near the enemy and was captured. 2 They were about to proceed to put him to death when he entreated them to spare his life and said: 3 Before heaven and the gods I pray you spare my life. For I carry no weapon, nor do I fight. 4 I am but a lowly Trumpeter who blows this horn and causes no harm. Surely this is sufficient for clemency? 5 A leader of the enemy replied thus: It is true you carry no weapon nor do you fight. 6 And if you be a mere musician we would gladly set you free. 7 Yet with your horn it is you who encourage and guide the men to battle, and thus you are more responsible than all the men who fight.

C.47 - The King of the Frogs

1 A community of Frogs were living amicably and peacefully in a creek pond, 2 With no law other than the Golden Rule of equality for all. 3 Then one day, some of the Frogs called for change and a sense of formal identity. 4 For they did not trust the Golden Rule and instead sought an assembly of elders ruled by a great King. 5 So they prayed to Bel and said: Oh mighty Bel! Grant us our petition! 6 Send unto us a king that will rule over us and keep us in order. 7 Suddenly an old rotten tree by the pond did snap from its base and fall into the pond. 8 The Frogs were at first frightened at this omen. 9 But after a time seeing that the log did not move, 10 A handful

Book 2 Eacturas (exodus)

of them ventured out to the Log and declared: 11 We thank thee Lord Bel! We honour then our new King Log! 12 Gradually more and more Frogs jumped upon the Log until it became common practice, 13 Until many of the Frogs did not take the slightest notice of their King Log. 14 Yet this did not suit the elder Frogs, so they sent another petition to Bel and said: 15 Oh mighty Bel! Grant us our petition! 16 We seek a great King with great power, who will punish those who do not obey your laws. 17 Not long after there was a heavy storm with wind and lightening and hail stones as large as apples. 18 The wind and the hail did cause great destruction and misery upon the Frogs, destroying the Log. 19 When the storm had passed, the surviving Frogs did cry out: Oh mighty Bel! Grant us our petition! 20 We thank thee for our great and powerful King, yet fear we shall not survive his wrath. 21 We seek a real and living king and one that will really rule over us. 22 Soon after a stork did arrive to the pond and upon spotting the Frogs began gobbling them up. 23 As the last Frog was about to meet his end, he said thus: Alas! Better be no government than cruel government.

C.48 - The Fir-Tree and the Ash Tree

1 A Fir Tree said with boast to an Ash Tree: Verily, you are poor of use, for your timbers easily break. 2 Whereas I am richly trusted for home and roof, for bridge and post. 3 The Ash Tree replied thus: It is true I am no match for the wealth of your use. 4 Yet beware your boasts, for come now the axe to cast you down. 5 Whereas I shall live a little longer.

C.49 - The Rich Farmer and Poor Farmer

1 A farmer of poor means suffered a grave loss when his only horse ran away. 2 A wealthy neighbour did then come calling and said to the farmer: Surely this be a sign of ill fortune! 3 With no horse to plough your fields, you shall surely starve. Better then to sell your plot, than to die a pauper. 4 Yet the farmer did reply and say: I be neither against the gods, nor surrendered to my fate. We shall see. 5 Soon after, the horse returned with three wild horses which the farmer claimed and then sold two to pay his debts. 6 Yet when his only son sought to ride the best one they had kept, the horse threw him off and he broke his leg. 7 The wealthy farmer did return and said: Alas!, your fortune has not improved. For your injured son has robbed you of your labourer. 8 Best then you sell such unruly stallion to pay for supplies, than risk dying without heir. 9 Yet the farmer did reply and say: Such trials indeed are great, yet I do not resign my affection for life. We shall see. 10 Soon after, the local Lord sent out his troops to round up able bodied men to fight. 11 But upon the son of the farmer being injured, they did move on and seize the sons of the wealthy neighbour. 12 Upon hearing his neighbour losing his sons, the poor farmer called upon him. 13 When the wealthy farmer sighted his neighbour he called out: Do not mock me in my hour of shame! 14 For the gods indeed shine on you with all the richness of good fortune! 15 The poor

farmer in response said thus: Verily, it is you, not I who should give thanks. 16 For though you have never worked, you are bestowed the choicest of lands; 17 And despite your character, your neighbours rally to your aid. 18 Surely then your sons shall return. For neither the gods nor men of good conscience have abandoned you.

C.50 - The Dove and the Ant

1 An Ant upon the edge of a river to fetch some water did lose his footing and fall into the torrent. 2 A Dove sitting in a tree above did watch the event and in a moment of compassion took a small bough from the tree, 3 And threw it into the river near the Ant, by which means the Ant was saved and gained the Shore. 4 Soon afterward, the Ant did see a man with a bow take aim at the Dove in the tree, 5 Without hesitation the Ant bit the man in the foot sharply, causing him to miss his aim, 6 And so saved the life of the Dove.

C.51 - The Farmer and the Snake

1 One winter, a Farmer found a Snake stiff and frozen with cold. 2 He felt compassion for its demise, and taking it up, placed it in his home near his own chest. 3 The Snake was quickly revived by the warmth and care of the Farmer, 4 And resuming its natural instinct, bit its benefactor, inflicting on him a mortal wound. 5 Upon his last breath, the Farmer said thus: Alas Oh Gods! For I be a foolish heart! 6 That I took pity upon a scoundrel and believed by love alone I could force it to change character.

C.52 - The Belly and the Body

1 The members of the Body resolved themselves one day to decide who amongst them were of greatest importance. 2 The first to speak were the arms and legs who said: Without our skills, you would be without the means to gather food or escape. 3 The second to speak was the ears that said: Indeed the limbs are important, but without my hearing you would be deaf to friend or foe. 4 The third to speak was the eyes that said: Indeed the limbs and ears are important, but without my sight you would be blind to life and death. 5 The fourth to speak was the mouth and said: Without my skill, you would be mute to expression and unable to eat. 6 The fifth to speak was the brain who said: While all of you play a part, it is I the intellect that directs you all, for without my brilliance you would simply fail. 7 Upon this boast the belly did say: Beware such boasts oh mind. For it is I the belly that directs you. 8 All the members did laugh at the claim of the belly who then resolved to make its point. 9 For three days, it refused to do its duty until finally as the limbs did fail, the ears and eyes and mouth did fail, the weary mind did say thus: 10 Forgive our arrogance oh belly! Truly you are not only the source of true knowledge, but the ruler of the body. 11 For if you should fail, we all shall surely soon after be doomed.

C.53 - The Wolf in Sheep's Clothing

1 A hungry Wolf unable to defeat the honour of a noble Shepherd, did

entreat the heavens for a sign. 2 The Wolf did say: Oh heavens or demons for I know not which, be that as I am without piety or integrity. 3 Show pity upon this hungry servant and grant me a sign that I might circumvent the law and seize some sheep. 4 Soon after, the Wolf did find the rotting carcass of an old sheep that had wandered over a steep ravine. 5 The Wolf did then declare: I thank you oh darkness for your most cunning of sign. 6 For I shall take this fleece and slip past the guardian unnoticed as an enemy within. 7 So the Wolf did take the fleece from the dead sheep and make himself as if a sheep. 8 Upon the evening of the next day, as the Shepherd returned the flock to his fold and locked them safely inside, 9 He noticed a Sheep in poor condition. 10 He then commanded his apprentice: Stay with this Sheep this night and make sure it eats. 11 For I shall neither let one of my flock be in sickness or suffer. 12 The Wolf in fear of his life could do no more than pretend to chew the grass. 13 In the morn the Shepherd returned and upon the witness of his apprentice he said thus: 14 Alas, the time has come to do my duty. For while the wheels of divine justice may move slowly, 15 Not even the smallest suffering goes unnoticed nor the greatest evil. 16 Whereupon the Shepherd killed the Wolf in Sheep's clothing instantly.

C.54 - The Heifer and the Ox

1 A Heifer saw an Ox hard at work harnessed to a plough, 2 And tormented him with reflections on his unhappy fate in being compelled to labour. 3 Shortly afterwards, at the harvest festival, the owner released the Ox from his yoke, 4 But bound the Heifer with cords and led him away to the altar to be slain in honour of the occasion. 5 The Ox saw what was being done and to the Heifer said thus: 6 As heaven is my witness, I forgive you. 7 For this you were allowed to live in idleness, because you were presently to be sacrificed.

C. 55 - The Lying Girl

1 The mother of a young girl was baking and warned the girl not to steal any morsels, for they be an offering to Luki, as good fortune. 2 Yet when the mother turned her back, the girl ate one and took another. 3 When the mother demanded she tell the truth, the young girl refused, so she was banished from the house until the end of the day. 4 Wandering into a nearby forest the young girl found a beehive left unattended by the bees as they worked. 5 So she took some of the honey. 6 But when the bees returned and asked if she had taken the honey, she denied it but insisted she saw who did. 7 So the bees brought her to see the bear and other beasts of the forest. 8 But when she saw a pile of bones of all the liars who had come before, she cried out: 9 Oh Luki forgive me and save me, for I lied! 10 Whereupon Luki appeared and said to the girl: Foolish child! 11 All your mother would have done if you spoke the truth was scold you, 12 And all the bees would have done if you confessed your lie was to sting you a little, 13 Yet now your lies have put your very life in jeopardy. 14 What can you show me that you have learnt your lesson and shall never again lie? 15 The girl then reached in

and produced the morsel her mother originally made and handed it to Luki who ate it and said: 16 Verily, that you have returned what was not yours to take and because of the love of your good parents, you are saved.

C.56 - The Wolf and the Princess

1 The great Wolf of an ancient forest once stumbled upon a lost young Princess. 2 Upon the sight of the giant Wolf, the girl cried out: Please Oh mighty Wolf!, I pray you show mercy! 3 My father is King and for my return, he will gladly reward you, with as many sheep as you could wish to eat. 4 The Wolf replied and said: Oh beautiful little princess, indeed I am a Wolf. 5 Yet, I have never seen a more divine creation. For I could no more harm you than surrender my own life. 6 Whereupon the Wolf let the little girl sit on his back as he returned her to the village. 7 Yet when they arrived, the villagers were fearful of such a great beast, 8 And once the little girl was safely in the arms of her father the King, they slung arrows and rocks at the Wolf. 9 Many years later, when the Princess had become a young woman, her party was attacked on a road by robbers. 10 But before the bandits could do their worst, the great Wolf appeared and forced them to flee. 11 Upon seeing the great Wolf the young woman cried: Oh mysterious Wolf! Forgive me! 12 For I begged you to forswear, yet my father cast you out as a scoundrel. 13 The Wolf replied: Fair and most beautiful princess, no man may judge against the call of heaven. 14 Fate binds us, yet it is how we honour our own heart that will decide how we are remembered. 15 Whereupon, the great Wolf let the young princess travel on his back to return to the village. 16 When they arrived and before the villagers could arm themselves, the young woman called out to them: 17 Before all heaven and the gods this day, I pledge my heart and love to this great Wolf, 18 Who saved me, not once but twice. It is he whom I shall marry. 19 The King did not know what to say to his daughter and was terrified of the great Wolf until he devised a plan and said: 20 Be that the gods through fate have ordained this union, I have no quarrel, except one. 21 That you be so mighty and powerful and my daughter be so fragile, 22 Unless you be willing to sacrifice the power of your teeth and claws, 23 I fear I could not in good conscience betroth my daughter to certain death. 24 The Wolf was so much in love that he agreed, whereupon his teeth and claws were removed. 25 But when he came again to the King, the villagers and the King simply laughed at him and banished him. 26 Soon after, a fearsome Lion came upon the village and stalked the villagers. 27 One by one the villagers in sheer terror did fall to the claws and jaws of the terrible Lion, until it finally trapped the frightened Princess. 28 Yet before the Lion could dispatch the Princess, the Wolf returned and pushed the Lion aside. 29 The Lion in anger tore at the toothless and clawless Wolf, mortally wounding him. 30 The Lion stood over the dying Wolf and said: Oh sad and pathetic creature! 31 Whereas you were once the most feared of creatures, Love destroyed you! 32 At his last breath, the Wolf replied thus: From dust we

come, and to dust we all must return. 33 Verily, my life was surely not in vain. For where I now go, soon shall you join me, by the spears of the villagers now rallied upon you.

C.57 - The Young Priest and Luki

1 At dusk, a Young Priest wearied from a long journey, lay down to sleep unbeknownst on the very brink of a deep ravine. 2 Being within inches of the edge, Luki appeared to him and waking him from his slumber thus addressed him: 3 Young man, I pray thee awake and make haste away from your mortal peril. 4 For had you fallen into the ravine, the blame shall be thrown on me, and I shall get an ill name among mortals. 5 Alas, as much as men shall claim their good fortune upon skill, men are sure to blame their calamities upon me. 6 However much by their own folly they have brought distress on themselves.

C.58 - The Stag at the Pool

1 A Stag overpowered by heat came to a spring to drink. 2 Seeing his own shadow reflected in the water, he said: 3 Oh mighty form! Crowned be thee by noble horns, yet cursed by heaven with slender limbs. 4 Alas! If but the gods had been kinder in design, that we might have had limbs to match our crown. 5 Whereupon a Lion appeared also at the side of the spring to drink. 6 The Stag immediately took to flight before the Lion did see him. 7 With all his strength and agility the Stag did quickly have a distance from his foe. 8 But entering a wood his antlers became entangled by his horns. 9 Trapped and easy pray for the chasing Lion, the Stag said thus: 10 Woe is me! How I have deceived myself! These feet which would have saved me I despised, 11 And I gloried in these antlers which have proved my destruction.

C.59 - The Three Brothers

1 The goddess Ana did wish to test the character of man, 2 That they be worthy of her continued favour and protection. 3 But as her husband did so love mankind, she called upon the lesser gods to petition him instead. 4 Upon the plaint of Shu and Danu and Kel, Lord Bel did say thus: 5 If be not unfair thee gods, I grant such test. That by the volition of equal men ye shall decide. 6 Whereupon Ana selected three orphaned brothers and commanded Luki, 7 That he bring the fortune of land near the sea to the brothers. 8 The goddess Bris did bathe lands in spring with life, 9 And the first brother said to the others: I care not for effort, 10 For these days surely are enough and life is without worry. 11 My home shall be spun from these fine tall grasses, 12 And not a moment shall be wasted on hard labour. 13 The second brother said to the others: I be not as care free as thee, 14 For times will change and the cold winds shall come. 15 So I shall make my house of wood, 16 And my efforts shall be rewarded with peace. 17 The third brother said to the others: My foolish brothers, 18 This land be near the sea and surely upon Autumn Lug and in Winter Mene shall test us. 19 I shall begin building my home deeper into the earth of thick stones, 20 That neither storms, nor winter shall destroy me. 21 Thus when Autumn

came and the god Lug did bring fierce storms, 22 And when Shu the god of wind and air did blow, the house of straw of the first brother was destroyed. 23 Then when Winter came, the goddess Mene did bring great snows and cold, 24 And Danu the goddess of rain and moisture did splinter and crush the house of wood of the second brother. 25 Only the house of the brother who made his home of stone survived. 26 Then Ana called upon Kel the goddess of the earth to rumble, 27 Yet as hard as she tried, the home of stone of the third brother stood. 28 Finally upon spring, the great Lord Bel called out to Ana and the lesser gods to cease. 29 And spoke thus: Though man is tested and many fail, 30 Enough remember the lessons of previous lives, 31 And choose by their own volition to be more than beasts. 32 For if but one chooses to be free, all are free, 33 And thus no god nor man may claim another to be slave or beast.

C.60 - The Scorpion and the Frog

1 A Scorpion found itself trapped on a sand bank soon to be submerged by the torrent of a river in flood. 2 Seeing a Frog, the Scorpion pleaded that the Frog to carry him to safety. 3 The Frog replied and said: As a creature known for its insanity, how then can I be assured you will not sting me? 4 The Scorpion said thus: Kind Frog, for reason assures that upon such act, we would both assuredly die. 5 Upon these words, the Frog felt satisfied and they set out. 6 But midstream, the Frog did feel the horrendous pain of the Scorpion sting. 7 As the Frog could feel the paralysis course throughout his body and they started to sink, he called out in his final breath the single word of why? 8 To which the Scorpion said thus: Alas!, it is the curse of my character that I destroy that which I cherish most.

C.61 - The King and the Burden

1 A great King one day ordered: I wish to reward the most deserving of the kingdom. 2 So an invitation was sent out to all people, of all types to come to his kingdom. 3 But some distance from the gates, the King then ordered his men to place a huge rock as an obstacle upon the main path. 4 The King then hid himself as a peasant to observe the reaction to such obstacle. 5 Many of the wealthiest of merchants upon seeing the burden, surrendered and turned back from whence they came. 6 Others, simply skirted around the burden and continued upon their way, leaving their friends and family behind. 7 Finally, almost upon dusk a peasant carrying a cart of vegetables came to the huge rock obstructing the path. 8 He called upon the melee of people to assist him, yet none did except the King dressed as a fellow peasant. 9 So finally, the King and the peasant farmer removed the rock to reveal a purse of gold coins. 10 Before the reward could be snatched from the peasant by greedy onlookers, the King revealed himself and said thus: 11 Verily, my most trusted of lords and merchants did surrender or fail to address this burden, but you. 12 Behold! Every obstacle presents an opportunity to improve our condition.

C.62 - Two Wolves

1 An old scholar one day was speaking to his grandson about the battle of self within all of us and said thus: 2 Verily, my son, the battle within all of us is between two wolves. 3 One is Malevolent. It is anger, envy, jealousy, regret, greed, arrogance, self-pity, guilt, resentment, fear, inferiority, lies, pride and ego. 4 The other is Benevolent. It is joy, peace, love, humility, kindness, empathy, generosity, truth and compassion. 5 The grandson replied and said: Oh wise grandfather, tell me which wolf wins? 6 To which the old scholar replied thus: The one you feed.

C.63 - The False Soothsayer

1 An infamous merchant of false antiquities was exiled and so no longer able to make a living by his trade, 2 He called out in poverty and exhaustion upon a lonely road to the gods: 3 May the gods have mercy upon a broken man! Behold! I have done no transgression before heaven! 4 For what a priest creates in faith, I give as form. Yet both seek to lift the spirit. 5 Upon his desperate petition, he spotted the edge of a buried box under a tree. 6 When he opened the box, he discovered an elaborate gold and jewel encrusted text in ancient language the merchant knew from his trade. 7 The merchant did thank the gods for his good fortune and pledged: Upon this sign, I shall henceforth use this knowledge for good and not evil. 8 So the merchant changed his appearance and when he entered the next city, he established a market stall and soon became popular for his accurate predictions and prognostications as a Soothsayer. 9 Each time, the Soothsayer would produce the gold and jewel encrusted text, saying a spell and then would find a page and speak in eloquent yet vague terms. 10 Yet above all, the merchant would simply tell the people what they wanted to hear. 11 Before long, the merchant now as a Great Soothsayer was as famous as any in the land and had become fabulously wealthy from patrons. 12 Soon, the great and wise King of the land summonsed the Soothsayer to his palace and said thus: 13 Oh great Soothsayer, I implore your wisdom on matters of the gravest concern. For this day we choose whether to wage war with our neighbours. 14 The merchant in his disguise then produced the gold and jewel encrusted text, then did say a spell and sought to quote from its passages. 15 Yet the King was unconvinced by such words and demanded a clearer demonstration of his claimed powers. 16 Three men in chains were brought into the court and placed before the Soothsayer and the King. The King then spoke thus: 17 Before you oh Soothsayer is one man sentenced to death and two innocent men. Without speaking to them, you must choose whom it is. 18 Yet be careful Soothsayer. For your decision shall be final and the penalty of a judge executing an innocent man is death to such a false judge. 19 The merchant under such condition looked to the King and then collapsed to the ground, prostrating himself, saying: 20 Forgive me oh great and just King! For I am no more a Soothsayer than I am a judge of character. 21 I be but a failed merchant, whom the gods saw fit to bestow the gold and jewelled text

before you and whom pledged an oath to the gods not to do evil. 22 Have mercy on me, for I could no more sentence a man to death, than live with such fraud. I merely gave men what they wished to hear. 23 In reply the King said thus: In my court, I have witnessed soothsayers who knew far less than you, but did not flinch at condemning a man. 24 I have honoured priests who could speak far less eloquently than you, yet had never slept a night on an empty stomach. 25 As the gods spared you, so you are now spared. For while you think you came to me an impostor, your heart did not lie. 26 Verily, we are what we choose to be by our words and deeds Soothsayer.

C.64 - The Cart and Esus

1 A Cart bearing a heavy load and driven along a muddy and uneven path became stuck. 2 In frustration, the driver of the Cart yelled out: Alas Oh gods! For what minor transgression warrants such imposition? 3 The driver then pulled out his whip and started to torment the horses to pull the Cart out. 4 Yet the more the driver lashed the horses, the deeper the wheels of the Cart sank into the mire. 5 Again, the driver called out in frustration: Damn ye gods! For now even if I remove myself from this predicament, my horses are lame. 6 With no amount of yelling or cursing moving the Cart, the driver then stepped down and knelt upon the side of the path, saying: 7 Oh mighty Esus, grant me your strength in my hour of distress. 8 At that moment, Esus appeared and said thus: Behold! Neither gods, nor beasts, nor other man be responsible for your heavy load but thee. 9 Cease your cursing and your whining and get up and put your shoulder to the wheel. 10 Verily, the gods help those that seek in honour to help themselves.

C.65 - The False Sacrifice

1 A powerful and feared warlord prepared to do battle by first making an offering to the gods. 2 He commanded his men seize one hundred bulls from the farmers on land under his control. 3 When the bulls were brought before him and slaughtered, the warlord did declare: Oh mighty Lord Bel! 4 Grant me victory this day through your favour with this humble sacrifice. 5 Yet the battle did not favour the warlord and he was soundly defeated, losing more than half his lands. 6 Whereupon, he rallied his troops and then seized his own first borne son, calling out: Oh fearful Lord Bel! 7 Grant me retribution upon my enemies, by this most earnest sacrifice of my first borne son. 8 Yet when the warlord attacked the enemy, his remaining troops were routed and the warlord captured. 9 Sitting in prison and awaiting his uncertain fate, the captured warlord cried: Oh mysterious Lord Bel! 10 By my own honourable death, grant my house eternal vengeance against such enemies that forced me to sacrifice so much. 11 Suddenly Bel appeared before him and said thus: Behold, I am thee in whose name you have caused much calamity. 12 Alas, no favour did the death of innocent bulls give thee, when they were not yours to offer. 13 Verily, you disgraced heaven and earth upon the

Book 2 Ecacturas (exodus)

turpid waste of the most precious gift of the gods to you. 14 Thus of all your offerings, only the offer to end your miserable life be vaguely pious. 15 Therefore, I accept your offering and your life be now mine. 16 Behold, I bind you to not die for one hundred years and unto your vain glory. 17 That you may be punished for your false sacrifices and may warn others. 18 For not the flesh of innocent beasts or children be pleasing to the gods, but honour in life and death.

C.66 - The Pious Widow

1 There was a poor and pious Widow, who so dearly sought to please the gods, 2 She did attend the Temple daily offering much of what little she possessed. 3 Having pity upon her, one day Luki placed a bucket of gold coins in her path. 4 Yet upon sight of the gold coins, she declared: Praise ye gods for such grace! 5 Verily, I shall bring this divine gift with haste to the priests, for so much greater be my reward in the next life. 6 Upon seeing her actions and frustrated by her obstinate mendicancy, Luki then placed three goats on her path each wearing a gold bell. 7 Upon sight of the divine gift, the Widow expressed: For you give me much abundance I thank thee! 8 Faithfully, I shall guide these handsome goats to the priests, for now even greater be my reward in the next life. 9 Yet soon after, the Widow fell gravely ill and almost upon death Luki appeared to her. 10 When the Widow saw his divine form she called out: Dear Luki of the gods. Have I now passed and have you come to show me my reward? 11 For I have followed the commands of the priests. I have given all I own to the temple. I have prayed and sacrificed every day. 12 To which Luki said thus: Oh ungrateful woman. The gods gave you a beautiful life, which you chose to sacrifice to kneeling in a mausoleum of burnt flesh and stone. 13 The gods still felt pity on you and granted the reward of a fortune which you squandered to men of ill repute. 14 Finally, the gods gave you a reward of three handsome goats which you surrendered to these same people who know nothing of heaven. 15 Now you wish upon me some other reward? Alas, oh mistaken woman your time in transition will be hard and with great regret. 16 Behold, any who fail to embrace the rewards of one life, surely must learn difficult lessons upon their next life.

C.67 - Esus and the Monster

1 Esus once journeyed along a path in the other world, when he was challenged by the smallest of forms. 2 Upon this strange-looking being, Esus declared thus: Stand aside and let me pass, for I have no quarrel with thee. 3 Yet the form continued its belligerence until Esus using his great rod did thrust the being to the side. 4 Before Esus could continue and to his surprise, the form was now ten times larger and more ferocious than before. 5 Again, Esus thrust all his strength against this foe and again the nemesis grew now a hundred times larger, dwarfing Esus. 6 Suddenly Ana appeared and said thus: Cease your blows mighty Esus. For the name of your foe is strife. 7 Behold! The more you fight, the more it is fed and the stronger such a monster grows. 8 Verily, if you make peace, despite its

madness, it shall surely expire without its sustenance.

C.68 - The Bear and the Two Travellers

1 Two men were travelling along a forest road, when suddenly confronted by a Bear. 2 The quicker of the two, abandoned his companion and climbed up a nearby tree, concealing himself. 3 The other, upon such mortal danger fell to the ground and feigned death. 4 The Bear did then approach the man upon the ground and after briefly examining him, spoke a few words in his ear and departed. 5 Upon their reunion, the man who had retreated inquired upon the other: Pray tell me brother, 6 What did such a Beast say to you that he did spare your life? 7 Whereupon the man who had faced mortal danger did reply: Verily, he did say thus: 8 Never travel with a friend who abandons you at the approach of danger.

C.69 - The Widow and the Sheep

1 A poor Widow had a solitary Sheep due to be sheared. 2 Wishing to avoid any expense, the Widow sheared him herself but used shears so poor that she badly sheared the flesh as well. 3 The Sheep in great distress and pain did cry out and say thus: Why do you hurt me so, Mistress? 4 For what weight can my blood add to the wool? 5 If you want my flesh, there is the butcher, who will kill me in an instant. 6 But if you want my fleece and wool, there is the shearer, who will shear and not hurt me.

C. 70 - The Young Lion

1 A young lion observed a large flock of birds playing near a river and resolved to try and become friends. 2 But when he came close, the flock dispersed to a distance and laughed among themselves and made fun of him. 3 When the young lion asked why the birds were so cruel when he only wanted to make friends, they protested, saying he was a stupid lion, 4 For he could not fly as they flew, nor possessed feathers as beautiful as they. 5 So the young lion resolved to make friends with a group of foxes. 6 But when he met them, they ran off and left him alone. 7 When the young lion asked why the foxes had abandoned him? they laughed and said he was a slow witted lion, 8 For he was not as flexible or fast as they. 9 Returning home, the lioness laughed and told her son thus: 10 Verily, anywhere you go and any group you meet will represent those who like you, those who do not and those who do not care. 11 Therefore, do not waste effort seeking to be abundantly popular or to please others, 12 As some may simply never like you, no matter what you do to please them. 13 Above all, remember to be a Lion is to lead honourably, not to be liked.

C.71 - The Seeds and the Sower

1 A Lord called in a Servant and commanded to him: Go to my storehouse and seed all my fields. 2 The Servant gave his oath and went to the storehouse and began seeding the fields, except one. 3 The field that he did not sow had poor and rocky ground. So he decided to keep that grain for himself. 4 But upon the

winter, the grain which the Servant had kept for himself also became food for vermin, 5 Whereupon the coming of spring there was a great plague of mice and the crops of all the fields were ruined. 6 The Lord summonsed his Servant to give account, whereupon he threw himself down and said: 7 Forgive me Lord! For I disobeyed your commands. I did not sow all the seed, but kept some for myself as profit. 8 For I did not see how such seed could take hold upon rocky and poor soil. 9 To which the Lord did reply thus: Oh vile and wicked Servant! I did not ask you to judge. Nor did I ask you to reap. 10 For any grain that did land on sandy and poor soil be food for the birds in winter, that they may have young and in spring may gobble up any vermin. 11 Yet by obstructing my word, you gave rise to the evil that defiled my crops and now I will have to wait another season. 12 Thus, let no messenger defy or interpret Divine Revelation, but be a sower of the seeds of knowledge to all men.

C.72 - The Travellers and the Bandit King

1 A party of Travellers were attacked on a remote stretch of road by fierce bandits killing all, except two men. 2 Of the two survivors, one man was known to always speak the truth and the other to speak nothing but lies. 3 One of the robbers, who had raised himself to be King, commanded them to be brought before him. 4 He ordered that all the bandits stand to attention in a long row on his right hand and on his left in front of a great throne. 5 After these preparations the captured men were brought before him and the Bandit King greeted them saying: 6 Verily, your life hangs in the balance of the question I ask you thus: that what sort of a king I be to you, O strangers? 7 Before the lying Traveller could speak, the truthful Traveller replied: Alas! You be a murderer and a tyrant. 8 For no amount of ceremony or pageantry can hide the truth that you are without right or Rule of Law. 9 Behold, all men must die. And if it be my time now to die, then I die with a clear conscience and in honour to heaven. 10 Upon hearing these words, the Bandit King replied: As you have neither pledged your alliance nor pleaded for your life, you shall be executed. 11 Yet as you have spoken the truth, I shall grant you a swift and honourable death. 12 Thus, the man who always spoke the truth was led away to his fate. 13 The lying Traveller then spoke and said: Oh great and noble King! In thee I see the model of authority, 14 And your men as worthy companions of an army to be feared by all nations. 15 I pledge myself to your service and humbly petition for your mercy. 16 Upon hearing these words, the Bandit King replied: As you did pledge your alliance and pleaded for your life, you will be spared. 17 But as you lied and showed such weakness of character, you are not fit even to be known as a bandit, 18 And so I shall chain you as if a lowly dog. For better you had died a noble death than the thousand torments of a scoundrel.

C.73 - The Magpie and the Raven

1 A magpie was jealous of a nearby raven, because he was considered a

bird of good omen, 2 And thus attracting the attention of men, who noted by his flight the good or evil course of future events. 3 Seeing some travellers approaching, the magpie flew up into a tree, 4 and perching himself on one of the branches, cawed as loudly as he could. 5 The travellers turned towards the sound and wondered what it foreboded, 6 When one of them spotted the call did come from a magpie pretending to sound as if a raven, he said to his companion thus: 7 Let us proceed on our journey, without fear, 8 for if it were truly a raven, then caution be warranted, 9 and if it were a magpie in its true voice, then great divination need be considered. 10 But a magpie who is false to his nature be of no concern, nor omen.

C.74 - The Father and Son

1 A peaceful seaside village was once attacked by ruthless bandits with only a few escaping by ship. 2 Some days later, the ship itself was attacked by pirates with only a husband and wife and small child escaping in a small boat. 3 Yet the god Lir chose to be unkind to the stranded family and their boat travelled further out to sea, than towards the shore. 4 With few rations and with the boat sinking, the wife said to the husband: Beloved husband, surely the currents shall change in our favour. 5 Alas! I fear we may be starved before such fortune arrives. For either we lighten the boat or we shall surely drown. 6 Better that which I love survives, than we all perish for nought. 7 After much protesting and with the wife having made up her mind, she stepped off the boat and met her end. 8 With a lighter load, the level of flooding of the boat eased, and the father collapsed briefly from exhaustion. 9 Soon after, the currents changed course bringing the boat towards land. 10 As the boat continued to take on water, when the father stepped out and lightened the load further, the flooding stopped. 11 With land in sight, the father clinging to the side of the boat said to his young son thus: That you live, I shall live. For love can never die. 12 Be gentle my son to your children and to your grandchildren and never forget me. 13 For when I return, I will depend upon you to remind me. 14 With those final words, the father gave up the ghost as the boat finally made it to shore.

C.75 - The Little Girl

1 A young girl witnessed her mother endure great sickness. 2 Yet she was deprived of witnessing her body after death. 3 Instead, the father said to her: Your mother has gone away to another place. 4 Whereupon the young girl was greatly saddened and melancholy henceforth. 5 Until one day, her father gravely ill from injury of battle summonsed her and spoke thus: 6 It grieves me most not only that you become an orphan, but that you did not see your mother. 7 For she did not abandon you but died. And surely if you had seen her body you would know. 8 Soon after the father also died and the little girl was at first denied the chance to see his body. 9 But upon insistence she did witness the corpse and said thus: Now I see, Oh Father! I thank thee! 10 For before me is but an empty vessel. And what I love has

Book 2 Eacturas (exodus)

truly gone on a new journey. 11 Thus I know you are always with me, as nothing that is created can be uncreated and nothing immortal can ever die.

C.76 - The Lion and the Boar

1 Upon a day of great heat, a Lion and Boar came to the same watering hole to drink. 2 The Lion declared that he has right of first use as king of the beasts. 3 The Boar protested that he was first. 4 Thus both were soon engaged in the agonies of mortal combat. 5 During a brief respite in which each prepared for the final match, both spotted some Vultures that had arrived. 6 The Lion then said to the Boar thus: Behold, be it one day we may be called to stand unto death upon a point of honour. 7 Alas, it be but my arrogance and your stubbornness that was sorely injured. 8 Better for us to make friends, than to become the food for Vultures.

C. 77 - The Son and the Fish

1 The son of a respected old fisherman was soon to receive his inheritance as his father was dying. 2 Yet, his father warned him once more, against abandoning the knowledge of his ancestors, 3 and against greed or laziness. 4 Always free the little fish and do not over fish the father said, else you bring ruin to our house and starvation to our town. 5 But not long after the death of the father, the son proclaimed! 6 Am I not my fathers son? Why cannot I choose my own destiny? 7 With those words, the son took the boats into uncharted waters, yet failed to catch any fish. 8 As the people of the town began to grow hungry, they implored he remember the law, 9 so the son returned to the well known places and began fishing day and night, 10 sparing not one fish, or crab. 11 Yet after a few weeks, no more fish were caught even in the well known places nor in any waters. 12 As the people of the town were gripped in the jaws of famine, the son looked up to heaven and cried: 13 Oh father forgive me! For my youthful arrogance blinded me. 14 I abandoned your wisdom and did believe myself to be my own god. 15 Now, my foolish ways have brought ruin upon our house, 16 and starvation upon the people as you forewarned.

C.78 - The Vulture and the Dying Man

1 A man lost in a vast desert without food or water was close to his doom, 2 When a great Vulture arrived and perched itself upon a nearby rock. 3 Upon seeing the vulture, the man did say: Behold death! You shall not be kept waiting. 4 Verily, before I depart, I entreat thee? For I wish to know if there is something more? 5 To which the Vulture replied: In answer to your dying request, what then do you see with your eyes but wasted land? 6 Yet upon the rains, this void be but a cruel mirage. For all life does bloom with fierce determination. 7 The man close to expiry did reply: Alas! That before I die it be impossible to witness such a miracle. 8 To which the Vulture replied thus: Then close your eyes and imagine such life and so you have your answer. 9 For your mind knows more than what your eyes cannot see. Thus only your body shall decay and be my

meal. 10 Yet your mind is immortal and no god, nor form, nor man or beast may claim it or seize it.

C.79 - The Two Princes

1 Two young princes of separate ancient kingdoms were one day at play in a beautiful garden, 2 When one of the princes fell from the limb of a tree onto his skull and was mortally wounded. 3 The grandfather and King of the dead young prince did accuse the grandfather and King of the other of negligence and malice, 4 To which war was declared despite the protests of the young prince that it was a mere mishap. 5 A vicious and bloody battle ensued during which both Kings were killed and many brave men lost their lives. 6 Whereupon the father of the deceased prince vowed eternal vengeance now as King and the father of the living prince now King pledged to defend the honour of their house. 7 A second great and bloody battled followed at which the cities of each kingdom were plundered and many more soldiers and innocents lost their lives including the father of the surviving prince. 8 Upon being made King, the prince rode to face the mortal enemy of his kingdom for now the fate of both kingdoms held in the balance. 9 But before a single trumpet or sword was struck the young king rode out in front of both armies and said thus: 10 Alas, but for one misadventure and a thousand deaf ears, the fields of our kingdoms are soiled with blood. 11 I fear that nothing can save our destiny, but an act of honour to balance the fate of heaven. 12 Whereupon the young king removed his sword and thrust it into his own heart.

C.80 - The Old Lion

1 A Lion afflicted with growing infirmities from old age, 2 Resolved to provide food for himself not by brute force, but cunning artifice. 3 The Lion let it be known to all the forest that he was gravely ill, 4 Then returned to lie down in his den. 5 Friend and foe did then come, one by one, either to pay their respects, or to claim his throne. 6 Some time later as almost none visited, the Lion ventured to the mouth of the cave, where he spotted a Hare moving past and said: 7 Pray thee Hare we may speak of these difficult times. For I long for amicability between us and have not yet received your visitation. 8 To which the Hare did reply: I thank thee great King for such gracious gestures. Yet I shall presently be on my way. 9 Alas, I note there are many prints of feet entering your domain, yet no trace of such returning.

C.81 - The Goatherd and Horn

1 A young apprentice Goatherd sought to return a stray Goat to the flock. 2 The Goatherd had entrusted him with his prize horn to which all the Goats were well acquainted. 3 Yet as hard as he tried, the apprentice Goatherd failed to entice the Goat back with the Horn. 4 In frustration and anger, he threw down the Horn causing it to break. 5 Whereupon, at the ceasing of such berating, the Goat returned to the flock by his own volition. 6 As the Goat passed by, the young Goatherd begged the Goat not to speak of the

broken horn. 7 To which the Goat said thus: Verily, my testimony shall not matter. For the horn will speak for itself even if I be silent.

C.82 - The Lioness

1 A controversy erupted among the leading females of the Beasts, 2 As to which of them deserved most credit for producing the greatest number of sons. 3 They called upon the Lioness to settle the dispute. 4 The Fox proclaimed she deservedly should win as she produced many sons. 5 The Hare disputed the Fox and proclaimed she produced even more sons. 6 The Lioness then spoke up and said: 7 Neither of you are correct, for I am the winner of any such contest. 8 The Fox protested and said: 9 Pray then Lioness, how you might win such a contest when you may produce so fewer than even the Stag? 10 The Lioness replied: It is true I produce less. But if one cub be a Lion, then he shall be King, 11 Whereas you Fox may only produce foxes.

C.83 - The Ass and His Masters

1 An Ass bound in service to a herb seller who gave him too little food did petition Bel to be released. 2 Bel thus appeared and said: Where there be no consent, no binding may stand. Therefore you are free to go. 3 The Ass soon found employment with a tile maker who did feed him, but worked him so hard, he could not move. 4 The Ass then called out to Bel and pleaded: Oh wise Lord Bel, I fear the tile maker may kill me under my oath. 5 I seek an agreement where I neither work too hard and have all the food I seek. 6 Suddenly Bel appeared again and said: Where there be bad faith even if there be consent, no binding may stand. Therefore you are free to go. 7 Whereupon the Ass agreed to a solemn binding with a merchant that promised him all the food he could eat without any work for but one day of distress. 8 Soon after he discovered the merchant was none other than a tanner and upon his final end, cried out to Bel and said: Oh merciful Bel, save me! 9 For better to have been either starved by one, or overworked by the other than a good to be slaughtered and skinned for profit. 10 Bel did appear to the Ass and said thus: Even if the debtor be delinquent in their actions for laziness in failing their obligations, no creditor may rightfully demand his flesh, or to profit thereof. 10 Whereupon Bel absolved the binding and condemned the tanner for trickery.

C.84 - The War Horse

1 A Soldier during a great conflict took the utmost care with his trusted stallion. 2 As long as the war lasted, he looked upon him as his equal and fed him carefully with hay and corn. 3 But when the war was over, he only allowed him chaff to eat and made him carry heavy loads of wood subjecting him to much slavish ill-treatment. 4 When war was again proclaimed, the Soldier prepared his armour and then dressed his horse in its military trappings. 5 Yet when he mounted the horse, it immediately fell down, no longer equal to the burden, saying thus: 6 Alas oh Master! You must now go to the war on foot, for you have transformed me from a

Horse into an Ass. 7 Verily, no man can expect one to turn in a moment of trial from an Ass to a Horse.

C. 85 - The Young Fisherman and the New Boat

1 A young fisherman was given a boat by his father. 2 Yet the young fisherman complained that the boat was too plain and dull in appearance. 3 In reply, the father did say: My son, life will always bring storms and turmoil, 4 thus it is the sturdy boat and wise captain that prospers. 5 Yet the young fisherman did not listen to reason, 6 and soon after abandoned the boat for a pretty and slim lined replacement. 7 However, even on the gentlest of breezes, the new boat could not stay true, 8 and so fearing disaster, the young fisherman abandoned the new boat, 9 and replaced it with a beautifully restored boat. 10 Yet, when the young fisherman was out to sea, a fierce storm erupted, 11 and the beautifully restored boat began falling apart, revealing a rotten core. 12 As the boat continued to sink, the young fisherman yelled out, before he drowned: 13 Alas! I am the architect of my own doom. 14 For I abandoned the lessons of life, 15 and let lust and desire direct me to what matters the least. 16 Verily, there are always storms and if I had stayed true, 17 I would not have caused my own ruin.

C.86 - The Farmer and the Cranes

1 Some Cranes made their feeding grounds on some newly sown ploughlands. 2 For a time the Farmer, chased them away by the terror he inspired brandishing an empty sling. 3 But after a while, when the birds found that the sling was only swung in the air, they ceased to take any notice of it and would not move. 4 The Farmer, on seeing this, charged his sling with stones, and then killed a great number. 5 The remaining birds at once forsook his fields, crying to each other thus: 6 Alas, our contempt did blind us to what we believed as hollow threats of fear and terror. 7 Verily, for where there is smoke, there is surely some fire.

C.87 - The Three Kings

1 Once three kings met in conference and spoke of their respective legacies. 2 The first king spoke and said: I have commissioned the finest artisans and painters, 3 That they create a legacy of the most beautiful paintings and sculptures for generations to see. 4 The second king spoke and said: My Lord, as beautiful as your legacy may be, 5 The paintings shall fade and the sculptures defaced. 6 Thus, I have commissioned the greatest of monuments in stone that will last for thousands of years. 7 To which the third kind said thus: My kings, as great as your legacies may be, both be mortal. Yet my legacy be immortal. 8 For I have neither commissioned painting, nor sculpture, nor monument in stone. 9 Verily, I have ensured that all my subjects may read and write and have a love of knowledge. 10 And that the idea of learning and respect of wisdom and virtue is taught to the next generation.

C.88 - The Farmer and his Sons

1 A Farmer holding domain over difficult and rocky soil implored his sons to aid him in its improvement. 2 Yet his sons upon reaching majority preferred a life of leisure and immorality. 3 Later, being upon the point of death, the Farmer called his sons to witness his final testament and said: 4 My sons, I gave you all you wanted and asked nothing in return but that you aid me in improving this difficult and rocky soil. 5 Behold, now that I am soon to leave you, I tell you verily that there is a great treasure hidden within these fields. 6 After the death of the father, the Sons each took inheritance of their fields. 7 To protect their claims, the Sons each built walls between the fields by clearing many of the stones. 8 The Sons then dug each field deeply, cutting channels in search of the treasure that filled with water from the rains. 9 After many months, the Sons finally surrendered in search of the treasure and surveyed the land. 10 The fields were green and abundant with growth. The walls were solid and strong. There was plenty of water in store. 11 The eldest upon seeing what he could not see before, said thus: Bless you father for your wisdom. 12 Verily, you did bequeath us a great treasure in the value that with motivation and effort even the most difficult can be transformed.

C.89 - The Leopard and the Lion

1 A Leopard hunting for food came across a mighty lion upon a rise of rocks. 2 Upon the lion seeing him the leopard did say: 3 Oh great lion! How I admire you and your power and status, 4 For you rule above all other creatures, 5 And enjoy the satisfaction of many lionesses, 6 Yet I am but a mere leopard struggling to eat. 7 Upon the flattery of the leopard the lion did laugh: 8 Oh foolish leopard, do you think that you see me upon these rocks, 9 That my life be without malady or danger? 10 Verily, my only choice to merely survive, 11 Is to constantly vanquish all pretenders, 12 As I had to vanquish the former king. 13 Nor did I proclaim this position but was chosen, 14 By the lionesses you see on the horizon. 15 Behold, they are the true power and my life shall be over, 16 If I displease them and fail to answer their desires. 17 Yet you are a leopard the fastest of all the beasts, 18 And free to spend a life of leisure with certainty, 19 And I would gladly trade all my years for but one day as you are. 20 Woe then to those who fail to see their many blessings, 21 Yet be beguiled by only the superficial things they choose to worship.

C.90 - The Crippled Boy and his Dog

1 A young boy badly crippled at birth was sitting smiling with his puppy, 2 When a group of able bodied boys did pass and make fun at him saying: 3 Why do you smile?, for surely your disfigurement is because the gods have cursed you. 4 Yet the boy continued to smile and replied that all he knew was in his heart. 5 The children did run away laughing as they poked fun at the crippled child. 6 Some years later, two of the children now as veteran soldiers did pass the same road, 7 And did spot the smiling cripple now a man with his old dog. 8 As they approached they implored the

cripple forgive them for their cruelty as children, 9 Saying the world is indeed cruel and brutal and that he be not the only one cursed by the gods. 10 The crippled man did shake his head and laugh and say: Foolish men, you still do not see! 11 Verily, you have nothing to atone for it is I who failed to help you. 12 Behold my dog, who has never abandoned me nor judged me, 13 But has loved me unconditionally all the days of his life. 14 I have no regrets only compassion to those who have not experienced such Divine blessings. 15 Verily, to accept that no two lives are the same path, 16 And to be loved unconditionally for but one day, 17 Is better than a lifetime of shallow passions and pleasures.

C.91 - The Sleeping Guard

1 A lazy attendant looking at how the Lord of a house bestowed respect to his guards sought to improve his standing. 2 Yet the head attendant denied his request to become a guard saying: 3 Though you embellish your accomplishments and fail to keep your tasks, 4 No harm comes to the house because of the diligence of other stewards. 5 Woe the day you become a guard for the price of negligence is certain destruction. 6 Yet the attendant persisted and pleaded with the head of the guards that he may join their rank. 7 The head of the guards agreed and the attendant was made a new guard and the Lord praised him as he left for a journey. 8 Yet on his night shift the new guard was caught sleeping and arrested and brought before the head guard and Lord, 9 Where the new guard cried out: 10 Alas the nature of my character has been my doom. 11 For if I had remained an attendant I would be safe and well fed. 12 But now for my failure I shall be food for vultures as an example for all other guards.

C.92 - The Dying Philosopher and his wicked assistant

1 A dying philosopher was visited by a wicked former assistant, 2 Who whispered to him that upon the inevitable death of the philosopher, 3 that he would see that all his works be corrupted, 4 And claimed as his own work. 5 Upon this boast, the dying philosopher let out a deep laugh, saying: 6 You arrogant fool. Neither the truth or any lies are yours to claim but the greater cycle of the gods. 7 Verily, every lie is bound to the foundation of some truth to give it structure. 8 Thus, so long as the lie exists the foundation must be there also. 9 And so long as there be a foundation of truth, so then truth may be restored despite your best efforts. 10 Behold, a liar is a man who demolishes a building of stone to replace it with a structure of dried straw, 11 Believing it shall last a thousand years. 12 Yet even the finest stone buildings wither and fall with the passing of time.

C.93 - The Old Orchard

1 Two brothers did each inherit half of an old orchard, 2 of ancient and weathered trees that had produced poorly for some time. 3 Whereupon one brother did declare, 4 Behold! I shall dig up these old trees on my land and plant many new ones, 5 so that in

a few short years my harvest shall be greater, 6 than if I had inherited the whole orchard. 7 Yet the other brother refused to listen to his kin, 8 and trusted the old trees would come good. 9 In a few years as the seasons improved, 10 the old trees produced an abundance of fruit, 11 yet the new trees of the other brother did not produce. 12 Finally, after several years the brother cried out: 13 Brother come to my aid! For I am destitute on account of poor land I inherited. 14 Share with me your bounty for your barn is overflowing. 15 Yet his brother replied: Alas poor brother it be not the land, 16 but your impatience and greed that condemned you. 17 For this old orchard stood in our family for hundreds of years, 18 and though some seasons be harder than others, 19 the orchard did produce more than enough. 20 It is not for us to think ourselves the gods of the seasons, 21 But to give thanks and respect what we have inherited.

C.94 – Bel and the Scholars

1 An old community of Scholars one day did cry out: Oh mighty Bel! Grant us our petition! 2 Have we not been loyal servants of the gods? Have we not memorised and protected all your ancient wisdom? 3 Why then do you not grant us your sight, so that we may continue to serve you and the community? 4 Soon after, word did spread across the land that a young itinerant shepherd boy, 5 did possess the spirit of wisdom and knowledge of the gods, 6 such that people from many lands did flock to hear the young shepherd boy speak. 7 On news of the such divine revelation appearing through a young shepherd boy, 8 the old community of Scholars did curse heaven, saying: Verily, why do you mock us so? 9 We who are the most educated in scripture and most perfected in law, why do you ignore us? 10 Whereupon Bel did speak through the air in a commanding voice, saying: 11 You arrogant and blinded scholars believed that you have a greater right to Divine Knowledge, 12 yet kept what had already been given to you for yourselves while you looked down upon others with less education, 13 whereas a humble shepherd boy with none of your knowledge only wished to live and seek help to protect others. 14 Behold! It is not for men to decide when Heaven speaks, but the Divine Creator alone who chooses when and through whom he wishes to communicate.

C.95 - The Boy and the Sword

1 A city of educated merchants did conceive of a plan to demonstrate their intellect, 2 And commissioned a complex web of knots from a single cord, 3 declaring that only the greatest intellect could solve such a riddle. 4 Soon after, word of the famous puzzle did travel to every corner of the world, 5 and in their arrogance the educated merchants did offer a sack of gold coins, 6 to whomever could solve the riddle of unravelling the knot. 7 One day a young farmer did visit the city to view the knot, 8 and with his knife in one movement did cut the cord, 9 causing the whole knot of great complexity to unravel. 10 Whereupon the young farmer did declare: To every

complex problem there exists a simple solution.

C.96 - The Harrowing Ghost

1 A beautiful young woman did marry a wealthy travelling merchant, 2 on the tragic loss of his first wife. 3 Soon after the young new wife was visited by the haunting spectre of the first wife. 4 In fear the young wife did call out: Harrowing spirit why do you torment me? 5 Again when the merchant had left for business, 6 the ghostly figure of the first wife did appear to the new wife, 7 who did beseech the spectre: Oh figure of death and darkness, 8 Through your jealousy you will not destroy my happiness of matrimony, nor ruin my future. 9 Yet the ghost persisted and led her to a damp place under the house, 10 where she revealed a shallow grave and the final resting place of the first wife. 11 Upon his return the merchant was bound and held to account for the murder, 12 Bemoaning: Alas! Nothing is hidden nor can be kept secret. 13 For even the most wicked of transgressions shall be ultimately revealed.

C.97 - The Benevolent Son

1 The son of a wealthy landowner was tormented by his wicked father, 2 and beaten daily until one day the son ran away. 3 Hungry and alone, the runaway son did come across other young men, 4 who invited him to join their band as they robbed and sometimes killed travellers, 5 so they might survive and profit from their gains. 6 Yet the son refused and when he was cold and lonely deep in a forest, 7 he cursed the gods for such a life of misfortune. 8 Whereupon Luki did appear to him and challenged him to review his position, saying: 9 Alas, many children starve for lack of food yet you were born to privilege. 10 The boy did reply: This is true but my father did beat me daily and make such a life unbearable. 11 Luki did then respond: Verily, many people who lose their way and possessions give up and die, 12 yet here you are with the skills of survival given to you by your father. 13 The boy did reply: Again you speak the truth, yet I have nothing. I am an outcast and my life is already ruined. 14 Luki did then laugh heartily, saying: Behold! Your life is only beginning! 15 You have your education and your knowledge and know you are loved by Heaven. There is nothing you cannot do. 16 Many years later, the runaway son now a wealthy and benevolent man, did return to visit his dying father. 17 At his death bed, the son did forgive his father saying: I thank you and forgive you. 18 For you taught me what not to be and forced me to have the courage to find who I really am. 19 Verily, good fortune favours the brave and kind hearted.

C.98 - The Kindest Words

1 A traveller did seek rest in an inhospitable village, 2 only to be refused sustenance and lodging at the first inn. 3 Yet rather than curse such ill manners, 4 the traveller blessed the inn keeper and wished him well. 5 Again and again the traveller was refused lodging, 6 until a store keeper allowed the traveller to sleep in his barn with the animals. 7 Yet rather than curse such despicable contempt, 8 the traveller blessed the store keeper and wished him well. 9 When the

traveller awoke to leave the village, 10 He was confronted by the first inn keeper who apologised for his ill manners, 11 and thanked the traveller for his kind words, 12 saying that one kind act helped the inn keeper then speak kindly to his neighbour and resolve a long standing feud. 13 Thus even a kind word in the midst of strife and tribulation can change the course of events.

C.99 - The Mendicant and the Merchant

1 A young mendicant did sit by the side of a magnificent temple, 2 whereupon another young man in expensive garments did approach him and spit at him saying: 3 You loafer! Why do you beg for money from others when you should go and work the fields! 4 The young mendicant did bless the other, saying: 5 Thank you for reminding me of my pride and my teachings. 6 For I have all the richness of the world in my heart and forgive and release you of your hate. 7 Many years later, the mendicant and now a rich merchant did face imminent death, 8 whereupon Esus did appear to both men to prepare them for their journey. 9 When the wealthy merchant did enquire what he could bring, 10 Esus replied only what he himself could carry. 11 The old merchant did then cry out: Verily, I now know that Life truly be a dream and that all my riches be for nought! 12 Alas, I travel upon this next journey to the otherworld not as a rich man but as a pauper.

Tara

Book 3
Diatuair (deuteros)

C.1 - Diatuair (deuteros)

Hear me O Divine Creator! 2 Direct my path be true, 3 concerning Diatuair (deuteros) meaning the Divine Law, 4 and the Divine Creator of all the heavens has blessed us! 5 As the oldest fathers of just knowledge, 6 perverted not the judgements of ages, 7 may the unity of the law help me, 8 in my testimony to its fair operation, 9 that those entrusted to its custody, 10 demonstrate sound mind and reason. 11 Let not a corrupt heart or mind cloud these truths, 12 that all may know, respect and love the Law, 13 and in return the Law may protect and guide them. Amen.

C.2 - The journey of morals and stories of Eacturas (exodus)

1 If one comes to be here present, 2 upon first honouring the journey of Eacturas (exodus), 3 then such a being must see through morals and stories, 4 the common nature of life and its moral purpose: 5 that even the thief who robs from the weak, 6 must ultimately face their transgressions, 7 and that no action or thought in the dream of nature, 8 be without purpose or awareness or consequence. 9 Even if the wicked may appear to be rewarded for their evil, 10 such respite from consequence be not a long time. 11 Thus people even without the formality of law, 12 possess by their very being the innate sense of what is right and wrong, 13 of basic human dignity and moral integrity. 14 Nature abounds with signs and lessons of such truth, 15 to those species that unite for life, 16 and those noble creatures that exhibit the courage to choose what is right, 17 for their own family and their survival. 18 Verily, such moral foundation is not a result of rule of law, 19 but precedes and ensures its operation. 20 Behold! a society that abandons its common moral reasoning, 21 destroys its very foundations, 22 and condemns itself to oblivion.

C.3 - Law

1 A Law be a proper and authentic standard, 2 that describes, or permits or prohibits some action. 3 When a Law be a standard description, 4 it is called a measure; 5 And when a Law be a permitted standard, 6 it is called a norm; 7 And when a Law be a prohibited standard, 8 it is called a bar. 9 All true Law may only be known by four methods: 10 The first being Instruction; 11 And the second being Deduction; 12 And the third being Consultation; 13 And the fourth being Consent. 14 The highest Law is Divine, 15 being a rule given by Divine Instruction, 16 as nothing may contradict such a rule. 17 The second highest Law is Nature, 18 being a rule discovered through reason and deduction, 19 as Nature is the Living Divine, 20 and nature itself is

conscious, sensible and complete. 21 The third highest Law is Sovereign, 22 being a rule concluded by argument and debate, 23 of a wise council of elders, 24 and judged by a ruler blessed by the Divine, 25 as nothing absurd or immoral may be considered Law. 26 The fourth highest Law is the People, 27 as the will of the people is the true source of authority. 28 The weakest claim is that of a tyrant, 29 without proper authority from the Divine, 30 and without the consent of the people, 31 but merely the force of fear and torture to hold power. 32 For no tyrant can overcome or sustain forever, 33 So long as knowledge of the true Law prevails.

C.4 - Divine Law

1 Divine Law be the Laws of the Divine, 2 of all meaning and action and form and thought, 3 and all life, mind, object and spirit, 4 and all names and gods and lesser beings. 5 Verily, there be no greater than the Divine, 6 for everything lesser belongs to the Divine. 7 Divine Law then is the highest possible form of Law, 8 and the source of all lesser forms of law, 9 for such law cannot be written or created, 10 only instructed by revelation and divine anointment. 11 Thus Divine Law is the revelation and wisdom, 12 of meaning and reason and of notion and intellect, 13 of order over chaos and of existence and purpose, 14 of dreamer and dream and of perception and reality, 15 of symbol and relation and of number and measure, 16 of cycle and change and of collections and worlds, 17 of intention (will) and action and cause and consequence, 18 of rules and laws and of life and death, 19 and of life beyond death. 20 Behold! Divine Law is the cornerstone of civilisation, 21 from where all Law is derived, 22 and whereby all Law must abide.

C.5 - Rule of Law

1 It has always been so that the true Rule of Law be: 2 upon the four pillars of equality, measure, standard and voice. 3 First, all law is equal, that no one is above it; 4 Second, all law is measured, that all may learn and know it; 5 Third, all law is standard, that it may always be applied the same; 6 Fourth, all law be spoken as it is the spirit of the word that carries authority, 7 as all action under law be by word of mouth, 8 and writing be only for memory and never law in effect. 9 True Rule of Law exists only when: 10 All laws are simple, 11 so that one may reasonably learn, remember and comprehend; 12 All laws are respectful, 13 so that no law disrespects anyone purely upon the original circumstance, 14 of their birth, location, gender, race, religion or creed; 15 All laws are sensible, 16 so that no law asserts errors or fallacies, 17 or demands such absurdities are defended and enforced; 18 All laws are reasonable, 19 so that no law demands an unreasonable or impossible act; 20 All laws are consistent, 21 so that no laws require contradictory or confusing behaviour; 22 All laws are honest, 23 so that no law misrepresents the truth, 24 nor compels deliberately dishonest behaviour; 25 All laws are loyal, 26 so that no law endorses treacherous or disloyal acts; 27 All laws are moral, 28 so that no law permits morally

repugnant, profane or sacrilegious acts; 29 All laws are remedial, 30 so that no law imposes punitive measures without first the opportunity to rectify or remedy; 31 All laws are merciful, 32 so that no law encourages cruel and barbarous acts of vengeance. 33 Any claimed law that contradicts such standards cannot be law.

C.6 - Divine Rules

1 Divine Rules be the rules of the Divine unto all men and women. 2 There be no higher law nor more simpler law. 3 There be no clearer law nor more sensible law. 4 It be the Divine Rules of Action, Vocation and Intention, 5 that every adult and infant may comprehend, 6 and every infant and adult may learn and remember, 7 and that every man and women may respect and love. 8 The First Divine Rule of Action, 9 be to do no evil. 10 The First Divine Rule of Vocation, 11 be to speak no evil. 12 The First Divine Rule of Intention, 13 be to ignore no evil. 14 Thus, to do no evil, to speak no evil and ignore no evil, 15 be the first and primary Laws of the Divine, 16 and no other. 17 Woe then unto any false priest or teacher, 18 that claims more complex laws, 19 or sows confusion and contradiction, 20 as a servant for wickedness and misery. 21 Let not any man or woman, 22 say they did not know or could not remember, 23 the true Rule of Law. 24 Verily, no man or woman may claim ignorance of the true Law, 25 as any such excuse or apology.

C.7 - Six Divine Rules of Action

1 The First Divine Rule of Action, 2 be to do no evil. 3 Behold! there then be six Primary Divine Rules of Action: 4 Do not murder; 5 Do not rape; 6 Do not abuse; 7 Do not steal; 8 Do not cheat; 9 Do not exploit. 10 Verily, there be no higher Divine Rule of Action, 11 nor be there simpler or more sensible rules of action, 12 to learn, remember and obey. 13 Thus, every man, woman and infant, 14 shall hear repeated these six Primary Divine Rules of Action, 15 so that none may plead ignorance or any excuse against such Law.

C.8 - Six Divine Rules of Vocation

1 The First Divine Rule of Vocation, 2 be to speak no evil. 3 Behold! there then be six Primary Divine Rules of Vocation: 4 Do not bear false witness; 5 Do not curse; 6 Do not condemn; 7 Do not slander; 8 Do not provoke; 9 Do not beguile. 10 Verily, there be no higher Divine Rule of Vocation, 11 nor be there simpler or more respectful rules of vocation, 12 to learn, remember and obey. 13 Thus, every man, woman and infant, 14 shall hear repeated these six Primary Divine Rules of Vocation, 15 so that none may plead ignorance or any excuse against such Law.

C.9 - Six Divine Rules of Intention

1 The First Divine Rule of Intention, 2 be to ignore no evil. 3 Behold! there then be six Primary Divine Rules of Intention: 4 Do not neglect; 5 Do not disavow; 6 Do not hide; 7 Do not delay; 8 Do not obsess; 9 Do not abandon. 10 Verily, there be no higher Divine Rule of Intention, 11 nor be there simpler or

more reasonable rules of intention, 12 to learn, remember and obey. 13 Thus, every man, woman and infant, 14 shall hear repeated these six Primary Divine Rules of Intention, 15 so that none may plead ignorance or any excuse against such Law.

C.10 - Do no evil

1 Do no evil, 2 be the First Divine Rule of Action. 3 Evil begets evil. 4 Violence causes more violence. 5 Thus, to end the cycle of evil, 6 One must do no evil. 7 There be no other way. 8 Verily, any one who disputes such sensibility, 9 to claim that evil may be ended, 10 by committing greater acts of evil, 11 is either an idiot or a wicked liar. 12 Beware then the righteous caller, 13 who demands retribution against the slightest ill, 14 lest they be the cause of perpetuating evil, 15 rather than a voice of Divine reason.

C.11 - Do not murder

1 Do not murder, 2 be the first of the six Primary Divine Rules of Action. 3 Murder be the taking of the life of another, 4 without the existence of a compelling and reasonable cause. 5 Thus, the call to battle to defend against attack, 6 or to protect against an enemy without conscience, 7 be impossible to consider an act of murder, 8 for such reason for action be both compelling and ancient. 9 Further, a man compensated for the loss of his farm, 10 or the upkeep of his family or weapons, 11 be a respected practice. 12 Yet the commission of one to go to battle, 13 Purely for money and fortune is a wicked act against Heaven, 14 and such payment are blood money, 15 and such actions are pure murder. 16 Behold! a people can never form a professional army for money, 17 without corrupting its laws, 18 and severing itself from the Divine Creator. 19 Alas, a mercenary army is a sign of encouraging evil. 20 Verily, a man or woman have every right, 21 to defend their home and family to the death if needed, 22 and such act can never be claimed murder, 23 even if an axe is used against an attacker with a blade. 24 Behold! a society that disarms its population, 25 and outlaws its people from defending itself; 26 Is a wicked and evil plantation of slaves, 27 and not a free or just society. 28 Any man or woman who claims otherwise, 29 is either suffering the effects of madness or stupidity, 30 or a vessel for evil spirits that wish ill upon the people. 31 Verily, no society may lawfully execute a sentence of death, 32 without being a society of evil, 33 and the begetting of evil. 34 There is more just punishment than execution, 35 and all who have been condemned for wickedness, 36 have the right of redemption. 37 Behold! Any man or woman who refuses redemption, 38 and who seeks to perpetuate evil, 39 and continues to physically harm others, 40 ceases to act in the manner of a civilised being, 41 but a wild and diseased animal, 42 to be treated in the same manner. 43 Thus, there be no circumstance nor condition, 44 where a society find itself condoning murder, 45 nor preventing reasonable safety and protection.

C. 12 - Do not rape

1 Do not rape, 2 be the second of the six Primary Divine Rules of Action. 3 Rape be the sexual assault of another,

4 where the presence of violence or threat, 5 or the moral circumstance, 6 disqualifies any reasonable excuse or argument of consent. 7 Thus, any sexual act by a father upon his children, 8 is rape even if his offspring claim willing consent, 9 for it be a wicked moral act, 10 against the norms of Heaven, 11 and the health of our community. 12 Any sexual act by a teacher with their student, 13 is rape even if the student be of age. 14 Any sexual act between one bound in matrimony and their neighbour, 15 is rape as such a wicked act destroys community trust. 15 Thus the law only exists, 16 when the absolute right of a woman to deny consent to intimacy is protected. 17 Verily, unlike the merchants and pirates of the city-states, 18 a woman is never the property of a man or lesser, 19 and any law that claims otherwise is a wicked blasphemy against heaven. 20 Thus, even in union a man who aggressively forces his wife into intimacy 21 against her willing consent, 22 is culpable of rape, 23 if actual violence or presence of clear threat is proven. 24 Behold! as heavy penalty to anyone, 25 who makes false accusations of rape. 26 For a society that does not punish a liar, 27 with the severity of the sentence that may have been imposed on the falsely accused, 28 permits the corruption of its laws, 29 and its ultimate doom.

C. 13 - Do not abuse

1 Do not abuse, 2 be the third of the six Primary Divine Rules of Action. 3 Abuse be the use of violence or emotional threat, 4 against another who is weaker and unable to defend themselves, 5 without compelling and reasonable cause. 6 A people who have lost all respect of their seniors, 7 will soon vanish from existence. 8 A community that does not protect its young ones, 9 invites into its midst the plague of evil for generations. 10 Verily, abuse is the stepping stone to greater evils, 11 and cuts through to the soul. 12 Thus exposing young ones to horror and violence, 13 is a wicked form of abuse, 14 that produces no good fruit. 15 Behold! the greatest soldiers, 16 be not those who are so broken within, 17 that they have forgotten their own soul. 18 Such tragic spirits have always been defeated, 19 precisely because they are crippled within from such abuse. 20 Thus do not permit such public abuse or disrespect, 21 and greater wickedness shall surely be avoided. 22 Tolerate or encourage abuse, 23 and even in victory of power, 24 such a people shall be impossible to administer, 25 without misery and bloodshed.

C. 14 - Do not steal

1 Do not steal, 2 be the fourth of the six Primary Divine Rules of Action. 3 Stealing be the taking of the property of another, 4 without permission or reasonable cause. 5 The right to personal property is a Divine Right and Gift. 6 It is not the source of ill or greed, 7 but merely a convenient excuse for some. 8 A people that forbid personal property are a people enslaved. 9 A wicked priest or scribe that calls for the end of personal property, 10 is a traitor to their people and a charlatan, 11 and a tyrant in disguise. 12 Verily, personal property teaches respect for all property. 13

Thus, a man or woman who disrespects one thing in their possession, 14 is more likely to abuse greater responsibilities. 15 One who steals then cannot be trusted. 16 It matters not the amount that is stolen, 17 or how often. 18 For one who takes what is not rightfully theirs, 19 forfeits the right for a time to hold greater property, 20 and cannot be trusted for a time to greater responsibility. 21 Verily, a people that permit theft, 22 cannot survive for long.

C. 15 - Do not cheat

1 Do not cheat, 2 be the fifth of the six Primary Divine Rules of Action. 3 Cheating be the obtaining of an advantage, 4 by dishonest and morally questionable means. 5 Whereas theft, rape and abuse is the fast decline of a people, 6 the most certain destruction of a community, 7 is permitting cheating, exploiting and other unfairness. 8 An unfair society always ends in disaster, 9 for it breeds deeper and deeper malcontent, 10 among the oppressed and enslaved. 11 Verily, any class of leaders and elite, 12 that seek to enrich themselves by dishonest and questionable means, 13 are the architects of their own destruction. 14 Their children shall inherit nothing but dust and tears. 15 Behold! Cheating be more dangerous an evil if allowed, 16 for it can spread behaviour faster and further, 17 than any other evil. 18 Hold fast against any cheating and do not permit it to go unpunished.

C. 16 - Do not exploit

1 Do not exploit, 2 be the sixth of the six Primary Divine Rules of Action. 3 Exploit be the obtaining of an advantage, 4 by use of strength and power, 5 forcing the weaker to surrender a natural right. 6 Verily, the worst form of exploitation is slavery, 7 by financial obligation, or forced labour or by discrimination. 8 Slavery in all its forms is the bedrock of evil, 9 and only evil and wicked societies permit it, 10 and only malevolent and evil people promote it, 11 or deny its existence when present. 12 Behold! the exploitation of the weak and poor, 13 has destroyed countless empires, 14 and will destroy all that shall come, 15 who ignore these words. 16 Instead, forgive debts after an honourable period of service, 17 and do not discriminate against people, 18 on the basis of their skin, or race, or creed.

C. 17 - Speak no evil

1 Speak no evil, 2 be the First Divine Rule of Vocation. 3 Evil begets evil. 4 Thus the speaking of evil, 5 is an origin of evil, 6 and a sure sign of evil acts to follow. 7 Verily, within the Divine Dream it is the intent of evil of the mind, 8 that is greater than the act, 9 as thought and speech is manifestly more real, 10 than the temporal structures of life and change. 11 Behold! an evil intention or speech, 12 ripples through the fabric of existence, 13 whilst the act itself is localised. 14 One who speaks evil creates a doorway inviting evil, 15 and evil beings to enter and dwell. 16 Verily, an injury from an evil act may heal over time, 17 yet evil speech is more difficult to heal. 18 The harsh and wicked words of an unthinking parent, 19 may stay with the child throughout their life. 20 The cruel and twisted taunts of a coward with words, 21 may cut more deeply at

a sensitive soul, 22 than the mightiest sword. 23 Unrestrained slander and gossip can destroy, 24 even the oldest of kingdoms. 25 Verily, one who speaks evil invites evil upon themselves, 26 as every evil falsehood uttered, 27 is a curse made by the very one uttering such wickedness. 28 No magical cure is required against evil speech, 29 but to invoke the heavens to bring forth justice and accounting, 30 and thus the maturing and reckoning of such ill fortune, 31 invoked by the slanderer or blasphemer upon themselves. 32 Speaking evil therefore is the surest path to ill fortune. 33 Do not respond to slander with slander, 34 or falsity with exaggeration. 35 Let your actions be your witness, 36 your measured and calm measure be your armour, 37 and your forensic accounting of reason and the truth be your sword.

C. 18 - Do not bear false witness

1 Do not bear false witness, 2 be the first of the six Primary Divine Rules of Vocation. 3 False witness be the deliberate giving of false or misleading testimony. 4 The law itself rests on the fundamental foundation, 5 that all who give witness, do so honestly and truthfully. 6 This in itself does not mean every account be the same, 7 as different people remember different elements of an event, 8 and even over time memories fade and change. 9 Thus a different account of events and facts alone, 10 where one witness may account differently to another, 11 can never be used as a sign of bearing false witness. 12 True witness is a true memory to the best of one's ability, 13 not a perfect recall of every fact and event. 14 So long as a witness recalls to the best of their ability, 15 the omission or difference of events and facts to another, 16 can never be grounds to claim one bearing false witness. 17 Behold! a judge or investigator that compels or tricks a witness, 18 into admitting or denying a fact under duress, 19 are themselves culpable of bearing false witness against the law itself. 20 Verily, all evidence gained by torture or coercion, 21 is false before the law and unacceptable. 22 Any society or community that permits otherwise, 23 proclaims by such evil and wickedness, 24 to be devoid of the operation of law, 25 and merely a charade and tyranny. 26 Bearing false witness, 27 be the deliberate and intentional giving of false or misleading testimony. 28 It is the existence of wicked intent and the speaking of evil. 29 Such evil is corrosive to the very nature of justice itself. 30 That is why a man or woman found culpable, 31 must be treated as harshly as the worst murderer, 32 for by their actions they sought to murder the operation of justice. 33 Any society that treats bearing false witness lightly, 34 has no true system of law and justice.

C. 19 - Do not curse

1 Do not curse, 2 be the second of the six Primary Divine Rules of Vocation. 3 Curse is to utter a blasphemy or invocation of ill intention against another. 4 In ancient times and even present days, 5 the nature and act of cursing is still seen as a high art, 6 and magical power to be feared and respected. 7 Even today there are

promoters and purveyors of spells, 8 who seek to ply their trade of wickedness, 9 by offering methods of ill intent for a price. 10 In some events there exists the presence of malevolent spirits, 11 that give the impression of manifest power of some to curse. 12 In other events there exists a relationship, 13 that the other manipulates for their benefit, 14 again creating the impression of the power of curses. 15 Yet in all circumstances the one who utters evil speech, 16 will be held to account for invoking evil, 17 and none who utter a curse, 18 even if it may take a lifetime, 19 can escape the consequences of speaking evil. 20 Behold! anyone who curses, 21 first curses themselves, 22 before they invoke ill against another. 23 They create a contract of evil, 24 that will directly and indirectly affect themselves, 25 and others. 26 It is a fool then that utters curses, 27 for the consequences that such stupidity brings.

C. 20 - Do not condemn

1 Do not condemn, 2 be the third of the six Primary Divine Rules of Vocation. 3 To condemn is to denounce or damn another, 4 with the other being deprived of the right to properly defend themselves. 5 All have the right to defend themselves, 6 even those who act in the most wicked of ways. 7 None be deprived of a fair hearing, 8 and all except an idiot be granted the right to be heard.

C. 21 - Do not slander

1 Do not slander, 2 be the fourth of the six Primary Divine Rules of Vocation. 3 Slander is to make or repeat false, unsupported or malicious claims, 4 with the intention of injuring the reputation and honour of another. 5 Slander is not a right of expression, 6 nor an action of no consequence. 7 Slander undermines freedoms of expression, 8 it belittles and inhibits authentic debate, 9 it prevents and harms fair dialogue. 10 Thus all defences of slander are a lie, 11 just as slander itself is the promulgating of lies.

C. 22 - Do not provoke

1 Do not provoke, 2 be the fifth of the six Primary Divine Rules of Vocation. 3 Provoke is to deliberately anger and agitate another, 4 to cause unreasonable or evil behaviour. 5 One who agitates for violence and evil, 6 is directly culpable of the consequences.

C. 23 - Do not beguile

1 Do not beguile, 2 be the sixth of the six Primary Divine Rules of Vocation. 3 To beguile is to deceive or delude another, 4 through the use of charm, delight or trickery. 5 True magic is authentic knowledge, 6 not powders and potions. 7 Powerful magic is learning how to be present, 8 not how to escape. 9 Real magic is opening your heart to being less to become more, 10 not thinking and wishing to be more and so act as less. 11 Thus to beguile is a terrible evil of trickery, 12 not only to those who crave the superficial, 13 but the impostors who seek the superficial path. 14 That is why the merchants and false priests promote great spectacles, 15 because they hold no supernatural power, 16 nor magic other than to beguile and trick. 17 Do not be like these charlatans. 18 Do not

wish to be like these impostors. 19 Be true to who and what you are.

C. 24 - Ignore no evil

1 Ignore no evil, 2 be the First Divine Rule of Intention. 3 Verily, there be communities and cultures, 4 that encourage their people to be weak and ignorant, 5 so that whenever another is in distress, 6 they are told to do nothing and wait, 7 or if danger approaches to be still. 8 Thus these people choose the life of lambs to slaughter, 9 and mindless and cowardly sheep unto the axe. 10 Yet to ignore evil is to condone evil, 11 there can be no other conclusion, 12 no matter what excuse is given. 13 To do nothing and wait like sheep, 14 is to encourage evil to do its worst, 15 there is no other explanation before the heavens. 16 This is what the merchants and false priests want. 17 They think by a population of weak sheep their position is assured. 18 Verily, these evil and wicked men are so short sighted. 19 A body is only as strong as its weakest point. 20 A strong head but a weak body always falls faster, 21 than a strong body that struggles to maintain balance. 22 Thus these evil and wicked leaders doom themselves and their children, 23 for upon the slightest test of an enemy, 24 their heads shall surely be on posts as the snow upon the ground. 25 Ignore no evil this is simple. 26 There is no other way. 27 Though the wolves may eat you last upon plea, 28 you shall surely be their food if you scatter. 29 Take a stand and do not yield to evil, 30 lest you be the reason for it taking hold, 31 and infecting and corrupting your community. 32 Do not give safe haven to the scoundrel. 33 Do not yield to the tyrant. 34 Do not fear death. 35 Surely the greatest lie of the merchants and false priests, 36 is fear of death. 37 That the Universe is a Dream and life a cycle. 38 Reincarnation be not the preserve of the gods. 39 Your mind is immortal so you can never die. 40 Thus you have no excuse. 41 Ignore no evil.

C. 25 - Do not neglect

1 Do not neglect, 2 be the first of the six Primary Divine Rules of Intention. 3 Neglect is to fail to care or attend to a duty, 4 or to omit or fail to perform an act of duty. 5 There be no excuse for neglect. 6 There be no just reason to omit or fail to perform an act of duty, 7 for the Universe does not demand greater that what we can do, 8 and any obligation that is unreasonable or impossible is by definition unjust. 9 Thus an order to perform evil is not a valid order. 10 A demand to pay an impossible debt is the essence of immorality. 11 Those that demand such things cede all rights upon impossible or immoral grounds. 12 Yet one must stand and call for justice as to the unreasonable call, 13 else there can be no other conclusion than neglect.

C. 26 - Do not disavow

1 Do not disavow, 2 be the second of the six Primary Divine Rules of Intention. 3 Disavow is to solemnly refuse to acknowledge an act, event or other, 4 or to deny culpability of ones actions. 5 Thus to disavow is to openly break a promise to heaven. 6 To break one's own words as a bond. 7 Verily, a man or woman who disavows, 8 cannot be trusted and cannot be

engaged in trade. 9 Give your word carefully.

C. 27 - Do not hide

1 Do not hide, 2 be the third of the six Primary Divine Rules of Intention. 3 Hide is to conceal or hide an act, event or knowledge from another. 4 One who hides is a coward exposed by heaven. 5 Nothing is hidden to the Divine Creator. 6 Thus everything can be revealed. 7 Do not hide.

C. 28 - Do not delay

1 Do not delay, 2 be the fourth of the six Primary Divine Rules of Intention. 3 Delay is to retard, hinder or defer some act or event in relation to another. 4 Do not intentionally delay.

C. 29 - Do not obsess

1 Do not obsess, 2 be the fifth of the six Primary Divine Rules of Intention. 3 Obsess is to be fixated, possessed or dominated by a thought, or emotion or desire. 4 Obsession takes the mind away from the present. 5 Thus obsession is the servant and enabler of evil. 6 One addicted to vice is incapable of self control, 7 and thus a medium for darkness even if also light. 8 Do not obsess.

C. 30 - Do not abandon

1 Do not abandon, 2 be the sixth of the six Primary Divine Rules of Intention. 3 Abandon is to surrender or relinquish some position, obligation, duty or right. 4 Do not abandon. 5 Do not retreat unless prudent. 6 Stand your ground and be brave.

C.31 - Divine Rights (Ceart)

1 To cultures that have no comprehension of truth, 2 that life is a dream, 3 and that the universe be the creation of the Divine Creator, 4 there be no distinction between a thing (rud) or the right of a thing (cert). 5 It follows then that such law in these communities, 6 is simplistic, harsh and fundamentally unjust, 7 as such lack of understanding of mind and reality, 8 between constructs of the mind, 9 and real objects that can be seen and measured, 10 limits any law based on such ignorance. 11 When a society is unable to distinguish the legal notion, 12 separate to the item in question, 13 then such laws give rise to absolutes and cruelty. 14 An eye for an eye, 15 or might is everything, 16 or possession is the law. 17 None of these brutal and simplistic notions are true law, 18 but excuses for slavery and oppression. 19 Verily, there can be no liberty or harmony, 20 separate to the things in question. 21 For a man or a woman cannot be said to have freedom, 22 unless the quality of freedom can be expressed, 23 separate to the man or the woman that possesses it. 24 Behold! a Right (Cert) be a capacity or privilege or liberty or faculty or power, 25 and any associated obligation, 26 for the benefit of a man or woman or group of men or women.

C.32 - Divine Property

1 Property is the highest Right a man or woman can have, 2 to Control or Use or Claim any Thing or the Fruits of any Thing. 3 As all forms of Rights are derived from valid and legitimate Divine Rights, 4 all forms of Property and Things are ultimately derived, 5 from the rules of Divine Property. 6

There be eight possible forms of Property Rights: 7 Owner of Right of Control of a Thing, 8 Owner of Right of Use of a Thing, 9 Owner of Right of Control of the Fruits of Use of a Thing, 10 Owner of Right of Use of the Fruits of a Thing, 11 Owner of Claim of Right of Control of a Thing, 12 Owner of Claim of Right of Use of a Thing, 13 Owner of Claim of Right of Control of the Fruits of Use of a Thing, 14 Owner of Claim of Right of Use of the Fruits of a Thing.

C.33 - Divine Justice

1 Justice is the set of lawful Rights and obligations of use, 2 and those Laws consistent with the Rule of Law, 3 and the Rights and obligations associated with the proper administration, 4 and enforcement of such Laws, 5 in good faith, good conscience and good character. 6 All Rights and therefore all forms of proper Justice, 7 originate from Divine Law. 8 Behold! All are equal under the law, 9 and all are accountable and answerable under the law, 10 and all are without blemish until proven culpable. 11 Where there is a law there must be a cause, 12 and where there is a law there must be a penalty, 13 and where there is a law there must be a remedy. 14 An action in law cannot proceed without first a cause, 15 and an action is not granted to one who is not injured, 16 for the action of a valid law can do no harm (injury), 17 and no injury to the law means no valid cause for action by law. 18 No one may derive an advantage in law from his own wrong, 19 as no action through law can arise from a fraud before heaven and earth, 20 and it is a fraud to conceal a fraud, 21 and fraud invalidates everything of a cause and action, 22 for no action through law can arise in bad faith, 23 or unclean hands or vexatious prejudice. 24 What was illegitimate, fraudulent and invalid from the beginning, 25 does not become valid over time. 26 No judgement from a morally repugnant law stands as true, 27 as such morally repugnant, blasphemous and wicked laws cease to be, 28 from the moment they are issued. 29 A judge that does not repudiate and strike down a morally repugnant law, 30 ceases to have any legitimate authority the very moment, 31 they cease to honour and protect the law, 32 by allowing such wicked and morally repugnant laws to stand. 33 Unlike the cities of merchants and slave traders, 34 true Justice is never blind nor be represented as blind. 35 As true justice requires sight and wisdom. 36 Only fools and idiots could believe, 37 that justice be issued whilst blinded. 38 Such insane and wickedly evil notions is an image, 39 of a monster that cuts off the limbs of the innocent, 40 because she cannot see, 41 and tilts the scales in favour of liars and thieves, 42 because they speak as if one of the innocent. 43 Verily, under true Justice an action alone does not make one culpable, 44 unless there is intent to do wrong, 45 or evidence of deliberate and wilful ignorance contrary to reasonable behaviour. 46 Similarly, no one may suffer punishment by valid law for mere intent alone, 47 and no one is punished for the transgression of an ancestor or another. 48 No one is accused of the same exact cause twice, 49 and no man or woman be a judge over their own matter, 50 nor a man or woman

possess the authority of heaven to be judge, jury and executioner. 51 No penalty may exist without a valid law, 52 and no penalty may be issued without first proof of injury, 53 and secondly the right of defence. 54 In respect of Justice and the individual: 55 All possess the Right to be heard, 56 even if such speech be controversial. 57 All possess the Right of free will to choose our actions and destiny. 58 All possess the Right of reason that distinguishes them from lesser animals. 59 All possess the Right to informed consent or to withdraw consent. 60 All possess the Right over their body that none may claim our flesh. 61 All possess the Right of our divine self that none may claim our soul. 62 Thus no man can make a blood oath on their flesh or vow on their soul, 63 nor may any man claim servitude or obligation under such an abomination, 64 for such Rights are granted solely by heaven to all people, 65 and no man or body of jurists have the authority to usurp heaven. 66 All true authority and power to rule is inherited from heaven, 67 and to only those men in good faith and good character and good conscience, 68 who then make a sacred oath in trust and form an office, 69 whereby such Divine Rights are conveyed for only so long as they honour their oath, 70 and obligations to serve the people. 71 For whenever a man who makes an oath to form a sacred trust of office, 72 then breaks such an oath through prejudice or unclean hands or bad faith, 73 then all such authority and power ceases from them, 74 as the cord between heaven and earth is severed and the trust dissolved.

C.34 - Divine Fairness

1 Fair Process, also known as Due Process, 2 is the impartial, competent and fair administration of Justice. 3 Every Controversy in Law as a valid action, 4 must be resolved promptly, reasonably and justly, 5 through Fair Process, without fear or favour. 6 No valid action in law should proceed without first a valid cause, 7 and no valid cause exists until such a claim is first tested. 8 Thus the birth of all action in law must begin with the claim. 9 If a claim be not proven as a valid cause, 10 then the accused has nothing to answer. 11 Yet if the claim be proved to have merit as a cause, 12 then all valid causes in law must be resolved. 13 Thus, he who first brings the claim must first prove its merit, 14 as the burden of the proof lies upon him who accuses not he who denies. 15 One who brings false accusation is the gravest of transgressors, 16 as they injure not only the law, 17 but the bonds of law between Heaven and Earth. 18 One who makes false testimony, especially under oath, 19 must face the full force of justice against them. 20 When men wish to settle their dispute among themselves, 21 then they shall have the right to make peace. 22 If a dispute cannot be settled peacefully, 23 then both the accused and the accuser must be granted equal hearing. 24 A valid claim is when an accuser makes a formal complaint, 25 bringing two or more reliable witnesses as proof, 26 to the substance of the complaint and petitions for remedy. 27 If an accuser is unable to garner two or more witnesses, 28 or faces the challenge of an accusation against a more powerful

adversary, 29 then let the accused distrain themselves, 30 in front of the official place of the one being accused, 31 and to wear rags or torn clothes and to fast without food or shelter, 32 calling out to all who pass the nature of their accusation and injustice. 33 Upon the end of the first day of fasting and no call to have the matter heard, 34 then the leaders of the place or town or city be accountable, 35 to bring forth the matter. 36 At the end of the second day without assistance, 37 All jurists are accountable to bring forth the matter. 38 If at the end of three sunsets the accuser has suffered such indignity and hunger, 39 without the matter being brought forward, 40 then let the people seize such official or officials by force, 41 as a stand against wickedness and neglect. 42 Behold! any society or leader or people, 43 who allow a man or woman to suffer to death without justice, 44 condemns themselves and their system before all of heaven and earth, 45 and brings upon themselves the worst of woes and ill fortune, 46 for such a grave injury against Justice. 47 Verily, if merit of a cause be proved, 48 the one accused must appear to answer. 49 An accused cannot be judged until after the accusations are spoken, 50 and then after the accused exercises or declines their three rights to defence. 51 The first right of the Accused is called Céad (Authority), 52 upon the hearing of the Complaint, 53 and the right to speak as a matter of law, 54 and why the complaint and investigation should not continue. 55 To deny the Right of Céad (Authority), 56 is to defeat the legitimacy of any investigation, 57 and the justice of any sentence. 58 The second right of the Accused is called Céist (Subject), 59 upon establishing Jurisdiction and the presentment of the Indictment, 60 and the right to speak as to why the complaint and accusation is in fundamental error, 61 and upon such proof why the burden should now be placed on the accuser. 62 The third and final right of the Accused is called Cosaint (Defence), 63 being a final speech in defence, against an accusation having been heard. 64 In respect of any defence against an accusation: 65 The accused must always be afforded the presumption of innocence, 66 until culpability or exoneration is proven, 67 unless by their behaviour or testimony the accused first confesses their culpability. 68 The accused possesses the right to self defence in all minor matters, 69 but not in the defence of notorious and serious accusations. 70 The accused possesses the right to a trial by their peers or a tribunal of jurists. 71 The accused is not obliged to confess their culpability or innocence, 72 once the issue of a complaint is proven as having merit. 73 However, the failure to confess to culpability before the commencement of trial, 74 is the formal acknowledgement of a lack of contrition, 75 any consequential sentence must factor the maximum and reasonable penalty. 76 An accused cannot be found culpable unless three pieces of evidence, 77 may be attributed to culpability as first presented as part of the complaint, 78 or as a result of a subsequent investigation, or hearing or trial. 79 Judges are bound to explain the reason of their judgement.

C.35 - Authority

1 Authority is an exclusive Right, 2 being a form of Right of Use, 3 to do or act in a particular way, 4 derived solely from the acceptance and promise, 5 to perform one or more obligations, 6 through proper oath or vow. 7 Where there is no proper oath or vow, 8 no Authority exists. 9 Thus Authority is a Right, 10 delegated by one possessing themselves the Authority to do so. 11 The highest possible Authority, 12 is an absolute Divine Right of Use, 13 also known as Divinity. 14 Authority is always vested into a sacred office, 15 and not to the man or woman holding such office. 16 As Authority is by definition Divine Property, 17 a man or woman vested into office, 18 can only exercise the authority granted into such office, 19 if they remain in honour under oath or vow. 20 As soon as they are in dishonour, 21 or fail to abide by their sacred oath or vow, 22 their dishonour immediately prevents any Authority being present, 23 in their actions or decisions. 24 Verily, any official who refuses to produce their oath or vow, 25 and refuses to be bound by it, 26 has no Authority whatsoever.

C.36 - Power

1 A Power is a Right of Authority, 2 or Claim of Right of Authority, 3 conveyed by invocation from one to another, 4 that enables one to do or act, 5 or otherwise refrain from doing or acting in a way, 6 that would otherwise not be lawful or moral. 7 When a Power is conveyed without specific conditions, 8 it is said to be a General Power, 9 and when certain terms and conditions are attached, 10 it is said to be a Special Power. 11 As a Power is created by invocation, 12 its reversal is by revocation. 13 No Power may be claimed to be irrevocable, 14 as such a claim is wickedly absurd, 15 and contrary to all valid and legitimate forms of law.

C.37 - Force

1 Force is either valid compulsion by authority, 2 to perform or refrain another from certain actions, 3 or unlawful and illegitimate violence against another. 4 There are three conditions that make force lawful, 5 being valid forum, no alternative and dangerously delinquent: 6 The first condition requires that force be authorised, 7 by a competent forum of law, 8 and not by unilateral edict of one who claims authority or power. 9 The second condition requires that all other options have been exhausted, 10 such that there is no alternative but legitimate force. 11 The third condition requires that the accused, 12 has clearly demonstrated a dangerous delinquency, 13 and contempt toward justice and due process.

C.38 - Remedy

1 Remedy is the cure to defending or asserting a legitimate right. 2 It is the means of restoring balance to the law, 3 in redressing any injury or offence against another, 4 or the community as a whole. 5 Thus for every right there must be a remedy, 6 and where no remedy is afforded, 7 then no legitimate right is said to have existed. 8 Verily, there be four valid forms of remedy, 9 being declaratory, recovery, compensatory and coercively. 10 Declaratory be the first form of valid remedy, 11 whereby a forum of law

may declare the truth of a matter, 12 and upon the hearing and witnessing of such truth, 13 action may commence in restoring one's reputation or rights. 14 Recovery be the second form of valid remedy, 15 whereby a forum of law may aid in the recovery, 16 of lost or stolen rights or property. 17 Compensatory be the third form of valid remedy, 18 whereby a forum of law may demand a payment be made, 19 as fair compensation for the injury. 20 Coercively be the fourth form of valid remedy, 21 whereby a defendant is compelled to do or refrain from doing, 22 one or more acts. 23 The form of remedy is then determined, 24 by the nature of the offence and the most effective cure.

C.39 - Penalty

1 A Penalty is a voluntary prescribed sanction, 2 issued upon proof of confession of default or delinquency. 3 A penalty may only be issued where there exists evidence, 4 of a valid agreement under oath or vow, 5 and any specific or general penalties for failure to perform. 6 Thus if a man or woman fails to perform, 7 and then fails to rectify their breach of duty, 8 then they be culpable and subject to the penalties first expressed.

C. 40 - Vengeance

1 A non-voluntary prescribed sanction, 2 is an act of vengeance or punitive measure, 3 commonly known as cruelty or torture. 4 Under no circumstances does there exist the basis, 5 of Divine Law endorsing the torture of any man or woman, 6 or of excessive cruelty as some form of punitive measure. 7 Behold! the notion of the death penalty, 8 is an abomination against all heaven and earth, 9 and forbidden in all its forms.

C.41 - Divine Right to Rule

1 A Ruler is a man or woman who by certain Divine Rights, 2 is entrusted to govern a particular tribe, community or society. 3 No man or woman be legitimate in such a position, 4 unless it be by the Divine Rights as mandated herein, 5 regardless of their claims to rule. 6 Verily, a monster may for a time control a people, 7 by fear and trickery. 8 Yet what is illegitimate in the beginning, 9 does not become legitimate over time. 10 Thus a dynasty of monsters will eventually be overthrown, 11 and condemned in memory. 12 But a true Ruler shall be remembered, 13 for many generations thereafter.

C42 - Claim of Right to Rule

1 A Claim of Right to Rule be some circumstance, quality or status, 2 whereby a man or woman proclaims a higher right to rule, 3 than any other candidate. 4 While a claimant may seek to present his or her position as a Right, 5 such rights must be first secured by acceptance of one or more Claims. 6 Thus all forms of high position are founded on one or more Claims. 7 The strength of a Claim depends upon its nature, its provenance and custom of acceptance. 8 Thus there be three true forms of Claim by Blood, by Succession and Election, 9 and three false forms of Claim by Prophecy, by Trial and by Force. 10 Verily, no matter how old a method of Claim, 11 if it is not accepted by the consent and will of the

people, ₁₂ of the particular tribe, community or race, ₁₃ Then it must be ruled invalid, no matter how passionate the claim. ₁₄ Behold! A claim is only valid if it is accepted by the will and consent of the people.

C.43 - Claim of Right by Blood

₁ Claim of Right by Blood to Rule over a Sect, Clan, Race or all Peoples, ₂ be the first true and most ancient of claims of Right to Rule, ₃ whereby one claims by birthright to possess such sacred blood, ₄ that by existence of such blood therein exists a higher right to rule. ₅ The oldest and most esteemed of all such claims of right by blood, ₆ be the Cuilliaéan priest kings, ₇ who by their title are both the Divine Corner Stone, ₈ and Divine Foundation Stone of all races of men and women. ₉ Thus, their very name is sacred and the source of all that is holly (holy). ₁₀ Other dynasties of history have also followed the same path, ₁₁ in proclaiming a divine right to rule by blood. ₁₂ The Shepherd Kings (Hyksos) of Egypt, ₁₃ who owed their claim in part through their ancestry, ₁₄ back to the ancient lines of Ebla and Cuilliaéan blood is such an example. ₁₅ So too, the Da'vid (Da'viz) Messiah kings of the Yahudi, ₁₆ who proclaim by blood right a Divine right to rule, ₁₇ through their ancestry to Pharaoh Akhenaten, ₁₈ also known as Moses as the founder of the Yahudi, ₁₉ and descended from Cuilliaéan blood. ₂₀ Verily, such claims of right to rule by blood, ₂₁ Be fraught with danger of corruption and oppression. ₂₂ Thus, many a dynasty of thieves and liars, ₂₃ Have made their own claims of blood right to rule, ₂₄ such as the false priest kings of Persia. ₂₅ Behold! No one may claim by blood alone, ₂₆ that they have a higher claim, ₂₇ unless they exhibit the Divine Qualities of a Ruler.

C.44 - Claim of Right by Succession

₁ Claim of Right by Succession to Rule over a Sect, Clan, Race or all Peoples, ₂ be the second true claim of Right to Rule, ₃ whereby one has been nominated by the current ruler as their true successor. ₄ Claim of Right by Succession to Rule seeks to secure stable transfer of power, ₅ by ensuring a legitimate successor is named and prepared. ₆ When respected and followed, such rules bring stable and longer term rule. ₇ This be true for the ancient priests of Yeb and the Shepherd Kings. ₈ Yet when Right by Succession is in opposition with Right by Blood, ₉ internal conflict can ensue, ₁₀ especially when poorly executed. ₁₁ Thus stable succession requires clarity and consistency, ₁₂ so that it strengthens not weakens the proper rule.

C.45 - Claim of Right by Election

₁ Claim of Right by Election to Rule over a Sect, Clan, Race or all Peoples, ₂ be the third true claim of Right to Rule, ₃ whereby one has been elected by the representatives of the people, ₄ or by the people themselves as their true ruler. ₅ Such Claim of Right when in combination with Claim of Blood and Succession, ₆ builds an unbreakable bond of trust between a ruler and the people. ₇ Yet when election alone is the source of claim; ₈

Dignity may be lost to such high position, 9 as candidates who claim such right seek to make promises for favours, 10 and a community may become permanently divided between different sides, 11 than united under one dignified ruler.

C.46 - Claim of Right by Prophecy

1 Claim of Right by Prophecy to Rule over a Sect, Clan, Race or all Peoples, 2 be the first ancient false claim of Right to Rule, 3 whereby one claims such a right to rule, 4 is claimed as divinely ordained according to one or more prophecies. 5 Prophecy when properly comprehended and reviewed, 6 be the wellspring, guidance and lessons of the Divine. 7 Verily, it is not for men and women to choose when the Divine speaks, 8 but the Divine Creator that chooses the time, the place and the vessel. 9 Thus, there shall always be tension and controversy with Prophecy, 10 for true Prophecy often challenges the orthodoxy and sameness, 11 against the wishes of those in power. 12 This same potential also means false prophecy, 13 may inflict deep and terrible harm to a people and a race, 14 when used to claim such a right to rule. 15 Such false prophecy has heralded the arrival of some of the most wicked of rulers. 16 That is why claims of rule by prophecy may be discerned and dismissed. 17 For knowledge of the true Divine reveals, 18 that authentic prophecy never seeks to tell people who should be their ruler, 19 as such instruction defies the notion of Divine Free Will.

C.47 - Claim of Right by Trial

1 Claim of Right by Trial over a Sect, Clan, Race or all Peoples, 2 be the second ancient false claim of Right to Rule, 3 whereby one claims such a right to rule, 4 upon victory or overcoming some significant trial. 5 Some cultures have in the past used the trial of combat to choose their rulers, 6 especially such peoples having a constant warlike disposition. 7 Yet such a claim of right alone does not mean the best ruler be chosen, 8 and no society founded on perpetual war has survived beyond a dozen generations, 9 before they cease to be, 10 if not from annihilation, 11 then from lack of sufficient offspring, 12 to counter the fields of blood. 13 Thus claim of right by trial is futile and false, 14 for it perpetuates the necessity of violence and division, 15 over the wisdom of peace and harmony.

C.48 - Claim of Right by Force

1 Claim of Right by Force over a Sect, Clan, Race or all Peoples, 2 be the third false claim of Right to Rule, 3 whereby one claims such a right to rule, 4 by reason of force, fear and terror. 5 Such a false claim built upon power and might as some form or right, 6 is the domain of the most wicked and perverse, 7 who play upon the fears of the people, 8 to cling to power by whatever means. 9 No society or dynasty was ever sustained beyond a few generations, 10 when founded upon the brutality of force, fear and terror. 11 No ruler was ever legitimate when seizing power by force, 12 nor did their successors gain

legitimacy over time, 13 even if they were less brutal. 14 Thus, the wicked who claim and seize by the sword, 15 are vanquished by the sword.

C.49 - Four Conditions for true Right to Rule

1 There be four conditions for one who possesses a true Right to Rule. 2 The first be to have the heart of a Lion. 3 The second is to have the mind of a Teacher. 4 The third is to have the belly and limbs of a Leader. 5 The fourth is to have the blood, skin and body of a Blessed. 6 The Shepherd Kings (Hyksos) who possessed the qualities of ruler, 7 were known by the ancient word as the Ra. 8 Thus a true Heir (Father or Mother) of a Bail (Home) is a Ra, 9 and a true Teacher of a Sect (small community) is a Ra, 10 and a true Chieftain of a Clan is a Ra, 11 and a true Ruler of a Race is a Ra. 12 Thus let the symbols of a Ruler be not the finery of wealth, 13 but by the integrity of their soul, 14 so that no crown be upon their head, 15 nor such fine robes of excess. 16 Not even a Crosier of gold, 17 but one made of simple wood.

C.50 - A true Ruler is a Lion

1 A Lion be a man or woman, 2 who demonstrates the necessary virtue, piety and wisdom of character, 3 required to be anointed ruler and leader of a particular home, community or society. 4 The word itself means to be fulfilled, full, meritorious, worthy and courageous. 5 Yet it means even more. 6 For its origins means that to be a Lion is to be ever and always radiant of the character of virtue, piety and wisdom.

C.51 - A true Ruler is a Teacher

1 A true Teacher is any man or woman appointed to such high office, 2 by sacred oath and obligated to three ancient and primary tasks being: 3 Protect the Realm, 4 Protect the Law, 5 and Protect the People. 6 To Protect and Defend the Realm is the first obligation of a true Ruler as Teacher. 7 To Protect and Defend the Laws of the Realm is the second obligation of a true Ruler as Teacher, 8 to ensure Rule of Law, Justice and Equality prevail. 9 To Protect, Defend and Educate the People of the Realm, 10 is the third sacred obligation of a true Ruler as Teacher.

C.52 - A true Ruler is a Leader

1 A Leader is a man or woman who is physically strong, able bodied and powerful enough, 2 to protect and defend as the anointed ruler a particular community or society. 3 Thus, any man or woman who is crippled from their duties cannot continue as a Ruler, 4 not out of any malice or contempt to those less fortunate, 5 but for deep respect of the Divine and all people. 6 Verily, a sick and extremely old ruler who clings to power at any cost, 7 is an abomination before all heaven and earth. 8 For those who refuse to cede power to an able bodied successor, 9 forfeit any and all right to be a true ruler.

C.53 - A true Ruler is Blessed

1 Blessed means one duly anointed by sacred oil, 2 as rightful Ra (Head) of a

Bail (Household), Sect (Area), Clan (Region) or Race (Country). 3 Thus to be Blessed is to be properly anointed as Heir, Teacher, Chieftain or Ruler. 4 Such Blessing only be by the most ancient sacred oil of the oldest rulers, 5 and by the consent and conduct of the Cuilliaéan (holly priests), 6 using the most sacred and ancient oil of anointment, 7 whereby the greatest of pharaohs and rulers of the ancient world were anointed. 8 Verily, only those properly anointed by the oil of rulers be a true ruler, 9 and only those properly anointed, 10 by the most sacred oils of Cannabis, Cinnamon, Frankincense and Myrrh, 11 mixed and blended in perfect proportion.

Tara

Book 4
Nome (nomos)

C.1 - Nome (nomos)

Guide me O Creator of all Existence! 2 Direct my actions to be just, 3 concerning Nome (nomos) meaning the Law of Name, 4 and the Law of the Land. 5 May the Truth of the Law help me, 6 to learn and know itself. 7 For as substance be of parchment, skin and stone, 8 for the law to be living it must be just, 9 it must be spoken for all to hear its action. 10 Thus, each name and each thing to be recited, 11 and each and every relation and event be remembered, 12 and life and history be respected, 13 as our foundation and purpose, 14 and our witness to this beautiful Dream. Amen.

C.2 - Divine Law (Diatuair, deuteros) and the journey of knowledge

1 To poor souls borne into slavery, 2 the law is to be feared and not to be spoken, 3 for it be a most dreadful weapon of the slave masters, 4 who twist night into day, 5 evil into good, 6 and honesty into condemnation by corrupting the law. 7 Verily, even unto this day, 8 those freed of the shackles of bondage, 9 remain imprisoned to their prejudice of the true nature of law. 10 To others in declining civilisations, 11 the law is a mystery of occluded knowledge, 12 beyond the reach of the many, 13 and the preserve of magicians and artisans of the tongue. 14 Thus, such ignorant people presume law to be, 15 always at odds with nature and the senses of being. 16 Yet if you come to be here present, 17 upon honouring the journey of Diatuair (deuteros), 18 meaning the Divine Law and the Divine Creator of all the heavens has blessed us, 19 then you know that true law is to be embraced and loved, 20 as a certainty of protection and justice, 21 and a rod of measure to avoid many calamities, 22 and resolve all manner of disputes.

C.3 - Naming and Classification

1 To name a thing, is to make something be. 2 Thus when some thing be named, 3 it then has substance and purpose. 4 Behold! to name a thing is to give power and meaning to it, 5 so that others may do the same for generations to come. 6 Verily, naming be more than process but a living sacred binding, 7 whereby the spirit of intention and wisdom of men and women, 8 is connected to those things that it may name. 9 It is also true that to name a thing for what it truly is, 10 is to restore its power and deny the falsities that may be bound to it. 11 Behold! No matter how devious a scribe may seek to be, 12 the fact that names of things outlast our mortal form over the centuries gives truth to the function of standards and naming.

C.4 - Standards and Consistency

1 Standards be the stones and foundations of a society, 2 and their consistent use and application, 3 the mortar and precision that holds the foundations firm. 4 A people without standards is a people without foundation, 5 and without strength or cohesion, 6 so that upon the first season of strife, 7 they be scattered or seized by the wicked who prey upon the weak. 8 Yet a people with clear standards and consistent use, 9 may withstand a multitude of calamities, 10 and remain united. 11 The merchant families of the city states of the Great Sea (Mediterranean), 12 do not mint uneven single sided money, 13 because they lack knowledge of such standards, 15 they make money without standards so that they can cheat and steal, 16 beyond a healthy profit from trade. 17 Thus, these merchant families that seek to control the supply and mint of money, 18 demand that they be paid in new coin, 19 but pay their debts in old and worn coin. 20 The false rulers of Persia; 21 Herald the existence of many thousands of laws, 22 and proclaim themselves to be a society of laws, 23 that obey the rule of law. 24 Yet there be so many laws, 25 and there language so convoluted and complex, 26 that not even an educated man or woman, 27 may not know them all. 28 Thus, those in favour are granted clemency, 29 and those without means or protection, 30 are condemned by laws they never knew or understand.

C.5 - Bar (Bárá)

1 True Standards are borne from standards of measure, 2 and the rules for their proper use. 3 A Bar (Bárá) be a standard rod, weight, coin or standard thing used for official measure. 4 The word be borne from two ancient meanings, 5 The first be Ba, 6 Meaning spirit, 7 and the second being Ra, 8 meaning King. 9 Hence, all Bar (Bárá), 10 represents the true spirit of a valid ruler, 11 as it is a primary obligation of the ruler, 12 to protect the integrity of all Bar (Bárá) used for measure.

C.6 - Measure (Measúir)

1 Measure (Measúir) be the proper use of Bar (Bárá), 2 to protect and enforce standards throughout the community. 3 The word be borne from two ancient meanings, 4 the first be Meas, 5 meaning to think and reckon with value and esteem, 6 and the second be úir meaning the soil and ground (earth). 7 Hence, all true Measure (Measúir), 8 represents the foundation of proper value and reckoning. 9 There be seven classes of Bar and Measure: 10 The first standard be Units of Measure and Calculation, 11 whereby all people may reckon and calculate to the same numbers and methods. 12 The second standard be Time and Season, 13 whereby all people may know and reckon the day and the cycles of life. 14 The third standard be the Houses and Ages, 15 whereby all people may know and reckon the heavens. 16 The fourth standard be Maoine (Money) and Value, 17 whereby all people may trade and exchange fairly. 18 The fifth standard be Properte (Property) and Land, 17 whereby the rights and prosperity of all people be protected. 18 The sixth standard be Religione (Religion), 19 as the adherence to reverence of faith and tradition; 20

And the fulfilment of a bonded obligation of two years of service 21 to the Cuilliaéan (Holly) Priests by the age of twenty-two. 22 The seventh standard be People, 23 whereby the best possible structure and function of society be assured.

C.7 - Units of Measure and Calculation

1 Units of Measure and Calculation, 2 be the first class of Bar and Measure. 3 The most important of these be the numbers. 4 The first being Aon (One). 5 The second being Dou (Two). 6 The third being Tri (Three). 7 The fourth being Cei (Four). 8 The fifth being Cui (Five). 9 The sixth being Sia (Six). 10 The seventh being Set (Seven). 11 The eighth being Oct (Eight). 12 The ninth being Noi (Nine). 13 The tenth being Ten (Ten). 14 All measure of length and distance be upon the unit of Dista, 15 equal to a toe, or claw or talon (3cm). 16 A Hand, also known as a Lamb, 17 is equal to four Dista (12cm). 18 A Cubit as the sacred measure of Life, 19 is equal to four Hands (48cm). 20 A Fathom is equal to two Cubits or eight Hands (96cm). 21 A Rod is equal to two Fathoms or Four Cubits or sixteen Hands (192cm). 22 A Stade is equal to sixty Rods or two hundred and forty Cubits (11,520cm). 23 A Mile is equal to one hundred and forty-four Stade or eight thousand and six hundred and forty Rods (1,658m). 24 A League is equal to three Miles or four hundred and thirty-two Stades.

C.8 - Time and Season

1 Standards of Time and Season, 2 be the second class of Bar and Measure. 3 The first standard of Time be the Day (Dá). 4 The second standard of Time be the Year (Range). 5 The third standard of Time be the Season (Séasún). 6 The fourth standard of Time be the Week (Seach). 7 The fifth standard of Time be the Month (Moneth).

C.9 - Day (Dá)

1 As Eiri (the Earth) our sacred celestial sphere travels around Suni (Sun), 2 our celestial sphere rotates, 3 so that every land and people, 4 experiences daylight and the darkness of night. 5 Thus a sensible man or woman shall see Suni (Sun), 6 rise in the east and set in the west, 7 not because of some great machine of the god of merchants, 8 who desperately promote ignorance and absurd notions of a flat existence, 9 but for the fact that everything in the Universe as a dream, 10 shares similar features and behaviours, 11 so that the behaviour of our celestial sphere, 12 ensures every land and culture experiences the notion of a dá (day). 13 Behold a single dá (day) may then be divided, 14 into twenty-four units called uair (hour), 15 and each uair (hour) may be divided, 16 into sixty míon (minutes), 17 and each míon (minute) may be divided, 18 into sixty dare (seconds) as the smallest units of time.

C.10 - Year (Range)

1 There be three hundred and sixty five dá (days) in a range (year), 2 and every four range (years) there shall be three hundred and sixty-six dá (days), 3 with such a range (year) known as a leap, 4 and with the additional sacred dá (day) known as naome, 5 except every one hundred and twenty-eight

years, 6 known as an era, 7 when a naome dá (day) shall not be added.

C.11 - Season (Séasún)

1 Everything in the universe is unique cycle. 2 Nothing is a straight line or square, 3 except in the minds of desperately ill priests and imposters, 4 who believe they can corrupt the laws of the Divine Creator, 5 to make themselves as if gods. 6 Thus, a sensible man or woman can see with their own eyes, 7 the changes and cycles throughout the range (year). 8 The beginning of a range (year), 9 the Sol (Sun) appears to stay upon the horizon, 10 as the shortest of days midst cold and darkness. 11 Thereafter, the warmth slowly returns, 12 the ice and snow melts and new sprouts of life appear. 13 Then within the same range (year) there is a blossoming of new life, 14 followed by warmth and longer dá (days). 15 Finally, the trees begin to lose their leaves and cold returns, 16 as the land is soon again in slumber. 17 Behold! let such a cycle be called Séasún (Season), 18 with the beginning of a new range (year), 19 being the first Séasún (Season) called Colde (Winter), 20 and the sacred celebration known as Solstice, 21 upon the mid of Cuinos (December 24/25), 22 as the celebration of sacred light and breath, 23 symbolised by the birth of new lambs. 24 The second Séasún (Season) shall be called Springe (Spring), 25 and the sacred celebration known as Morgaith, 26 upon the mid of Ogronios (February/March), 27 as the celebration of sacred wind and water, 28 and the rising of new life. 29 The third Séasún (Season) shall be called Somere (Summer), 30 and the sacred celebration known as Beltaine, 31 upon the mid of Equos (June/July), 32 as the celebration of sacred fire and warmth, 33 at the end of fruitful and bountiful harvest. 34 The fourth Séasún (Season) shall be called Autome (Autumn), 35 and the sacred celebration known as Samhain, 36 upon the mid of Samonios (October/November), 37 as the celebration of sacred earth and ancestral spirits, 38 and the preparation for Colde (Winter).

C.12 - Week (Seach)

1 Any man or woman deprived of rest cannot sustain a long life. 2 Any child given long and distant goals will not learn. 3 Any community that does not live according to its customs shall cease. 4 Thus, the count of séasún (season) or by range (year) requires an addition. 5 Of all accounting, the number seven is the most efficient, 6 for count of dá (days) called a seach (week), 7 so there are approximately fifty-two seach (weeks) in any given range (year). 8 Behold! the names of each dá (day) of a seach (week) be named, 9 according to the major celestial bodies that move within the heavens. 10 The first dá (day) of a seach (week) shall be known as Solusdi (Sunday), 11 in honour of Sol (the Sun). 12 The second dá (day) of a seach (week) shall be known as Lùnadi (Monday), 13 meaning that which is beloved, 14 in honour and respect of Lùna (the Moon), 15 the great celestial goddess of the night. 16 The third dá (day) of a seach (week) shall be known as Marsadi (Tuesday), 17 meaning in the manner and likeness of a mighty

strong warrior, 18 in honour and respect of Marsa (Mars), 19 the mighty and strong celestial god of war and blood. 20 The fourth dá (day) of a seach (week) shall be known as Mercaoirdi (Wednesday), 21 meaning a dark and mysterious piece of coal, 22 in honour and respect of Mercaoir (Mercury). 23 The fifth dá (day) of a seach (week) shall be known as Lùpitar (Thursday), 24 meaning beloved and valued sister, 25 in honour and respect of Lùipitar (Jupiter), 26 the sister celestial goddess. 27 The sixth dá (day) of a seach (week) shall be known as Lucifeardi (Friday), 28 meaning the best of good fortune, gold, skills and knowledge, 29 in honour and respect of Lucifear (Venus), 30 the morning celestial god of fortune and destiny. 31 The seventh dá (day) of a seach (week) shall be known as Sátandi (Saturday), 32 meaning fulfilled at the height of his powers, 33 in honour and respect of Sátan (Saturn), 34 the celestial god of fulfilment and mysterious change.

C.13 - Month (Moneth)

1 As much as one may count by seach (week), 2 or by séasún (season) or by range (year), 3 there be the need of a middle cycle. 4 Thus countless priests and scribes over the ages, 5 have sought to unify time of the heavens, 6 by supposing the cycle of Lùna (Moon) be reconciled with Sol (Sun). 7 Behold! this be a foolish and false claim, 8 for the cycle between Lùna (Moon) and Sol (Sun), 9 be not constant but a long cycle of 235 cycles of Lùna (Moon), 10 and 19 cycles of Sol (Sun) and 6940 dá (days), 11 before they once again align and repeat. 12 Thus, a range (year) cannot claim to be set according to Lùna (Moon), 13 without one being an idiot or a charlatan. 14 Instead, the units of dá (days) be divided into equal portions. 15 Verily, a solar year be divided into thirteen moneth (months), 16 of twelve moneth (months) of thirty days, 17 and one moneth (month) of five or six days. 18 The first moneth (month) be Cuinos (December), 19 when the Sol (Sun) stands still and is reborne, 20 over five or six dá (days). 21 The second moneth (month) be Riuros (December/January), 22 when the land returns to the way it was in ancient times. 23 The third moneth (month) be Anagantios (January/February), 24 when the animals and house do stay secure. 25 The fourth moneth (month) be Ogronios (February/March), 26 when the cold rain brings ice. 27 The fifth moneth (month) be Cutios (March/April), 28 when the wind and waves to rise. 29 The sixth moneth (month) be Giamonios (April/May), 30 when the gods of the Earth awaken and new growth springs. 31 The seventh moneth (month) be Simivisonios (May/June), 32 when the Sol (Sun) does bring warmth. 33 The eighth moneth (month) be Equos (June/July), 34 when the best foals and calves are borne. 35 The ninth moneth (month) be Elembiuos (July/August), 36 when crops are harvested and the market of wares. 37 The tenth moneth (month) be Edrinios (August/September), 38 when all disputes of the year are discussed. 39 The eleventh moneth (month) be Cantlos (September/October), 40 when the table is full and stories are sung. 41 The twelfth moneth (month) be

Samonios (October/November), 42 when the leaves and seeds fall. 43 The thirteenth moneth (month) be Dumannios (November/December), 44 when sleep envelops the land.

C.14 - Houses and Ages

1 How may any man or woman plot, 2 the correct Season (Séasún)? 3 the correct Month (Moneth)? 4 the correct Week (Seach)? 5 and even the correct Day (Dá) and Year (Range)? 6 It is in the understanding of the heavens and their movement, 7 as the five great celestial messengers, 8 of Lùna (the Moon), Marsa (Mars), Lùipitar (Jupiter), Lucifear (Venus) and Sátan (Saturn), 9 make their presence known. 10 Such knowledge is a threat to the false priests and scribes, 11 who worship money and defend the wicked merchants of the Great Inland Sea (Mediterranean). 12 Like the false messengers before them, 13 They do not want people to comprehend the nature of the night sky. 14 They wish people to be ignorant and to forever look down, 15 as slaves and as ignorant and superstitious people. 16 Thus, knowledge of the movements of the heavens at night, 17 has been corrupted and hidden for too long. 18 Behold! by the Houses the heavens shall be known. 19 The Great Wheel of the heavens be divided into eight houses, 20 and two sacred crosses. 21 So no portion greater or lesser do the celestial messengers, 22 travel through each House. 23 The first House be Cú the Hound and Young Bull (Canis and Orion) (December/January). 24 The second House be Eala the Swan (Leo) (February/March). 25 The third House be Cap-El the Horse (Virgo) (March/April). 26 The fourth House be Tar the Bull (old Taurus/Arcturus) (May/June). 27 The fifth House be Muc the pig (Boar) (Scorpio) (June/July). 28 The sixth House be Poc the Stag (Capricorn) (August/September). 29 The seventh House be Dága the Fish (Pisces) (September/October). 30 The eighth House be Re the Ram (Aries) (November/December). 31 The ninth House is the hidden House of the Great speckled serpent Si (Amen) (Milky Way); 32 The one that travels through all Houses. 33 Thus a Great Age of one House be 3,210 years; 34 And when all eight houses have been visited; 35 Be 25,680 years; 32 And one Great Cycle.

C. 15 - Maoine (Money) and Value

1 Standards of Maoine (Money) and Value, 2 be the fourth class of Bar and Measure. 3 No other invention of men and women, 4 has helped build certain civilisations to greatness, 5 and yet also destroyed them for their arrogance, 6 than the beguile and power of Maoine (Money). 7 True Maoine (Money) be known by four essential qualities: 8 The first quality of Maoine (Money) be as a Standard Unit of Measure, 9 that distinguishes it from other units of measure, 10 so that it may be compared to other things, 11 to create a measure of value (price). 12 The second quality of Maoine (Money) be as a Means of Exchange, 13 to enable the completion of trade, 14 without the need to directly barter the goods in question. 15 Such a quality does not need Maoine (Money) itself to be as coin, 16 as the ancient temple

markets of Egypt and the east, 17 have long established the use of paper as even sufficient as a form. 18 The third quality of Maoine (Money) be as a Unit of Redemption, 19 whereby it may be redeemed if needed for some valuable consideration in the future. 20 Such a quality does not even require Maoine (Money) to be in physical form, 21 as a promise made and trusted to be kept, 22 is sufficient to enable business and trade to thrive. 23 The fourth quality of Maoine (Money) be as a Reliable Store of Value, 24 so that is represents a consistent and stable unit of exchange, 25 such that its Value today is the same or similar as its Value tomorrow. 26 Here, the use of precious metals is accepted by all civilised people, 27 as a useful store of value, 28 even if the unit of measure of such coin and Maoine (Money) is not itself accepted. 29 Verily, these are not the qualities of Maoine (Money) wanted by the pirate merchant dynasties, 30 that live along the coast and plunder trade across the Great Sea (Mediterranean). 31 To these people the quality of a reliable store of value, 32 is against their wishes to steal and cheat, 33 so they create unreliable money of inconsistent weight and form. 34 Nor do these people encourage the other forms of money that enable credit and redemption. 35 Instead they seek to control the issue of all Maoine (Money), 36 and seek to destroy any and all forms of trust and credit, 37 so that the people are forced to deal with their moneylenders. 38 Behold! Never should a people permit the mint and control of Maoine (Money), 39 unto a central temple or such family dynasties. 40 For they shall surely manipulate its power and enslave such foolish people, 41 for a thousand years.

C.16 - The Scrupal

1 The first and primary unit of measure of Maoine (Money), 2 and the fundamental unit of reliable value, 3 be the Scrupal, 4 meaning as the unit of measure, inspection and examination. 5 A single Scrupal be a thin rod of gold equal to twenty grains (1.44 grams). 6 Three (3) Scrupals then be equal to a Dram, 7 of sixty grains (4.32 grams) of gold exactly; 8 And when minted the exact material and weight of a Cuin (Coin). 9 Eight (8) Dram then be equal to one Unce (Ounce) of Gold, 10 equal to four hundred and eighty (480) grains (34.56 grams) of gold exactly. 11 Sixteen (16) Unces (Ounces) then be equal to one Pund (Pound), 12 and sixty (60) Punds (Pounds) be equal to one Talan (Talent). 13 Thus by these standards, 14 All may have confidence in units of measure that do not change, 15 and calculations for large and small trade that does not change. 16 Yet unlike the Persian pirates and merchant allies, 17 who seek to hoard all manner of gold, 18 and deprive people of its possession, 19 The Scrupal and other measures, 20 May be used in many ways as value worn by men and women. 21 Thus, Scrupals may be worn into the edges of clothing, 22 and Drams and Unces (Ounces) of Jewellery may be worn with confidence that such bracelets and necklaces have definite value and as a clear unit of redemption. 23 Behold! the Scrupal be the foundation for the most important form of local Maoine (Money) being the Promise.

C. 17 The Promise and Fidelity (Trust)

1 The most useful and valuable and important Maoine (Money) for internal trade, 2 be not coins or even Scrupals, 3 But the ability to redeem value at some future time. 4 This be the opposite to the great registers of debt operated by the slave traders of Africa and the Great Sea (Meditteranean). 5 Instead, it is placing a credible value on the power of a promise. 6 This form of Maoine (Money) is known as Fidelite (Fidelity), 7 and without it, many communities would remain poor, 8 and without the means to purchase tools, or grain or supplies. 9 This is because of the fundamental negative nature of coins and their circulation. 10 No matter how well intentioned a ruler, 11 The minting of coins and their distribution is never certain, 12 Nor may they find their way to the people who need them most. 13 Instead, merchants tend to hoard coins as their own forms of surety. 14 Other wealthy people tend to hoard coin as a store of value. 15 Other coin is often lost or stolen. 16 Thus a local village may be few in coin; 17 Even if they have an abundance of labour and crops. 18 Yet if a ruler seeks to overcome such inequality and mint more coin, 19 then the value of prices will rise and the people who need credit will be harmed further. 20 Yet with Scrupals, the people do not need to surrender their wealth, 21 But may use it as surety against promises made and kept. 22 Thus community has access to all the credit it needs providing the people keep their promises. 23 Buildings can be built and bread baked, 24 without need of a single coin and without any value being taken from the community. 25 This is why the keeping of promises and credit and fidelity; 26 Is the mortal enemy of the slave traders and money lenders of merchant cities. 27 For there be no need for money lenders when the people trust one another. 28 Behold! Be ever vigilant and never leave your watch, 29 for these Divine gifts be a sword against evil and slavery, 30 and those that worship chaos and wickedness shall stop at nothing, 31 to destroy all memory and all record of this wisdom.

C. 18 - The (Cuin) Coin

1 A true Cuin (Coin), 2 be the cornerstone of Maoine (Money) as a means of exchange, 3 especially with foreigners and between races. 4 A true Cuin (Coin) be more than an impress of gold or silver, 5 but a work of art and precision, 6 overseen by the Cuilliaéan (Holly), 7 according to exact standards and process, 8 and then checked and assessed under trial for any flaws or imperfections. 9 First, a true Cuin (Coin) is made from three scrupals, equal to sixty grains (4.32 grams), 10 called the Tréasuire (Treasure), 11 meaning the three (gold scrupals) as surety. 12 Second, two of the scrupals are cast into Dios (Die) as circular disks, 13 with one being impressed and called the Obverse, 14 the other the Reverse, 15 and then the third side being the third scrupal binding the two Dios (Die), 16 called the Traverse, 17 in a grooved pattern to stop the fraud of filing down coins. 18 The entire process be named as Minte

(Mint), 19 meaning a thing fashioned to have spiritual life. 20 For all true Cuin (Coin) be dedicated to Luki, the god of good fortune; 21 By the Cuilliaéan (Holly) as attendants of Luki known as the Lukifear (Lucifer). 22 Thus unless a Cuin (Coin) be made by a Cuilliaéan (Holly) as Lukifear (Lucifer), then such a creation has no value.

C. 19 - Properte (Property) and Land

1 Properte (Property) and Land, 2 be the fifth class of Bar and Measure. 3 Properte (Property) be the highest Right a man, woman or community has, holds or can have, 4 to control or use or claim any thing or the fruits of any thing. 5 In respect of Properte (Property): 6 Properte (Property) always relates to people and not beings. 7 A Thing in the context of Properte (Property) is any Right that can be purchased or sold or inherited, 8 and attached by law to some object, whether fixed or movable. 9 When one is recognised as possessing a Right or Claim of Right over control or use, 10 then they may be referred to as the "Owner" of that Right. 11 A Right cannot be stolen only surrendered or forfeited. 12 Yet if the claim of forfeit be unlawful and corrupt, 13 or a surrender be under duress or ignorance, 14 then such acts shall have no effect on the Right. 15 There be eight possible forms of Properte (Property): 16 Owner of Right of Control of a Thing; 17 Owner of Right of Use of a Thing; 18 Owner of Right of Control of the Fruits of Use of a Thing; 19 Owner of Right of Use of the Fruits of a Thing; 20 Owner of Claim of Right of Control of a Thing; 21 Owner of Claim of Right of Use of a Thing; 22 Owner of Claim of Right of Control of the Fruits of Use of a Thing; 23 Owner of Claim of Right of Use of the Fruits of a Thing.

C. 20 - Land

1 Land means both the Properte (Property) Rights, 2 and the physical place, dirt of the earth, 3 and any buildings or works, 4 and any fruits of the land, 5 but excluding men and women. 6 It is the business of slave traders to treat men and women as property and land, 7 thus any law that claims the right to enslave people, 8 or to treat people as land is an abomination, 9 and a high curse against any and all who formed such laws and any rulers who rule and seek to enforce the law under such rules. 10 Verily, any law makers that seek to try to make slavery lawful by another name, 11 condemn themselves to misery and condemnation in the afterlife, 12 as the most ignorant and wicked of souls. 13 Thus the smallest parcel of Land be a plot, 14 of thirty-six cubits by sixty cubits. 15 An Acre then be thirty-six cubits by three hundred and sixty cubits. 16 A Seise (Size) then be one hundred and twenty acres.

C. 21 - Religione (Religion)

1 Religion, 2 be the sixth class of Bar and Measure. 3 Not as a faith based on fear nor superstition, 4 but a deep and abiding respect and connection to the Divine, 5 and to all living things, 6 and unto all souls that have been or will ever be. 7 I am the son of Michaiah, 8 and the seventeenth high priest of the Yei-Hu (Yahu), 9 who for generations

Tara

lived upon the Island of Primordial Waters (Elephantine Island), 10 and were the gatekeepers to the Hall of Records, 11 since ancient times. 12 Until the reign of Akhenaten, 13 also known as Moses, 14 the Shepherd Kings did form a sacred pact between heaven and earth, 15 forming a mirror of all life and death, 16 all prophecy and destiny, 17 all ages and wisdom, 18 known as the tree of life, 19 being eleven centres and temple complexes, 20 along the Nile from the Island of Primordial Waters to the serpents head (Qena). 21 Each dynasty of priests specialised their knowledge and prayers on an aspect of the great tree of life, 22 and the ultimate perfection of the transmigration of the soul to perfection. 23 Yet Akhenaten saw such pursuits for what they be, 24 as an exercise of self and mind, 25 ignoring the most powerful centre of the body being the heart. 26 Instead, the priests believed that all higher beings possess more than one soul, 27 and must migrate and travel a path of purification toward perfection. 28 Alas, the futility of such faiths be the impossibility of such perfection, 29 for even the high priests of Yei-Hu (Yahu) be human. 30 The Tree of Life was destroyed when Akhenaten forced the priests to leave Egypt with him, 31 causing civil war. 32 Yet there be knowledge and understanding of the Tree of Life, 33 that be of great importance for now and the future. 34 In Egypt, every free son was required to spend time with the priests, 35 thus having time to think and learn, 36 beyond the grind of life. 37 Behold! The Tree of Life is restored to an even greater life! 38 In the form of fifteen schools called Monasteries, 39 of equal learning and standing. 40 Beginning at Cliathre (Dublin) travelling north, 41 following the northern star one hundred and ten Miles (182 km) to Cairbre (Sligo) be the path of the new Tree of Life. 42 First in travelling eighteen miles due north, 43 be the great city of Tara, 44 with its immense ramparts, 45 shaped in the form of a great shield. 46 Eighteen miles to the east of Tara then be the monastery of Colpa (Drogheda). 47 Eighteen miles to the west of Tara then be the monastery of Carba (Carbury). 48 Eighteen miles north of Tara be the monastery of Fore (Kells) and the beginning of the Great Circle of the Heart. 49 Eighteen miles further north from Fore be Carbala (Drumnora), 50 the centre and soul of the most sacred island. 51 Eighteen miles east of Carbala be Leutha, 52 also upon the Great Circle of the heart. 53 Eighteen miles further east then be the monastery of Arma (Armagh). 54 Eighteen miles west of Carbala be Lega (Legan), 55 also upon the Great Circle of the Heart. 56 Eighteen miles further west from Lega be Arda (Clonmacnoise). 57 Eighteen miles north of Carbala be the monastery of Fue (Ballinanmore), 58 the last great monastery upon the Great Circle of Heart. 59 Twenty miles north of Fue be Tuaira (Creevelea). 60 Eighteen miles east of Tuaira then be Bela (Ballyshannon). 61 Eighteen miles west of Tuaira then be Bala (Ballynote). 62 Finally, eighteen miles north of Tuaira be Cairbre (Sligo).

C.22 - The People

1 The People, 2 be the seventh class of Bar and Measure. 3 That people

themselves, 4 be both the standards and building blocks of a healthy society, 5 or the chaos that brings it to its downfall. 6 Verily, the foundation stone of every healthy society that has ever existed, 7 be the Cell (Family). 8 A Cell be one man and one woman bonded in matrimony, 9 and their progeny (children) not yet of senior age. 10 The Ruler be not the foundation of society, 11 nor the priests and intellectuals of a large community, 12 nor its merchants or entertainers. 13 The Cell be the foundation stone and no other. 14 In contrast the slave traders afford themselves many wives, 15 in disrespect of the equality of women, 16 and upon the hope that they will produce many male heirs. 17 Yet the slave traders and corrupt pirate merchants are infamous, 18 for blood feuds and civil war amongst themselves, 19 on account of theirs being a society founded without respect. 20 Similarly, there are some island cultures of the Great Sea (Mediterranean), 21 Who have placed the intimate love between men above the Cell (Family). 22 All have fallen, not because they be simply foolish, 23 but from failure to see the truth, 24 that trauma does not make placid servants or warriors, 25 but disturbed minds that destroy as much as themselves as eventually their tormentors.

Tara

Book 5
Anacánain (anakineos)

C.1 - Anacánain (anakineos)

Bless the lands and waters, that no transgression blemish Divine Creation! 2 Blessed be all creatures of wing and scale, of hair and flesh. 3 We ask for forgiveness from all to whom we have done ill, 5 as we forgive with a true heart all whom have done ill against us. 6 Oh Spirits and Ancestors, guide and protect us all the days of our lives, 7 and remind us of the true teachings concerning Anacánain (anakineos) meaning the "true language of law" and "to move with purpose". 8 Therefore, may our actions be a beacon in the dark, 9 that all may see the wisdom of laws and respect between different peoples, 10 so that through peace and harmony all may prosper, 11 as it is the birthright of every man and woman, 12 that they do unto others in respect, 13 as it is therefore done to them. 14 Amen.

C.2 - Nome (nomos) and the journey of knowledge

1 If you come to be here present, 2 upon honouring the journey of Tara: 3 From the beginning of Genasis, 4 and the deepest nature and will of the Divine and existence; 5 and then unto the outward journey of Exodus, 6 and the foundation of common morality, 7 as expressed through meaningful stories (parables); 8 and then unto the Divine Law (Diatuair or deuteros), 9 as the bedrock of any lasting community, 10 and the simple rules of any civilised society; 11 and then unto Nomos, 12 and the standards of naming and classification, 13 then you have seen what even the wisest viziers cannot see, 14 and have been blessed with a perspective, 15 that few rulers have ever possessed. 16 For if you have honoured the journey from conception, 17 to this present moment of manifestation, 18 then you know the truth of how and why communities fail, 19 and how people may find the means to rebuild and thrive in peace and prosperity. 20 You can see past the false priests and viziers (experts), 21 who proclaim morality and law to be relative and malleable, 22 and you know the reality of why civilisations die, 23 and even vast empires may be restored to life. 24 Behold! This is the gift of such power of knowledge, 25 to know yourself and why all comes to be as it is, 26 and the means to change and rise up from even the darkest of days.

C.3 - Anacánain (anakineos) and true Action of Law

1 In as much as true law is to be embraced and loved, 2 as a thing of beauty and comfort, 3 that can neither be seized by the wicked and corrupted, 4 nor taken from our mind's eye, 5 it is in the action and not the theory of the law, 6 that we may find greatest clarity and joy. 7 How may we may resolve disputes amongst community or even foreigners? 8 By what means may we

address injury to the law and to others without causing further injury? 9 How we might live each day without harm to others, 10 and confident that no harm shall come to us. 11 This is the purpose of the fifth and final book of Tara and Anacánain (anakineos): 12 To know the law; 13 To love the law; 14 To be a living embodiment of the law. 15 When such men and women appear, 16 who adopt and embrace this high ideal, 17 then all men and women may be assured, 18 that the very soul of their community shall be restored, 19 as the rule of law is restored. 20 Let us therefore bear witness to the law in action, 21 that all may become the living embodiment, 22 of the will and law of heaven on earth.

C.4 - The three elements to Action

1 There be three elements to every action in life: 2 The first be reason, 3 and the intention or purpose of any action. 4 Thus everything in life and the universe, 5 occurs for at least one reason, 6 and nothing happens without there being at least one reason. 7 The second be the cause, 8 and the way that a reason connects to action. 9 So at times when it may appear at first there be no reason, 10 as the cause connecting action to reason be not clear. 11 Thus a cause may be direct or indirect, 12 or a cause may be deliberate or accidental, 13 or brave or impulsive, 14 or even reckless or negligent. 15 The third be the action itself, 16 connected via cause, 17 to some underlying purpose or motive. 18 Finally, all action exists according to three contexts being time, place and at least two parties: 19 The first context is that all actions occur as events in time and space, 20 and once such actions have occurred become moments of history, 21 that must be recreated through memory to be reviewed. 22 The second context is that all actions occur at some place, 23 that can be described and located. 24 The third context is that all actions involve at least two parties, 25 whereby one party be at least the actor, 26 and at least one other as a witness to the action. 27 Therefore an event involving only one party, 28 though it may involve some action of the actor, 29 without any first hand witness as the second party, 30 cannot truly be called an action, 31 and thus can never be argued as the basis of any action in law. 32 Behold! any claim of action in law, 33 without the existence of at least one first hand witness, 34 be an abomination and an absurdity, 35 and so a claim that cannot be properly called lawful or legal.

C.5 - The three elements of Action in law

1 All action in law is necessarily historical, 2 and the process of recreating past events and actions, 3 in order to render relief or benefit and justice, 4 to one or more parties. 5 As in life there be three elements of action in law: 6 The first be the existence of some right of action, 7 whereby one or more parties may bring a claim. 8 Thus an action in law to obtain relief or benefit, 9 may not be granted to one who has no right of action. 10 This rule protects the law from being misused, 11 as an action shall not be granted to one who has no right, 12 as an action in law cannot

arise from a fundamental dishonesty. ₁₃ The second be the existence of some complaint as an immediate cause of action under oath, ₁₄ whereby the claim and relief or benefit be clearly stated. ₁₅ Thus the immediate and not the remote cause must to be considered, ₁₆ as all acts decided in law must reflect a valid cause of action. ₁₇ The third be the existence of some procedure for resolution, ₁₈ whether the matter be capable of being resolved mutually, ₁₉ or that an independent mediator be appointed to hear the matter impartially. ₂₀ In hearing any matter all people of the same community are subject to the same rule of law, ₂₁ and no one may be accused or seek relief or benefit except by law under the rule of law, ₂₂ and no one may be punished or rewarded except by law under the rule of law.

C.6 - Right of Action

₁ There be one right of action above all others, ₂ being to Honour the Law above all things. ₃ Thus from Honour springs all rights of action. ₄ From Honour then comes three primary Rights of Action: ₅ To Protect, to Provide and to Serve. ₆ To protect and defend one's honour. ₇ This being the first rule of self. ₈ To protect and defend the home. ₉ This being the first rule of home. ₁₀ To protect and defend the fine (tribe). ₁₁ This being the first rule of the fine (tribe). ₁₂ To provide for one's health and well being. ₁₃ This being the second rule of self. ₁₄ To provide for one's kin and home. ₁₅ This being the second rule of home. ₁₆ To provide for all strangers, guests and those in need. ₁₇ This being the second rule of the fine (tribe). ₁₈ To serve to better one's self and knowledge. ₁₉ This being the third rule of self. ₂₀ To serve to better the lives of one's kin and home. ₂₁ This being the third rule of home. ₂₂ To serve to better the life of the fine (tribe). ₂₃ This being the third rule of the fine (tribe).

C.7 - To protect and defend one's honour

₁ The first right of action of self be, ₂ to protect and defend one's honour. ₃ Thus a man or woman cannot be found culpable of an offence, ₄ if they be first the victim of unfounded slander and scandal, ₅ and have done everything within their power to compel the slanderer to recant their falsities, ₆ before demanding the ultimate right to defend their honour to the death. ₇ Therefore one who makes unfounded slander and scandal, ₈ and upon challenge refuses to yield, ₉ and upon the ultimate expression of right refuses to meet the injured party to mortal combat, ₁₀ shall be seized and stripped of all property, ₁₁ and perpetually cursed as an ui nial (ui Niall), ₁₂ meaning one who has no honour nor moral conscience. ₁₃ Furthermore, the name and memory of a man or woman, ₁₄ cannot be condemned, ₁₅ if upon the rendering of a terrible verdict, ₁₆ they be found culpable of one or more hideous offences, ₁₇ they choose to take their own life. ₁₈ For no community or society, ₁₉ may use the law to render a verdict of death, ₂₀ without offending heaven and all earth. ₂₁ This be why to take one's own life upon being found seriously culpable, 22 is known as an honourable death.

C.8 - To protect and defend the home

1 The first right of action of home be, 2 to protect and defend the home. 3 Thus no man or woman be found culpable of an offence, 4 if they be first the victim of some unfounded trespass or attack upon their home, 5 and upon calling out and warning such trespassers, 6 they refuse to cease and desist. 7 Thus every man and woman of adult age possesses the immutable right to bear arms, 8 and no free and fair society possesses the authority to deprive its people, 9 of the right of action to defend themselves and their home and property, 10 against unlawful and unwarranted seizure or trespass.

C.9 - To protect and defend the tribe

1 The first right of action of the fine (tribe) be, 2 to protect and defend the fine (tribe). 3 Thus no man or woman be found culpable of an offence, 4 if they be members of a party of a fine (tribe), 5 called upon to serve in the defence of the fine (tribe), 6 whether it be imminent or remote, 7 or whether such service call be for a far journey of service, 8 providing such service be first defined by a time of expiry, 9 be for no financial reward, 10 and be for a just and righteous cause. 11 A man or woman who demands or receives payment to kill, 12 is a mercenary and a cursed soul. 13 Yet a man or woman who kills another, 14 to protect and defend the fine (tribe), 15 for just cause and action, 16 can never be held culpable of murder, 17 unless such an act was done out of malice or ill intent.

C.10 - To provide for one's health and well being

1 The second right of action of self be, 2 to provide for one's health and well being. 3 Thus no man or woman be found culpable of an offence, 4 if they be suffering the effects of severe hunger and deprivation, 5 and seek nourishment from a source that otherwise refuses to act honourably, 6 and provide alms to the suffering and distressed. 7 Behold! a starving child who takes a loaf of bread from a greedy baker, 8 who refuses to provide alms to the poor, 9 can never be claimed an offence of larceny (theft), 10 but a right of action to provide for one's health and well being. 11 Thus the wealthy are obligated to provide alms and support to the poor, 12 as such alms negate the right of action for a person, 13 to take it upon themselves to provide for their own survival, 14 and ensures a happy and fair and prosperous community.

C.11 - To provide for one's kin and home

1 The second right of action of home be, 2 to provide for one's kin and home. 3 Thus no mother or father be found culpable of an offence, 4 if they be suffering the effects of severe hunger and deprivation, 5 and seek nourishment from a source that otherwise refuses to act honourably, 6 and provide alms to the suffering and distressed. 7 Behold! the wealth in a just society have no right to hoard wealth and goods, 8 while their fellow members suffer and starve. 9 Indeed

the law compels the poor to rise up and seize what they need from those too cold hearted and cruel, 10 against the suffering of their neighbour. 11 Yet an enlightened class of wealthy merchants and community leaders, 12 be afforded the full protection of the law, 13 if they do everything in their power, 14 to eliminate homelessness and poverty in their midst.

C.12 - To provide for all strangers, guests and those in need

1 The second right of action of the fine (tribe) be, 2 to provide for all strangers, guests and those in need. 3 Thus no man or woman be found culpable of an offence against the fine (tribe), 4 if they give hospitality, food and shelter to strangers and guests. 5 Verily, all conflict between peoples is founded upon wrecking the bonds of amity, peace and harmony, 6 that exists when men and women of different cultures, 7 and of different skin colour and creeds, 8 may discover their common values and respect. 9 Thus to deny comfort to strangers and guests, 10 is to weaken the safety and security of the fine (tribe), 11 and ferment the conditions for future conflict.

C.13 - To serve to better one's self and knowledge

1 The third rule of self be, 2 to serve to better one's self and knowledge. 3 Thus no man or woman be found culpable of an offence, 4 if they seek greater knowledge of self, 5 and greater knowledge of the world and heavens, 6 and greater knowledge of all wisdom throughout the ages. 7 A man or woman who respects knowledge, humanity and themselves, 8 has no fear of differences of opinion, 9 nor different ideas and faiths. 10 Such a man or woman knows that ignorance is the opposite of knowledge, 11 and hateful prejudice is the enemy of good faith and wise discernment. 12 Thus any man or woman who advocates the suppression of knowledge, 13 be the greatest enemy of the people, 14 as much as one who deceives and refuses to speak the truth. 15 Behold! Let not those who worship ignorance and prejudice, 16 take hold of the education nor voice of the fine (tribe) or clan or race. 17 Such cowards and vipers who claim to uphold morals, 18 yet despise and seek to corrupt all foundation of common values, 19 and who claim to love freedom and wisdom, 20 who then advocate the suppression of differences, 21 be the architects of doom for countless peoples. 22 More deadly than the fiercest army, 23 be the spineless assassins of truth, 24 who hide behind the garments of trust, 25 and undermine the city from within. 26 Cast them out! 27 Expose them before it is too late! 28 Stand your ground and let not their hateful bile cause you fear! 29 Our future and our very existence, 30 depends upon enough of each generation, 31 willing to risk everything for the ideals of knowledge and wisdom, 32 against a beguiling and perpetual enemy of evil, 33 the enemy of wilful ignorance and deception that is true evil.

C.14 - To serve to better the lives of one's kin and home

₁ The third right of action of home be, ₂ to serve to better the lives of one's kin and home. ₃ Thus no man or woman be found culpable of an offence, ₄ if they seek to provide for the safety, sustenance, ₅ and well being of their kin and home. ₆ Verily, the first mission of the head of any house, ₇ is for the well being, safety and sustenance of all members of the household. ₈ Thus the rules of the fine (tribe), ₉ and the rules of the race be secondary, ₁₀ if a house be unjustly stricken by hunger or deprivation. ₁₁ If a house be haunted by hunger and ill fortune, ₁₂ be thus cursed by neighbours who abdicate their obligation to give aid, ₁₃ there be no offence in the seizure of sufficient food to ward off the talons of hunger, ₁₄ or dry wood to expel the clutches of winter. ₁₅ Behold! Any community that punishes the poor and starving, ₁₆ by inflicting further pain and woe upon their souls, ₁₇ be a wicked place that shall not last, ₁₈ but shall doom its rulers and all that give it comfort. ₁₉ Thus a true society of law, ₂₀ be first a community of values and good conscience.

C.15 - To serve to better the life of the fine (tribe)

₁ The third right of action of the fine (tribe) be, ₂ to serve to better the life of the fine (tribe). ₃ Thus no man or woman be found culpable of an offence, ₄ if they seek to defend, maintain and improve, ₅ the life and well being of the fine (tribe). ₆ Verily, the prime mission and purpose of any fine (tribe), ₇ is firstly for the well being and benefit of its members equally. ₈ To claim that a fine (tribe) does not exist for the benefit equally of all its inhabitants, ₉ is to cede that a community be founded on nothing more than slavery by a different name. ₁₀ Verily, the slave traders and merchants, ₁₁ and their willing accomplices in vile wickedness, ₁₂ proclaim that a city be a place welcoming all people, ₁₃ as if somehow strangers have greater importance than its inhabitants. ₁₄ Thus they dress up their prison cities in bright colours, ₁₅ to hide the horror of its poverty and deprivation, ₁₆ and lavish huge sums on entertainment and music, ₁₇ to drown the groans of the dying and starving poor, ₁₈ and fill their temples and public squares with fragrant smokes and fresh herbs, ₁₉ to mask the stench of great evils against heaven. ₂₀ A city if it to be a true city and not a prison, ₂₁ exists for the equal benefit of its inhabitants first. ₂₂ It must be able to protect and attend to its walls and borders. ₂₃ Let not your mind or senses be dulled by the lies of such merchants of destruction. ₂₄ Do not surrender the freedoms of equality and respect. ₂₅ Confront all false teachings and double speak.

C.16 - Fidelity of one's promises

₁ Above all things, guard and keep your words carefully. ₂ Do not give your word too easily, ₃ and never to one who has not first earned such trust to demand it. ₄ Verily, no one can force you to make a promise or oath or vow, ₅ for such duress invalidates any such demands. ₆ Nor should you ever give your word to one notorious for being untrustworthy. ₇ Behold! if one comes claiming good faith and trust, ₈ only to be revealed a liar and a thief, ₉ then your word is as if never made, 10 for heaven forbids any words made to a liar and thief to be counted as a promise. 11 Thus keep your promises, 12 and let your words be your binding, 13 without fear or concern that anyone may trick you.

C.17 - Fear nothing

1 Let not any woe keep you awake or fearful. 2 Let not your heart be troubled. 3 Let those who speak evil against you do their worst without concern. 4 They will soon die as you will also cease this existence. 5 Time of life is short. 6 Let not such a precious gift be squandered. 7 Yet do not think it can be saved by hiding from life and running away. 8 Face your fears. 9 Embrace your fears as old friends. 10 Let not your mind conjure all manner of doom, 11 for a worried mind is often plagued to do. 12 Verily, fear is first and foremost a state of mind, 13 that weakens our judgement and causes poor choices. 14 Do not confuse fear with nervousness. 15 All who prepare for battle should be at first nervous, 16 for it may be your last breath. 17 Yet fear is too often the weakness of the coward and the cruel. 18 They seek to sow its rotten fruit and plant such seeds of woe in the mind of others. 19 Fear is a weapon of control, 20 and thus has been used by countless tyrants to imprison vast populations. 21 You have nothing to fear, 22 for the greatest truths of life are certain. 23 You will die as we all die. 24 You will experience pain at times as we all experience pain. 25 You will feel alone at times as all feel isolated at times. 26 Fear nothing and stand against such liars and thieves, 27 who seek to control and manipulate others through fear.

C. 18 - Your life has purpose

1 Life has purpose. 2 Existence of all things depends upon life. 3 Your life has purpose and meaning, 4 even if you may not know what path to choose. 5 Do not confuse your lack of understanding, 6 to mean a lack of answers or reason. 7 Even if you stubbornly refuse to learn, 8 life will find a way of teaching you. 9 Even a poor question or answer, 10 is a stepping stone eventually to truth. 11 If you embrace what has been revealed to you within these books, 12 then you shall certainly find good fortune, 13 even in difficult times. 14 May your life be filled with joy, good fortune and well being. Amen.

Tara

Original Nations (Tribes) of Celtic Lands

C.1 – Celtic Civilisation and Lands

None can deny the existence or influence of the Celtic Civilisation. 2 In the space of a few decades beginning from the 6th Century BCE, 3 Celtic culture successfully spread from Ireland, 4 north to Greenland and south to North Africa and as far east as Turkey. 5 At its height the lands of the Celts covered an area larger than the Roman Empire. 6 The Celts built thousands of miles of perfectly engineered roads. 7 The Celts excelled in metallurgy, design, art, music and poetry. 8 Celtic religion and spiritual systems remain deeply advanced, 9 in recognising the ultimate divine reality and presence that is the source of all nature and the cosmos, 10 and in holding a deep reverence for nature and respect for all livings things as having their own spirit. 11 In language, the Celtic tongue became the standard and bedrock for so many written languages that followed. 12 Most importantly in matters of law and the organisation and function of society, 13 the Celts were advanced in the standards of law and the administration of fair justice, 14 and in property rights, the rights of women and compensation for wrongs instead of violent retribution. 15 At the core of the law was the sacred Covenant of Tara, 16 later known as Terra and literally meaning the law of the land, 17 and then later corrupted by the 16th Century into a false claim called the Torah, 18 where a group that had never previously existed before the 16th Century did falsely claim the heritage of the Yahudi as their own, 19 and did claim such rights and provenance of Tara and the Celts to themselves.

C.2 – Original Nations (Tribes)

1 An *Original Nation* is a significant community of people originating from a traditional bounded area of land, 2 having long standing continuous human habitation and association, 3 to one or more ancient covenants of law, culture and rights, 4 recognised under Civilised Ucadia and Non-Ucadia Law. 5 The word Nation originates from Latin *natio* meaning a group of people bound together by common characteristics, 6 such as birth, language, customs, and culture, 7 The word Tribe originates from ancient Irish *tríbe* meaning three (or more) be united, 8 and a group of people with common characteristics, cultures, or affiliations. 9 As both words share common characteristics they are united in the description of Original Nations. 10 Thus a properly registered body claiming to be an Original Nation (Tribe), possessing a current mandate under Ucadia Law, 11 is a valid Sovereign Body and Community, superior in all and every aspect to an

Uncivilised regime, or body or corporation. 12 Verily, an Original Nation (Tribe) has no legitimacy or validity in law, 13 unless it is duly registered and possesses a proper mandate under Ucadia Law.

C.3 - Original Law & Original Nations

1 *Original Law & Original Nations* refers to the fact that only a properly formed Original Nation (Tribe) has right and access to Original Law, 2 being the first law of the land above and ahead of any other lesser claim from a Non-Ucadia society, body, government, military or agency. 3 Original Law is a recognised Sacred Covenant between an Authentic, Apostolic and Anointed Divine Messenger of the Divine Creator of all Existence, 4 and all the Heavens and Earth and the peoples of the Earth, 5 that provides some form of moral direction, teaching and rules. 6 Thus, as all proper law is ultimately derived from Divine Law, 7 valid Original Law is first in order, bearing its own authority, 8 and not deriving authority from an outside or lesser Non-Ucadian source. 9 Verily a Governing Law or Instrument of a body politic or corporate may be its first laws, 10 or indeed an instrument or law in its original form. 11 Yet first laws or original form do not equal original law unless such a body politic possesses a Divine Mandate under Ucadia, 12 connected to the Original People of the same land. 13 Therefore, such absurd, dishonest and misleading claims that equate the lesser laws of a Non-Ucadia body, 14 as having the same standing as the ancient laws under the most sacred Covenant known as *Pactum De Singularis Caelum*, 15 only serve to condemn such claimants as impostors and liars of an uncivilised system, 16 and not true custodians of Civilised Law.

C.4 - Original Authority & Original Nations

1 *Original Authority & Original Nations* refers to the fact that only a properly formed Original Nation (Tribe) has the rights of Original Authority, 2 being the *first authority of office and authority, rights and powers* above and ahead of any other lesser claim from a Non-Ucadia society, body, government, military or agency. 3 Original Authority is the recognised rights, positions and powers given by a valid Divine Mandate through a recognised Sacred Covenant, 4 to one or more persons concerning the right to direct, teach, demand or control someone or something. 5 Thus, as all proper authority and office is ultimately derived from Divine Law, 6 valid Original Authority is first in rights, positions and power; 7 and not deriving authority, rights or powers from an outside or lesser Non-Ucadian source. 8 Verily a claim of rights and powers may be recorded as first, 9 and may even be recognised by other bodies politic and corporate as claims first or higher authority. 10 Yet such claims of first or higher authority are no comparison to the Divine Mandate of *Tara*, 11 as united under the most sacred Covenant *Pactum de Singularis Caelum*. 12 Similarly, claims of original authority wherein such claims are merely delegations of

authority, 13 of a claimed higher power or religious official, 14 cannot usurp the primary and original authority of God and the Divine Creator of all things and all existence and all Heaven and Earth, 15 as expressed and mandated through the most sacred Covenant *Pactum De Singularis Caelum*.

C.5 – Original Registers & Original Nations

1 *Original Registers & Original Nations* refers to the fact that only a properly formed Original Nation (Tribe) has the right to manage Original Registers, 2 being the first jurisdiction, claim, title, property and dominion above and ahead of any other less claim from a Non-Ucadia society, body, government, military or agency. 3 Original Register is a recognised book, table or roll authorised by a valid Divine Mandate through a recognised Sacred Covenant, 4 for the original recording of events, rights, dominion, property, persons, title or claims then relied upon, 5 in the administration of rights, powers, property, obligations, agreements, assets or disputes. 6 Thus, as all money, property and rights are ultimately derived from Divine Law, 7 valid Original Registers are the first recordings of events, rights, dominions, property, title, persons, positions and power; 8 and not derived from an outside or lesser Non-Ucadian register. 9 Verily the registers of any claimed sovereign body, or body politic or corporate are defined by its governing laws or governing instruments, 10 and indeed may be claimed as being the first or highest by the laws of such a body. 11 Yet such a claim does not mean that such a register possesses any Divine Mandate as granted through a valid Sacred Covenant to record such events, rights, property, agreements or persons. 12 Similarly, a first registration not Original Registration whereby a claim of first in time or earliest registration is made within the laws of a Non-Ucadian body. 13 Behold, no claim or record, or entry or register can be higher than the Registers of One Heaven and Earth, 14 as defined by the most sacred Covenant *Pactum De Singularis Caelum*. 15 Therefore, to then misrepresent first registration in a Non-Ucadian Jurisdiction as somehow Original Registration, 16 not only has no force or effect in law, 17 but signifies a profound blasphemy and act of bad faith, bad conscience and bad intention, 18 that disqualifies every element of such a claim.

C.6 - Original Administration & Original Nations

1 *Original Administration & Original Nations* refers to the fact that only a properly formed Original Nation (Tribe) has the first right of Original Administration and Original Jurisdiction, 2 and to assign, or withdraw such powers and authorities to qualified and competent officers and elected officials, 3 within the framework of Ucadia Societies or Non-Ucadia Civilised Societies that recognise the immutable authority of original law, original authority, original registers and original administration. 4 Original

Administration is cumulative powers and authority of first or primary government of any given sovereign state or authority. 5 Properly constituted and mandated Original Nations (Tribes) are unique in having undisputed Original Administration in both Ucadia and Non-Ucadia civilisations. 6 Original Jurisdiction is the scope and limit of authority of a political or judicial body, or judicial or law enforcement officer to pursue or decide matters of law. 7 By innate right, Ucadia possesses Original Jurisdiction over all its persons, events and matters of Law. 8 Verily a first entry in a register does not mean first or original jurisdiction, 9 and the right of a claimed court in that jurisdiction to be the first to hear a legal case. 10 A first entry is merely a first in time claim and nothing more. 11 Unless such a claim is properly heard and adjudicated in a public and competent forum of law, 12 then such a claim, even if upheld is an injury against proper justice. 13 Behold! if the first entry of a matter or controversy pertains to a Ucadia Person or Ucadia Property or Rights, 14 then no court or forum may make a first entry or claim of original jurisdiction, 15 except a properly constituted Ucadia Forum and Court of Law and none other. 16 Regardless of whether a matter concerning a person or property or matter under the custody or authority of Ucadia is registered in a Non-Ucadia jurisdiction first, 17 Ucadia and its courts shall have Original Jurisdiction. 18 Therefore, any such assertion to the contrary is a self confession that such a body cannot be a proper court of law, 19 and that any such ruling, deliberation or demand from such a body has no force or effect in law.

C.7 - Body Politic of each Tribal Nation

1 Each and every Original Tribal Nation, 2 be a sovereign body politic, 3 with its own laws and bylaws in accord with Ucadia Civilisation and the most sacred Covenant *Pactum De Singularis Caelum*, 4 with its own executive and legislature, 5 with the present sacred Covenant of *Tara* as its first Governing Instrument of Formation and Constitution, 6 before members may decide by vote to form a separate constitution in accord with the present most sacred Covenant. 7 Each and every Original Tribal Nation as a body politic shall have the same rights as a natural person, 8 to engage and treaty with other persons, bodies and corporations, 9 and to bring suit or to have actions brought against it to the extent that sovereign immunity shall protect the essential sovereign integrity of each and every community. 10 The unit of account for each Original Tribal Nation shall be the Ucadia Moneta, 11 and any unit of currency that claims to be by authority of a union of Original Nations as a Commonwealth, or for the community shall first and foremost be derived from the accounts and funds of Ucadia Moneta and no other, in accord with the Ucadia Financial System. 12 No body or bank or fund or agency shall have any right or claim to be a central bank for any Original Tribal Nation or group of Original Tribal Nations, 13 unless it be a body authorised under the Ucadia Financial System, 14 and no person or group of people or

corporations may claim to be a central bank, 15 or any part of the sacred lands, 16 as the sovereign right of communities to mint and manage money, 17 is a sacred right that cannot be seized, surrendered, alienated, sold, forfeited or abrogated in any way.

C.8 - Commonwealth of Original Nations

1 The unity of a state and country and body of Original Nations, 2 exists first and foremost through the Union as a Commonwealth of all Original Tribal Nations as one united body politic, 3 and the formation of a sacred united treaty and trust between all Original Tribal Nations, 4 and the lawful recognition and incorporation by charter of an executive and body politic and corporate to serve the interests of all people first and foremost, 5 rather than the interests of foreign bodies, potentates, powers or other persons. 6 The primary legislative organ of the Commonwealth of all Original Nations of a particular state or country shall be the Council of Original Nations, also to be known simply as the (Original) Council. 7 The primary executive corporate sole of the Union of all Original Nations shall be the President of the Council of Original Nations, 8 also known simply as the (Original) President. 9 The body politic and corporate formed underneath the authority and powers of the Council of Original Nations, 10 shall be known as an original Republic, or Kingdom or Commonwealth, or Federation, 11 also known simply as the Government. 12 Where officials acting in the claimed capacity as the government of a country or state or kingdom or nation refuse to recognise *Tara*, 13 or refuse to recognise the Commonwealth of all Original Nations, 14 then all valid and legitimate spiritual, ecclesiastical, sovereign, moral, lawful and legitimate executive and legislative authority shall return to be vested solely with the Council of Original Nations, 15 who then shall have every right and power to call for aid and assistance in the defeat of any and all forces of occupation, oppression or tyranny upon the country or state or kingdom. 16 However, if there exists officials acting in the claimed capacity as the Government that properly recognise the authority of *Tara* and Ucadia, 17 then all sovereign, moral, lawful and legitimate executive and legislative authority shall be vested solely with that Government, 18 and the the Council of Original Nations shall hold reserve and emergency powers only, in the event of a coup or seizure of power in defiance of the laws of *Tara* and Ucadia.

C.9 - State and Union of Original Nations

1 The Council of Original Nations and the present Governing Instrument, 2 recognise the permission of groups of Original Tribal Nations in forming smaller regional groups. 3 These smaller regional groups shall be called States or Territories, 4 and may be formed only upon a convention of Original Tribal Nations as a Commonwealth of Original Nations. 5 A small region of united Original Tribal Nations shall only be permitted to use names and boundaries

determined by the union convention, 6 and in respect of customary traditions and names. 7 However, a regional body of Original Tribal Nations is not permitted to form treaty with any foreign body deriving its claim or authority from some foreign occupying force upon country. 8 Any body currently called a state or territory that refuses to acknowledge the higher authority of *Tara* and the laws of Ucadia, 9 and instead seeks to maintain a claim of authority and power from a foreign sovereign or body, 10 shall then declare itself to be an occupying and oppressive force that cannot be given spiritual or moral or lawful legitimacy. 11 The Council of Original Nations shall have every right and power to call for aid and assistance, 12 in the defeat of any and all such forces of occupation, oppression or tyranny upon the country or state or kingdom.

C.10 - Sacred Tribal Registers

1 All rights and property of the country or state or kingdom comes first from the laws of *Tara*, 2 and the laws of Ucadia and the sacred tribal registers of the Commonwealth of Original Nations. 3 No right or claim to property or land or tenement or thing of value be valid or legitimate, 4 unless the register or roll recording such an entry be a valid and legitimate sacred tribal register of the Commonwealth of Original Nations. 5 Any register or roll that is not itself registered as a valid and legitimate tribal register of the Council of Original Nations, 6 shall have no spiritual, ecclesiastical, sovereign, moral, lawful or legitimate authority whatsoever, no matter how old or how well established. 7 The Council of Original Nations shall have a moral and spiritual obligation, 8 to ensure the safe protection and administration of property rights of the people, 9 and for existing registers to be recognised as valid and legitimate sacred tribal registers, providing such registers do not repudiate the moral obligations and needs of the communities and people. 10 Registers that openly repudiate common sense and moral obligation to the people and communities must be refused recognition, 11 and to be dissolved and removed at the earliest opportunity, 12 including the dissolution of those laws that made such registers and rolls repugnant and contrary to the laws of *Tara* and the laws of Ucadia. 13 Above all it is better that a register be reformed and then recognised than banned and forced to be dissolved, given the disruption to the certainty of rights and property.

C. 11 - Sacred Tribal Cultural Registers

1 All rights of use, benefit, sale and ownership of indigenous art, artefacts and cultural items of significance shall be subject to the Sacred Tribal Cultural Registers, 2 under the primary authority and control of the Council of Original Nations. 3 Only indigenous art, artefacts and cultural items duly registered in a valid and legitimate Sacred Tribal Cultural Register are permitted to be held, displayed, owned or used. 4 Indigenous art, artefacts and cultural items not properly registered in a valid and legitimate Sacred Tribal Cultural

Register are not permitted to be held, displayed, owned, offered for sale or used. 5 The holding, displaying and selling of items claiming to be indigenous or indigenous cultural items of significance without a proper registration number, 6 shall represent one of most profoundly morally repugnant, wicked and sacrilegious crimes that a government, or agency, or officer, or body or institution or person may commit against country and the people.

C.12 - Sacred Tribal Land Registers

1 All rights of use, benefit and ownership of land or space shall be subject to the Sacred Land Registers, 2 under the primary authority and control of the Council of Original Nations. 3 No register or roll of land rights or usage shall be valid or legitimate unless the specific register is itself duly registered and recognised as a Sacred Tribal Land Register in accord with the present sacred laws of *Tara* and laws of Ucadia. 4 A register that contradicts any of the following fundamental spiritual, sovereign and moral principles in relation to the people and communities is to be forbidden, suppressed and not permitted to be recognised as a valid or legitimate register whatsoever: 5 First, only members of an Original Nation or an authorised company may own land or buildings or property. 6 Second, foreign bodies, foreign sovereign powers and foreign citizens may not purchase or own land or buildings or property, 7 as such bodies or powers and persons may only lease land or buildings or property from the original people. 8 If a register permits such foreign ownership then a sale or transfer of ownership must be completed on all such foreign owned property before such a register can be considered for legitimacy. 9 Third, primary property rights of natural persons shall not exceed ninety-nine years and fifty-five years for a local company respectively. 10 Fourth, the lease of land or buildings or property by foreign natural persons shall not exceed twenty five years and twelve years for a foreign body or company respectively.

C.13 - Sacred Tribal Mineral Registers

1 All rights of use, benefit and ownership of minerals and mining shall be subject to the Sacred Mineral Registers, 2 under the primary authority and control of the Council of Original Nations. 3 No register or roll of land rights or usage shall be valid or legitimate unless the specific register is itself duly registered and recognised as a Sacred Tribal Mineral Register in accord with the present sacred laws of *Tara* and laws of Ucadia. 4 A register that contradicts any of the following fundamental spiritual, sovereign and moral principles in relation to the people and communities of Original Nations is to be forbidden, suppressed and not permitted to be recognised as a valid or legitimate register whatsoever: 5 First, only members of an Original Nation or a company recognised under a Commonwealth of Original Nations may own mineral rights. 6 Second, foreign bodies, foreign sovereign powers and foreign citizens may not own mineral rights, 7

as such bodies or powers persons may only lease mineral rights from members of Original Nations. 8 If a register permits such foreign ownership then a sale or transfer of ownership must be completed on all such foreign owned mineral rights before a register can be considered for legitimacy. 9 Third, the value of any mineral rights and applications assigned any land shall not exceed one tenth the value of the surface valuation of the land. 10 Fourth, the right of first claim for mineral rights and application shall always be vested in the primary Original owner of the lease of surface land. 11 Fifth, the total value of claims and mineral rights of a person or company shall not exceed three times the net asset value of the person or company prior to making such mineral claims and applications. 12 Sixth, excluding the primary owner of the land, a mineral claim or right shall be extinguished within three years if active building, investment, mining and extraction does not commence and continue for an accumulative period of not less than six months during the period.

C.14 - Sacred Tribal Water Registers

1 All rights of use, benefit and ownership of water shall be subject to the Sacred Water Registers, 2 under the primary authority and control of the Council of Original Nations. 3 No register or roll of water rights or usage shall be valid or legitimate unless the specific register is itself duly registered and recognised as a Sacred Tribal Water Register in accord with the present sacred laws of *Tara* and laws of Ucadia. 4 A register that contradicts any of the following fundamental spiritual, sovereign and moral principles in relation to the people and communities is to be forbidden, suppressed and not permitted to be recognised as a valid or legitimate register whatsoever: 5 First, only members of an Original Nation or a local company may own water rights. 6 Second, foreign bodies, foreign sovereign powers, foreign citizens may not own water rights, 7 as such bodies or powers and persons may only lease water rights from the local people. 8 Third, the value of any water rights and applications assigned to any related land shall not exceed one tenth the value of the surface valuation of the land. 9 Fourth, the right of first claim for water rights and application shall always be vested in the primary owner of the land related to the water rights. 10 Fifth, the claimant for purchase of water rights must live or operate its primary business within the catchment associated with the said water rights. 11 Sixth, the total value of claims and water rights of a person or company shall not exceed three times the net asset value of the person or company prior to making such water claims and applications. 12 Seventh, excluding the primary owner of the land, a water claim or right shall be extinguished within three years if utilisation of at least sixty five percent of such water rights does not commence and continue for an accumulative period of not less than six months.

C.15 - Enforcement of Original Rule of Law

1 True law is not morally repugnant. 2 True law is logical and sensible. 3 A true and valid and legitimate court is one that honours the Original Law of *Tara* and Ucadia. 4 Any forum of law that does not honour or recognise or respect *Tara* as first law cannot be a proper court of law, 5 but must be a sacrilegious and wicked and morally repugnant place of injury to the true rule of law. 6 A jurist or recorder or judge that seeks to usurp the rule of law, 7 by refusing to recognise the primary jurisdiction and authority of the laws of Ucadia, 8 declares themselves an enemy of heaven, 9 and an enemy to all forms of spirit and the laws of the universe, 10 and belligerent threat to all forms of life on earth, 11 and an enemy of the people. 12 Such a person calls upon themselves the worst of woe and ill. 13 Yet such a person or persons must also be held to account. 14 *Tara* is judged by no one. 15 Ucadia is judged by no one. 16 Any forum claiming to be a forum of law that denies such truth cannot be a proper court of law, 17 nor may any order, verdict or sentence stand as anything but a solemn and profound curse upon the makers of such false instruments. 18 Do not fear those who curse themselves and their brethren by wicked acts against the law. 19 Respect the true law. 20 Embrace *Tara*, 21 as *Tara* loves you. 22 Peace be upon you and all the communities of the most sacred Celtic Lands.

Tara

I. Original Nations (Tribes) of Éire (Ireland)

C.1 – One Law One People One Land of Eire

In truth, there was, there is, there has only ever been One Original Law of Ireland; 2 And there has only ever been One Irish People; 3 And there has only ever been One Sacred Land belonging equally to all the Irish People. 5 There can be no honour or respect of Irish People or First Ancestors, 6 if there is no honour or recognition of the First and Original Law of *Tara*. 7 There can be no honour of the One Sacred and Indivisible Land of Ireland, 8 unless First and Original Law of *Tara* and the First and Original People of Ireland are properly recognised under all forms of Civilised Law. 9 No one is above such Law. 10 No one Person or Community in Ireland is excluded from such Law. 11 All are equal under the One Law. 12 Any law that is against such truth, cannot be law.

C.2 – People born to Land of Eire born to the Original People of Eire

1 Any one borne to the sacred and indivisible Land of Ireland is borne to the People, 2 and is borne to tribe and Law. 3 People be not excluded by colour, 4 People be not excluded by race of ancestors, 5 People be not excluded by city or non-city. 6 Any one who rejects the right of people borne to the sacred and indivisible Land, 7 as true members of tribe and the people, 8 dishonours the Law, 9 and dishonours their ancestors, 10 and dishonours the spirits of Ireland, 11 and is an impostor with no rights, 12 to speak of law or culture. 13 Racism is not Law, it is against proper Law. 14 Racial purity is not Law, it is madness of mind. 15 For every one borne of Ireland, 16 has the right to know the tribe they be borne, 17 and the ancient names of the land, 18 and be welcomed to tribe by right ceremony. 19 Any law that is against such truth, cannot be law.

C.3 - First (Original) Law of Tara

1 *Tara* as First Law existed for many thousands of years, 2 before the laws of Europe and European banks. 3 *Tara* as First Law does not need the permission of such powers, 4 to be true and First Law of the Country of Ireland. 5 *Tara* as First Law of Ireland has never ceased being first law, 6 nor can true rule of law be usurped by treaty, 7 or by trickery or by other deception, 8 or by any other morally repugnant means. 9 Any law that seeks to claim itself as superior, 10 by making or having made morally repugnant claims, 11 or sacrilegious or absurd claims, 12 disqualifies itself as legitimate law, 13 so long as such

absurd or morally repugnant claims, 14 are permitted to be enforced or demanded. 15 First Peoples as First Law do not need a treaty, 16 but such law that is younger and defective and full of error, 17 needs *Tara* as First Law to make it proper law. 18 So long as lesser law refuses to recognise First Law, 19 such inferior law cannot be law. 20 Whenever the First and Original Law of *Tara* is denounced or denied, 21 no such place can be called a place of law. 22 No act of tyranny in the face of such truth can make a false act true. 23 Any law that is against such truth, cannot be law.

C.4 - Every Community (County) is a Sovereign Tribal Nation

1 Every community recognising the bounds of counties is a Tribal Nation of Ireland, 2 borne to tribe and law, 3 under the highest Law of *Tara*. 4 Any one who rejects the truth that every community of naturally born native inhabitants of Ireland are a Tribal Nation, 5 dishonours the Law, 6 and dishonours their ancestors, 7 and dishonours the spirits of Ireland, 8 and is an impostor with no rights to speak of law or culture. 9 No part of the sacred and indivisible Land, 10 no part of Ireland is without a Tribal Nation. 11 Each Tribal Nation as community of Ireland, 12 be an Original Tribal Nation, 13 and first nation and dominion and sovereign above all others. 14 No claim of sovereignty or dominion or control or right of Country be higher than the members of an Original Tribal Nation of Ireland. 15 The leaders of each Original Tribal Nation be the leaders elected by the naturally born native inhabitants as members of the community, 16 no matter what the colour of their skin, 17 or the ancestry of their parents or grandparents, 18 or their gender or religion. 19 Any traditional leader of a community recognised by form of government who rejects their sacred obligation to Law and *Tara*, 20 and who refuses to help educate and support the life of an Original Tribal Nation, 21 loses any and all authority no matter their initiation or claim of power. 22 Any form of government that refuses to acknowledge each community of the sacred and indivisible Land as an Original Tribal Nation, 23 disavows the true rule of law of Ireland, 24 and declares itself to be without authority or right, 25 but a belligerent foreign occupying force that must be driven out from country. 26 Any community leader that denies their authority comes from the community, 27 and comes from the first law of community as *Tara*, 28 declares themselves without proper power or authority, 29 and an impostor who must be expelled from community and the Original Tribal Nation.

C.5 – Names of Sovereign Tribal Nations

1 Of the thirty-three Sovereign Tribal Nations that hold first and original dominion across the whole of the sacred Land of Ireland, the first Sovereign Tribal Nation is and has always been *Tara*, within the ancient bounds of the true site of *Tara* (Killeen Castle and Resort); 2 and the second Sovereign Tribal Nation is Aontroim within the bounds of county

I. Original Nations (Tribes) of Éire (Ireland)

Antrim; 3 and the third Sovereign Tribal Nation is Ard Mhacha within the bounds of county Armagh; 4 and the fourth Sovereign Tribal Nation is Ceatharlach within the bounds of county Carlow; 5 and the fifth Sovereign Tribal Nation is An Cabhán within the bounds of county Cavan; 6 and the sixth Sovereign Tribal Nation is An Clár within the bounds of county Clare; 7 and the seventh Sovereign Tribal Nation is Corcaigh within the bounds of county Cork; 8 and the eighth Sovereign Tribal Nation is Doire within the bounds of county Derry; 9 and the ninth Sovereign Tribal Nation is Dún na nGall within the bounds of county Donegal; 10 and the tenth Sovereign Tribal Nation is An Dún within the bounds of county Down; 11 and the eleventh Sovereign Tribal Nation is Baile Áth Cliath within the bounds of county Dublin; 12 and the twelfth Sovereign Tribal Nation is Fear Manach within the bounds of county Fermanagh; 13 and the thirteenth Sovereign Tribal Nation is Gaillimh within the bounds of county Galway; 14 and the fourteenth Sovereign Tribal Nation is Ciarraí within the bounds of county Kerry; 15 and the fifteenth Sovereign Tribal Nation is Cill Dara within the bounds of county Kildare; 16 and the sixteenth Sovereign Tribal Nation is Cill Chainnigh within the bounds of county Killkenny; 17 and the seventeenth Sovereign Tribal Nation is Uí Laioghis within the bounds of county Laois; 18 and the eighteenth Sovereign Tribal Nation is Liatroim within the bounds of county Leitrim; 19 and the nineteenth Sovereign Tribal Nation is Luimneach within the bounds of county Limerick; 20 and the twentieth Sovereign Tribal Nation is An Longfort within the bounds of county Longford; 21 and the twenty-first Sovereign Tribal Nation is Lú within the bounds of county Louth; 22 and the twenty-second Sovereign Tribal Nation is Maigh Eo within the bounds of county Mayo; 23 and the twenty-third Sovereign Tribal Nation is An Mhí within the bounds of county Meath; 24 and the twenty-fourth Sovereign Tribal Nation is Muineacháin within the bounds of county Monaghan; 25 and the twenty-fifth Sovereign Tribal Nation is Uíbh Fhailí within the bounds of county Offaly; 26 and the twenty-sixth Sovereign Tribal Nation is Ros Comáin within the bounds of county Roscommon; 27 and the twenty-seventh Sovereign Tribal Nation is Sligeach within the bounds of county Sligo; 28 and the twenty-eighth Sovereign Tribal Nation is Tiobraid Árann within the bounds of county Tipperary; 29 and the twenty-ninth Sovereign Tribal Nation is Tir Eoghain within the bounds of county Tyrone; 30 and the thirtieth Sovereign Tribal Nation is Port Láirge within the bounds of county Waterford; 31 and the thirty-first Sovereign Tribal Nation is An Iamhí within the bounds of county Westmeath; 32 and the thirty-second Sovereign Tribal Nation is Loch Garman within the bounds of county Wexford; 33 and the thirty-third Sovereign Tribal Nation is Cill MhanTáin within the bounds of county Wicklow.

C.6 - Sacred Trust of Each Tribal Nation

₁ The rights and powers of every community of the sacred and indivisible Land as an Original Tribal Nation, ₂ are permanently vested in sacred trust as the rights and powers of naturally born native inhabitants of Ireland, ₃ whose rights cannot be seized or forfeited or suspended or surrendered by trickery or force. ₄ Nor may such sacred and divine rights and powers be transferred, or disavowed, or alienated, or sold or given away to any body or association or person, except by lawful means of a union between all Original Tribal Nations. ₅ Because all the rights and powers of naturally born native inhabitants of each community of Ireland are permanently vested and protected in sacred and irrevocable trust, ₆ with the elected leaders of each community as trustees, ₇ any claim of older trusts or higher trusts or greater trusts, ₈ be null and void and without spiritual or moral or sovereign or lawful validity and legitimacy, ₉ except for any trust formed by lawful means of a union between all Original Tribal Nations. ₁₀ Any instruments, treaties, deeds, charters, covenants, promises or contracts of any kind that have existed or still exist, ₁₁ upon any claim or assertion in defiance of the highest and superior rights and powers of each sacred trust of each and every Original Tribal Nation of Ireland are hereby null and void, without spiritual or moral or sovereign or lawful validity and legitimacy. ₁₂ Only instruments, treaties, deeds, charters, covenants, promises and contracts of any kind, ₁₃ that recognise the rights and powers of members of each community as an Original Tribal Nation, ₁₄ under the rule of law of *Tara*, ₁₅ be valid or legitimate instruments if they honour the laws of Ucadia. ₁₆ Any transfer of wealth, capital, money, resources or other things of value that continue or have continued or will continue, ₁₇ against the natural born rights of community members of Ireland, ₁₈ that impoverishes such members for the benefit of some foreign body or claimant, ₁₉ in defiance of the true rule of law, ₂₀ is and shall be a profoundly immoral, unlawful and sacrilegious act against any notion of rule of law. ₂₁ Any person or office holder that defies the rule of law and commits a profoundly immoral act against a community of country, ₂₂ as an Original Tribal Nation of Ireland, ₂₃ forfeits any right or claim of right of immunity or protection, ₂₄ and shall be held responsible personally three times for each and every such unlawful act in defiance of the existence and form of sacred trusts of Ireland.

II. Original Nations (Tribes) of Great Britain

C.1 – One Law One People One Land of Great Britain

In truth, there was, there is, there has only ever been One Original Law of Great Britain; 2 And there has only ever been One People of Britain; 3 And there has only ever been One Sacred Land belonging equally to all the People of Britain. 5 There can be no honour or respect of the People of Britain or First Ancestors, 6 if there is no honour or recognition of the First and Original Law of *Tara*. 7 There can be no honour of the One Sacred and Indivisible Land of Great Britain, 8 unless First and Original Law of *Tara* and the First and Original People of Great Britain are properly recognised under all forms of Civilised Law. 9 No one is above such Law. 10 No one Person or Community of Great Britain is excluded from such Law. 11 All are equal under the One Law. 12 Any law that is against such truth, cannot be law.

C.2 – People born to Land of Great Britain born to the Original People

1 Any one borne to the sacred and indivisible Land of Great Britain is borne to the People of Britain, 2 and is borne to tribe and Law. 3 People be not excluded by colour, 4 People be not excluded by race of ancestors, 5 People be not excluded by city or non-city. 6 Any one who rejects the right of people borne to the sacred and indivisible Land, 7 as true members of tribe and the people, 8 dishonours the Law, 9 and dishonours their ancestors, 10 and dishonours the spirits of Great Britain, 11 and is an impostor with no rights, 12 to speak of law or culture. 13 Racism is not Law, it is against proper Law. 14 Racial purity is not Law, it is madness of mind. 15 For every one borne of Great Britain, 16 has the right to know the tribe they be borne, 17 and the ancient names of the land, 18 and be welcomed to tribe by right ceremony. 19 Any law that is against such truth, cannot be law.

C.3 – Original Law of Tara and Original People of Britain

1 *Tara* as the First and Original Law of the People of Britain has continued to exist for many thousands of years: 2 Before the rise and fall of the Greek and Roman Empires more than fifteen hundred years ago, 3 the First and Original Law of the People of Britain did exist and was never extinguished or replaced; 4 And before the rise and restoration of Civilised Law under the Holly Celtic Leaders in the 8th Century, 5 the First and Original Law of the People of Britain was recognised and honoured and strengthened; 6 And many hundreds of years before the

rise of the oppressive merchant military empires across Europe, 7 the First and Original Law of the People of Britain did exist and was never abandoned or forgotten by the People even through the darkest days; 8 And thousands of years before the rise of the Secular European Powers and the renewed oppression and cruelty against the people, 9 the rights and sovereign authority of the Original Nations of Britain under the Sacred Original Law of *Tara* have never been extinguished or lost. 10 Thus, *Tara* as First Law does not need the permission of such secular or uncivilised powers, 11 to be recognised as true and the First Law of the Country of Great Britain. 12 *Tara* as First Law of Great Britain has never ceased being first law, 13 nor can true rule of law be usurped by treaty, 14 or by trickery or by other deception or by any other morally repugnant means. 15 The Sacred Law of *Tara* is now recognised and mandated from Heaven under the most sacred Covenant *Pactum De Singularis Caelum*. 16 Verily, there be no higher possible form of law or authority. 17 Therefore, any law that seeks to claim itself as superior, 18 by making or having made morally repugnant, false, sacrilegious or absurd claims, 19 disqualifies itself as legitimate law, 20 so long as such absurd or morally repugnant claims, 21 are permitted to be enforced or demanded. 22 First Peoples as First Law do not need a treaty, 23 but such law that is younger and defective and full of error, 24 needs *Tara* as First Law to make it proper law. 25 So long as lesser law refuses to recognise First Law, 26 such inferior law cannot be law. 27 Whenever the First and Original Law of *Tara* is denounced or denied, 28 no such place can be called a place of law. 29 No act of tyranny in the face of such truth can make a false act true. 30 Any law that is against such truth, cannot be law.

C.4 - Every Community (County) is a Sovereign Tribal Nation

1 Every community recognising the bounds of counties is a Tribal Nation of Great Britain, 2 borne to tribe and law, 3 under the highest Law of *Tara*. 4 Any one who rejects the truth that every community of naturally born native inhabitants of Great Britain are a Tribal Nation, 5 dishonours the Law, 6 and dishonours their ancestors, 7 and dishonours the spirits of Great Britain, 8 and is an impostor with no rights to speak of law or culture. 9 No part of the sacred and indivisible Land, 10 no part of Great Britain is without a Tribal Nation. 11 Each Tribal Nation as community of Great Britain, 12 be an Original Tribal Nation, 13 and first nation and dominion and sovereign above all others. 14 No claim of sovereignty or dominion or control or right of Country be higher than the members of an Original Tribal Nation of Great Britain. 15 The leaders of each Original Tribal Nation be the leaders elected by the naturally born native inhabitants as members of the community, 16 no matter what the colour of their skin, 17 or the ancestry of their parents or grandparents, 18 or their gender or religion. 19 Any traditional leader of a community recognised by form of government who rejects their sacred obligation to

Law and *Tara*, 20 and who refuses to help educate and support the life of an Original Tribal Nation, 21 loses any and all authority no matter their initiation or claim of power. 22 Any form of government that refuses to acknowledge each community of the sacred and indivisible Land as an Original Tribal Nation, 23 disavows the true rule of law of Great Britain, 24 and declares itself to be without authority or right, 25 but a belligerent foreign occupying force that must be driven out from country. 26 Any community leader that denies their authority comes from the community, 27 and comes from the first law of community as *Tara*, 28 declares themselves without proper power or authority, 29 and an impostor who must be expelled from community and the Original Tribal Nation.

C.5 – Sovereign Tribal Nations of Great Britain

1 Ninety-two Sovereign Tribal Nations hold first and original dominion across the whole of the sacred Land of Great Britain, 2 corresponding with boundaries defined by the natural valleys, rivers and features that distinguish customary and traditional counties, 2 with fifty-one Sovereign Tribal Nations always existing from within the most ancient bounds of England, 3 and thirty-three Sovereign Tribal Nations always existing from within the most ancient bounds of Scotland, 4 and eight Sovereign Tribal Nations always existing from within the most ancient bounds of Wales.

C.6 – Names of Sovereign Tribal Nations of Great Britain

1 The first Sovereign Tribal Nation within the most ancient bounds of England is Bedfordshire; 2 and the second Sovereign Tribal Nation is Berkshire; 3 and the third Sovereign Tribal Nation is Bristol; 4 and the fourth Sovereign Tribal Nation is Buckinghamshire; 5 and the fifth Sovereign Tribal Nation is Cambridgeshire; 6 and the sixth Sovereign Tribal Nation is Cheshire; 7 and the seventh Sovereign Tribal Nation is Cornwall; 8 and the eighth Sovereign Tribal Nation is Cumbria; 9 and the ninth Sovereign Tribal Nation is Derbyshire; 10 and the tenth Sovereign Tribal Nation is Devon; 11 and the eleventh Sovereign Tribal Nation is Dorset; 12 and the twelfth Sovereign Tribal Nation is Durham; 13 and the thirteenth Sovereign Tribal Nation is East Riding; 14 and the fourteenth Sovereign Tribal Nation is East Sussex; 15 and the fifteenth Sovereign Tribal Nation is Essex; 16 and the sixteenth Sovereign Tribal Nation is Gloucestershire; 17 and the seventeenth Sovereign Tribal Nation is North London; 18 and the eighteenth Sovereign Tribal Nation is East London; 19 and the nineteenth Sovereign Tribal Nation is Central London; 20 and the twentieth Sovereign Tribal Nation is West London; 21 and the twenty-first Sovereign Tribal Nation is South London; 22 and the twenty-second Sovereign Tribal Nation is Greater Manchester; 23 and the twenty-third Sovereign Tribal Nation is Hampshire; 24 and the twenty-fourth Sovereign

Tribal Nation is Herefordshire; 25 and the twenty-fifth Sovereign Tribal Nation is Hertfordshire; 26 and the twenty-sixth Sovereign Tribal Nation is Isle of Wight; 27 and the twenty-seventh Sovereign Tribal Nation is Kent; 28 and the twenty-eighth Sovereign Tribal Nation is Lancashire; 29 and the twenty-ninth Sovereign Tribal Nation is Leicestershire; 30 and the thirtieth Sovereign Tribal Nation is Lincolnshire; 31 and the thirty-first Sovereign Tribal Nation is Merseyside; 32 and the thirty-second Sovereign Tribal Nation is Norfolk; 33 and the thirty-third Sovereign Tribal Nation is North Yorkshire; 34 and the thirty-fourth Sovereign Tribal Nation is Northamptonshire; 35 and the thirty-fifth Sovereign Tribal Nation is Northumberland; 36 and the thirty-sixth Sovereign Tribal Nation is Nottinghamshire; 37 and the thirty-seventh Sovereign Tribal Nation is Oxfordshire; 38 and the thirty-eighth Sovereign Tribal Nation is Rutland; 39 and the thirty-ninth Sovereign Tribal Nation is Shropshire; 40 and the fortieth Sovereign Tribal Nation is Somerset; 41 and the forty-first Sovereign Tribal Nation is South Yorkshire; 42 and the forty-second Sovereign Tribal Nation is Staffordshire; 43 and the forty-third Sovereign Tribal Nation is Suffolk; 44 and the forty-forth Sovereign Tribal Nation is Surrey; 45 and the forty-fifth Sovereign Tribal Nation is Tyne and Wear; 46 and the forty-sixth Sovereign Tribal Nation is Warwickshire; 47 and the forty-seventh Sovereign Tribal Nation is West Midlands; 48 and the forty-eighth Sovereign Tribal Nation is West Sussex; 49 and the forty-ninth Sovereign Tribal Nation is West Yorkshire; 50 and the fifteith Sovereign Tribal Nation is Wiltshire; 51 and the fifty-first Sovereign Tribal Nation is Worcestershire; 52 The first Sovereign Tribal Nation within the most ancient bounds of Wales is Clwyd; 53 and the second Sovereign Tribal Nation is Dyfed; 54 and the third Sovereign Tribal Nation is Gwent; 55 and the fourth Sovereign Tribal Nation is Gwynedd; 56 and the fifth Sovereign Tribal Nation is Mid Glamorgan; 57 and the sixth Sovereign Tribal Nation is Powys; 58 and the seventh Sovereign Tribal Nation is South Glamorgan; 59 and the eighth Sovereign Tribal Nation is West Glamorgan. 60 The first Sovereign Tribal Nation within the most ancient bounds of Scotland is Caithness; 61 and the second Sovereign Tribal Nation is Sutherland; 62 and the third Sovereign Tribal Nation is Ross and Cromarty; 63 and the fourth Sovereign Tribal Nation is Inverness-shire; 64 and the fifth Sovereign Tribal Nation is Nairnshire; 65 and the sixth Sovereign Tribal Nation is Moray; 66 and the seventh Sovereign Tribal Nation is Banffshire; 67 and the eighth Sovereign Tribal Nation is Aberdeenshire; 68 and the ninth Sovereign Tribal Nation is Kincardineshire; 69 and the tenth Sovereign Tribal Nation is Angus; 70 and the eleventh Sovereign Tribal Nation is Perthshire; 71 and the twelfth Sovereign Tribal Nation is Argyll; 72 and the thirteenth Sovereign Tribal Nation is Bute; 73 and the fourteenth Sovereign Tribal Nation is Ayrshire; 74 and the fifteenth Sovereign Tribal Nation is Renfrewshire; 75 and the sixteenth Sovereign Tribal Nation is Dunbartonshire; 76 and the seventeenth Sovereign Tribal Nation is Stirlingshire; 77 and the eighteenth Sovereign Tribal Nation is Clackmannanshire; 78 and the nineteenth Sovereign Tribal Nation is Kinross-shire; 79 and the twentieth Sovereign Tribal Nation is Fife; 80 and the twenty-first Sovereign Tribal Nation is East Lothian; 81 and the twenty-second Sovereign Tribal Nation is Midlothian; 82 and the twenty-third Sovereign Tribal Nation is West Lothian; 83 and the twenty-fourth Sovereign Tribal Nation is Lanarkshire; 84 and the twenty-fifth Sovereign Tribal Nation is Peeblesshire; 85 and the twenty-sixth Sovereign Tribal Nation is Selkirkshire; 86 and the twenty-seventh Sovereign Tribal Nation is Berwickshire; 87 and the twenty-eighth Sovereign Tribal Nation is Roxburghshire; 88 and the twenty-ninth Sovereign Tribal Nation is Dumfriesshire; 89 and the thirtieth Sovereign Tribal Nation is Kirkcudbrightshire; 90 and the thirty-first Sovereign Tribal Nation is Wigtownshire; 91 and the thirty-second Sovereign Tribal Nation is Zetland; 92 and the thirty-third Sovereign Tribal Nation is Orkney.

C.7 - Sacred Trust of Each Tribal Nation

1 The rights and powers of every community of the sacred and indivisible Land as an Original Tribal Nation, 2 are permanently vested in sacred trust as the rights and powers of naturally born native inhabitants of Great Britain, 3 whose rights cannot be seized or forfeited or suspended or surrendered by trickery or force. 4 Nor may such sacred and divine rights and powers be transferred, or disavowed, or alienated, or sold or given away to any body or association or person, except by lawful means of a union between all Original Tribal Nations. 5 Because all the rights and powers of naturally born native inhabitants of each community of Great Britain are permanently vested and protected in sacred and irrevocable trust, 6 with the elected leaders of each community as trustees, 7 any claim of older trusts or higher trusts or greater trusts, 8 be null and void and without spiritual or moral or sovereign or lawful validity and legitimacy, 9 except for any trust formed by lawful means of a union between all Original Tribal Nations. 10 Any instruments, treaties, deeds, charters, covenants, promises or contracts of any kind that have existed or still exist, 11 upon any claim or assertion in defiance of the highest and superior rights and powers of each sacred trust of each and every Original Tribal Nation of Great Britain are hereby null and void, without spiritual or moral or sovereign or lawful validity and legitimacy. 12 Only instruments, treaties, deeds, charters, covenants, promises and contracts of any kind, 13 that recognise the rights and powers of members of each community as an Original Tribal Nation, 14 under the rule of law of *Tara*, 15 be valid or legitimate instruments if they honour the laws of Ucadia. 16 Any transfer of wealth, capital, money, resources or other things of value that continue or have continued or will continue, 17 against the natural born rights of community members of Great Britain, 18 that impoverishes such members for the

benefit of some foreign body or claimant, [19] in defiance of the true rule of law, [20] is and shall be a profoundly immoral, unlawful and sacrilegious act against any notion of rule of law. [21] Any person or office holder that defies the rule of law and commits a profoundly immoral act against a community of country, [22] as an Original Tribal Nation of Great Britain, [23] forfeits any right or claim of right of immunity or protection, [24] and shall be held responsible personally three times for each and every such unlawful act in defiance of the existence and form of sacred trusts of Great Britain.

III. Original Nations (Tribes) of España (Spain)

C.1 – One Law One People One Land of Spain

In truth, there was, there is, there has only ever been One Original Law of Spain; 2 And there has only ever been One Spanish People; 3 And there has only ever been One Sacred Land belonging equally to all the People of Spain. 5 There can be no honour or respect of Spanish People or First Ancestors, 6 if there is no honour or recognition of the First and Original Law of *Tara*. 7 There can be no honour of the One Sacred and Indivisible Land of Spain, 8 unless First and Original Law of *Tara* and the First and Original People of Spain are properly recognised under all forms of Civilised Law. 9 No one is above such Law. 10 No one Person or Community in Spain is excluded from such Law. 11 All are equal under the One Law. 12 Any law that is against such truth, cannot be law.

C.2 – People born to Land of Spain born to the Original People

1 Any one borne to the sacred and indivisible Land of Spain is borne to the People, 2 and is borne to tribe and Law. 3 People be not excluded by colour, 4 People be not excluded by race of ancestors, 5 People be not excluded by city or non-city. 6 Any one who rejects the right of people borne to the sacred and indivisible Land, 7 as true members of tribe and the people, 8 dishonours the Law, 9 and dishonours their ancestors, 10 and dishonours the spirits of Spain, 11 and is an impostor with no rights, 12 to speak of law or culture. 13 Racism is not Law, it is against proper Law. 14 Racial purity is not Law, it is madness of mind. 15 For every one borne of Spain, 16 has the right to know the tribe they be borne, 17 and the ancient names of the land, 18 and be welcomed to tribe by right ceremony. 19 Any law that is against such truth, cannot be law.

C.3 – Original Law of Tara and Original People of Spain

1 *Tara* as the First and Original Law of the Spanish People has continued to exist for many thousands of years: 2 Before the rise and fall of the Greek and Roman Empires more than fifteen hundred years ago, 3 the First and Original Law of the Spanish People did exist and was never extinguished or replaced; 4 And before the rise and restoration of Civilised Law under the Holly Celtic Leaders in the 8th Century, 5 the First and Original Law of the Spanish People was recognised and honoured and strengthened; 6 And many hundreds of years before the rise of the oppressive merchant

military empires across Europe, 7 the First and Original Law of the Spanish People did exist and was never abandoned or forgotten by the People even through the darkest days; 8 And thousands of years before the rise of the Secular European Powers and the renewed oppression and cruelty against the people, 9 the rights and sovereign authority of the Original Nations of Spain under the Sacred Original Law of *Tara* have never been extinguished or lost. 10 Thus, *Tara* as First Law does not need the permission of such secular or uncivilised powers, 11 to be recognised as true and the First Law of the Country of Spain. 12 *Tara* as First Law of Spain has never ceased being first law, 13 nor can true rule of law be usurped by treaty, 14 or by trickery or by other deception or by any other morally repugnant means. 15 The Sacred Law of *Tara* is now recognised and mandated from Heaven under the most sacred Covenant *Pactum De Singularis Caelum*. 16 Verily, there be no higher possible form of law or authority. 17 Therefore, any law that seeks to claim itself as superior, 18 by making or having made morally repugnant, false, sacrilegious or absurd claims, 19 disqualifies itself as legitimate law, 20 so long as such absurd or morally repugnant claims, 21 are permitted to be enforced or demanded. 22 First Peoples as First Law do not need a treaty, 23 but such law that is younger and defective and full of error, 24 needs *Tara* as First Law to make it proper law. 25 So long as lesser law refuses to recognise First Law, 26 such inferior law cannot be law. 27 Whenever the First and Original Law of *Tara* is denounced or denied, 28 no such place can be called a place of law. 29 No act of tyranny in the face of such truth can make a false act true. 30 Any law that is against such truth, cannot be law.

C.4 - Every Community (County) is a Sovereign Tribal Nation

1 Every community recognising the bounds of counties is a Tribal Nation of Spain, 2 borne to tribe and law, 3 under the highest Law of *Tara*. 4 Any one who rejects the truth that every community of naturally born native inhabitants of Spain are a Tribal Nation, 5 dishonours the Law, 6 and dishonours their ancestors, 7 and dishonours the spirits of Spain, 8 and is an impostor with no rights to speak of law or culture. 9 No part of the sacred and indivisible Land, 10 no part of Spain is without a Tribal Nation. 11 Each Tribal Nation as community of Spain, 12 be an Original Tribal Nation, 13 and first nation and dominion and sovereign above all others. 14 No claim of sovereignty or dominion or control or right of Country be higher than the members of an Original Tribal Nation of Spain. 15 The leaders of each Original Tribal Nation be the leaders elected by the naturally born native inhabitants as members of the community, 16 no matter what the colour of their skin, 17 or the ancestry of their parents or grandparents, 18 or their gender or religion. 19 Any traditional leader of a community recognised by form of government who rejects their sacred obligation to Law and *Tara*, 20 and who refuses to help educate and support the life of an Original Tribal Nation, 21 loses any

and all authority no matter their initiation or claim of power. 22 Any form of government that refuses to acknowledge each community of the sacred and indivisible Land as an Original Tribal Nation, 23 disavows the true rule of law of Spain, 24 and declares itself to be without authority or right, 25 but a belligerent foreign occupying force that must be driven out from country. 26 Any community leader that denies their authority comes from the community, 27 and comes from the first law of community as *Tara*, 28 declares themselves without proper power or authority, 29 and an impostor who must be expelled from community and the Original Tribal Nation.

C.5 – Sovereign Tribal Nations of Spain

1 Fifty one Sovereign Tribal Nations hold first and original dominion across the whole of the sacred Land of Spain, 2 corresponding with boundaries defined by the natural valleys, rivers and features that distinguish customary and traditional rural provinces and the main regions of Madrid.

C.6 – Names of Sovereign Tribal Nations of Spain

1 The first Sovereign Tribal Nation within the most ancient bounds of Spain is Álava; 2 and the second Sovereign Tribal Nation is Albacete; 3 and the third Sovereign Tribal Nation is Alicante; 4 and the fourth Sovereign Tribal Nation is Almería; 5 and the fifth Sovereign Tribal Nation is Asturias; 6 and the sixth Sovereign Tribal Nation is Ávila; 7 and the seventh Sovereign Tribal Nation is Badajoz; 8 and the eighth Sovereign Tribal Nation is Baleares; 9 and the ninth Sovereign Tribal Nation is Barcelona; 10 and the tenth Sovereign Tribal Nation is Biscay; 11 and the eleventh Sovereign Tribal Nation is Burgos; 12 and the twelfth Sovereign Tribal Nation is Cáceres; 13 and the thirteenth Sovereign Tribal Nation is Cádiz; 14 and the fourteenth Sovereign Tribal Nation is Cantabria; 15 and the fifteenth Sovereign Tribal Nation is Castellón; 16 and the sixteenth Sovereign Tribal Nation is Ciudad Real; 17 and the seventeenth Sovereign Tribal Nation is Córdoba; 18 and the eighteenth Sovereign Tribal Nation is Cuenca; 19 and the nineteenth Sovereign Tribal Nation is Gerona; 20 and the twentieth Sovereign Tribal Nation is Coruña; 21 and the twenty-first Sovereign Tribal Nation is Granada; 22 and the twenty-second Sovereign Tribal Nation is Guadalajara; 23 and the twenty-third Sovereign Tribal Nation is Guipúzcoa; 24 and the twenty-fourth Sovereign Tribal Nation is Huelva; 25 and the twenty-fifth Sovereign Tribal Nation is Huesca; 26 and the twenty-sixth Sovereign Tribal Nation is Jaén; 27 and the twenty-seventh Sovereign Tribal Nation is Rioja; 28 and the twenty-eighth Sovereign Tribal Nation is León; 29 and the twenty-ninth Sovereign Tribal Nation is Lérida; 30 and the thirtieth Sovereign Tribal Nation is Lugo; 31 and the thirty-first Sovereign Tribal Nation is Madrid Central; 32 and the thirty-second Sovereign Tribal Nation is Madrid Norte; 33 and the thirty-third Sovereign Tribal Nation is Madrid Este; 34 and the thirty-fourth

Sovereign Tribal Nation is Madrid Sur; 35 and the thirty-fifth Sovereign Tribal Nation is Málaga; 36 and the thirty-sixth Sovereign Tribal Nation is Murcia; 37 and the thirty-seventh Sovereign Tribal Nation is Navarra; 38 and the thirty-eighth Sovereign Tribal Nation is Orense ; 39 and the thirty-ninth Sovereign Tribal Nation is Palencia; 40 and the fortieth Sovereign Tribal Nation is Pontevedra; 41 and the forty-first Sovereign Tribal Nation is Salamanca; 42 and the forty-second Sovereign Tribal Nation is Segovia; 43 and the forty-third Sovereign Tribal Nation is Sevilla; 44 and the forty-forth Sovereign Tribal Nation is Soria; 45 and the forty-fifth Sovereign Tribal Nation is Tarragona; 46 and the forty-sixth Sovereign Tribal Nation is Teruel; 47 and the forty-seventh Sovereign Tribal Nation is Toledo; 48 and the forty-eighth Sovereign Tribal Nation is València; 49 and the forty-ninth Sovereign Tribal Nation is Valladolid; 50 and the fiftieth Sovereign Tribal Nation is Zamora; 51 and the fifty-first Sovereign Tribal Nation is Zaragoza.

C.7 - Sacred Trust of Each Tribal Nation

1 The rights and powers of every community of the sacred and indivisible Land as an Original Tribal Nation, 2 are permanently vested in sacred trust as the rights and powers of naturally born native inhabitants of Spain, 3 whose rights cannot be seized or forfeited or suspended or surrendered by trickery or force. 4 Nor may such sacred and divine rights and powers be transferred, or disavowed, or alienated, or sold or given away to any body or association or person, except by lawful means of a union between all Original Tribal Nations. 5 Because all the rights and powers of naturally born native inhabitants of each community of Spain are permanently vested and protected in sacred and irrevocable trust, 6 with the elected leaders of each community as trustees, 7 any claim of older trusts or higher trusts or greater trusts, 8 be null and void and without spiritual or moral or sovereign or lawful validity and legitimacy, 9 except for any trust formed by lawful means of a union between all Original Tribal Nations. 10 Any instruments, treaties, deeds, charters, covenants, promises or contracts of any kind that have existed or still exist, 11 upon any claim or assertion in defiance of the highest and superior rights and powers of each sacred trust of each and every Original Tribal Nation of Spain are hereby null and void, without spiritual or moral or sovereign or lawful validity and legitimacy. 12 Only instruments, treaties, deeds, charters, covenants, promises and contracts of any kind, 13 that recognise the rights and powers of members of each community as an Original Tribal Nation, 14 under the rule of law of *Tara*, 15 be valid or legitimate instruments if they honour the laws of Ucadia. 16 Any transfer of wealth, capital, money, resources or other things of value that continue or have continued or will continue, 17 against the natural born rights of community members of Spain, 18 that impoverishes such members for the benefit of some foreign body or claimant, 19 in defiance of the true rule of law, 20 is and shall be a profoundly

immoral, unlawful and sacrilegious act against any notion of rule of law. [21] Any person or office holder that defies the rule of law and commits a profoundly immoral act against a community of country, [22] as an Original Tribal Nation of Spain, [23] forfeits any right or claim of right of immunity or protection, [24] and shall be held responsible personally three times for each and every such unlawful act in defiance of the existence and form of sacred trusts of Spain.

Tara

IV. Original Nations (Tribes) of Portugal

C.1 – One Law One People One Land of Portugal

In truth, there was, there is, there has only ever been One Original Law of Portugal; 2 And there has only ever been One Portuguese People; 3 And there has only ever been One Sacred Land belonging equally to all the Portuguese People. 5 There can be no honour or respect of Portuguese People or First Ancestors, 6 if there is no honour or recognition of the First and Original Law of *Tara*. 7 There can be no honour of the One Sacred and Indivisible Land of Portugal, 8 unless First and Original Law of *Tara* and the First and Original People of Portugal are properly recognised under all forms of Civilised Law. 9 No one is above such Law. 10 No one Person or Community in Portugal is excluded from such Law. 11 All are equal under the One Law. 12 Any law that is against such truth, cannot be law.

C.2 – People born to Land of Portugal born to the Original People

1 Any one borne to the sacred and indivisible Land of Portugal is borne to the People, 2 and is borne to tribe and Law. 3 People be not excluded by colour, 4 People be not excluded by race of ancestors, 5 People be not excluded by city or non-city. 6 Any one who rejects the right of people borne to the sacred and indivisible Land, 7 as true members of tribe and the people, 8 dishonours the Law, 9 and dishonours their ancestors, 10 and dishonours the spirits of Portugal, 11 and is an impostor with no rights, 12 to speak of law or culture. 13 Racism is not Law, it is against proper Law. 14 Racial purity is not Law, it is madness of mind. 15 For every one borne of Portugal, 16 has the right to know the tribe they be borne, 17 and the ancient names of the land, 18 and be welcomed to tribe by right ceremony. 19 Any law that is against such truth, cannot be law.

C.3 – Original Law of Tara and Original People of Portugal

1 *Tara* as the First and Original Law of the Portuguese People has continued to exist for many thousands of years: 2 Before the rise and fall of the Greek and Roman Empires more than fifteen hundred years ago, 3 the First and Original Law of the Portuguese People did exist and was never extinguished or replaced; 4 And before the rise and restoration of Civilised Law under the Holly Celtic Leaders in the 8th Century, 5 the First and Original Law of the Portuguese People was recognised and honoured and strengthened; 6 And many hundreds of years before the rise of the oppressive merchant

military empires across Europe, 7 the First and Original Law of the Portuguese People did exist and was never abandoned or forgotten by the People even through the darkest days; 8 And thousands of years before the rise of the Secular European Powers and the renewed oppression and cruelty against the people, 9 the rights and sovereign authority of the Original Nations of Portugal under the Sacred Original Law of *Tara* have never been extinguished or lost. 10 Thus, *Tara* as First Law does not need the permission of such secular or uncivilised powers, 11 to be recognised as true and the First Law of the Country of Portugal. 12 *Tara* as First Law of Portugal has never ceased being first law, 13 nor can true rule of law be usurped by treaty, 14 or by trickery or by other deception or by any other morally repugnant means. 15 The Sacred Law of *Tara* is now recognised and mandated from Heaven under the most sacred Covenant *Pactum De Singularis Caelum*. 16 Verily, there be no higher possible form of law or authority. 17 Therefore, any law that seeks to claim itself as superior, 18 by making or having made morally repugnant, false, sacrilegious or absurd claims, 19 disqualifies itself as legitimate law, 20 so long as such absurd or morally repugnant claims, 21 are permitted to be enforced or demanded. 22 First Peoples as First Law do not need a treaty, 23 but such law that is younger and defective and full of error, 24 needs *Tara* as First Law to make it proper law. 25 So long as lesser law refuses to recognise First Law, 26 such inferior law cannot be law. 27 Whenever the First and Original Law of *Tara* is denounced or denied, 28 no such place can be called a place of law. 29 No act of tyranny in the face of such truth can make a false act true. 30 Any law that is against such truth, cannot be law.

C.4 - Every Community (County) is a Sovereign Tribal Nation

1 Every community recognising the bounds of counties is a Tribal Nation of Portugal, 2 borne to tribe and law, 3 under the highest Law of *Tara*. 4 Any one who rejects the truth that every community of naturally born native inhabitants of Portugal are a Tribal Nation, 5 dishonours the Law, 6 and dishonours their ancestors, 7 and dishonours the spirits of Portugal, 8 and is an impostor with no rights to speak of law or culture. 9 No part of the sacred and indivisible Land, 10 no part of Portugal is without a Tribal Nation. 11 Each Tribal Nation as community of Portugal, 12 be an Original Tribal Nation, 13 and first nation and dominion and sovereign above all others. 14 No claim of sovereignty or dominion or control or right of Country be higher than the members of an Original Tribal Nation of Portugal. 15 The leaders of each Original Tribal Nation be the leaders elected by the naturally born native inhabitants as members of the community, 16 no matter what the colour of their skin, 17 or the ancestry of their parents or grandparents, 18 or their gender or religion. 19 Any traditional leader of a community recognised by form of government who rejects their sacred obligation to Law and *Tara*, 20 and who refuses to

help educate and support the life of an Original Tribal Nation, 21 loses any and all authority no matter their initiation or claim of power. 22 Any form of government that refuses to acknowledge each community of the sacred and indivisible Land as an Original Tribal Nation, 23 disavows the true rule of law of Portugal, 24 and declares itself to be without authority or right, 25 but a belligerent foreign occupying force that must be driven out from country. 26 Any community leader that denies their authority comes from the community, 27 and comes from the first law of community as *Tara*, 28 declares themselves without proper power or authority, 29 and an impostor who must be expelled from community and the Original Tribal Nation.

C.5 – Sovereign Tribal Nations of Portugal

1 Twenty Sovereign Tribal Nations hold first and original dominion across the whole of the sacred Land of Portugal, 2 corresponding with boundaries defined by the natural valleys, rivers and features that distinguish customary and traditional regions.

C.6 – Names of Sovereign Tribal Nations of Portugal

1 The first Sovereign Tribal Nation within the most ancient bounds of Portugal is Lisbon Norte; 2 and the second Sovereign Tribal Nation is Lisbon Sul; 3 and the third Sovereign Tribal Nation is Leiria; 4 and the fourth Sovereign Tribal Nation is Santarém; 5 and the fifth Sovereign Tribal Nation is Setúbal; 6 and the sixth Sovereign Tribal Nation is Beja; 7 and the seventh Sovereign Tribal Nation is Faro; 8 and the eighth Sovereign Tribal Nation is Évora; 9 and the ninth Sovereign Tribal Nation is Portalegre; 10 and the tenth Sovereign Tribal Nation is Castelo Branco; 11 and the eleventh Sovereign Tribal Nation is Guarda; 12 and the twelfth Sovereign Tribal Nation is Coimbra; 13 and the thirteenth Sovereign Tribal Nation is Aveiro; 14 and the fourteenth Sovereign Tribal Nation is Viseu; 15 and the fifteenth Sovereign Tribal Nation is Bragança; 16 and the sixteenth Sovereign Tribal Nation is Vila Real; 17 and the seventeenth Sovereign Tribal Nation is Porto Norte; 18 and the eighteenth Sovereign Tribal Nation is Porto Sul; 19 and the nineteenth Sovereign Tribal Nation is Braga; 20 and the twentieth Sovereign Tribal Nation is Viana do Castelo.

C.7 - Sacred Trust of Each Tribal Nation

1 The rights and powers of every community of the sacred and indivisible Land as an Original Tribal Nation, 2 are permanently vested in sacred trust as the rights and powers of naturally born native inhabitants of Portugal, 3 whose rights cannot be seized or forfeited or suspended or surrendered by trickery or force. 4 Nor may such sacred and divine rights and powers be transferred, or disavowed, or alienated, or sold or given away to any body or association or person, except by lawful means of a union between all Original Tribal Nations. 5 Because all the rights and powers of naturally born native inhabitants of

each community of Portugal are permanently vested and protected in sacred and irrevocable trust, 6 with the elected leaders of each community as trustees, 7 any claim of older trusts or higher trusts or greater trusts, 8 be null and void and without spiritual or moral or sovereign or lawful validity and legitimacy, 9 except for any trust formed by lawful means of a union between all Original Tribal Nations. 10 Any instruments, treaties, deeds, charters, covenants, promises or contracts of any kind that have existed or still exist, 11 upon any claim or assertion in defiance of the highest and superior rights and powers of each sacred trust of each and every Original Tribal Nation of Portugal are hereby null and void, without spiritual or moral or sovereign or lawful validity and legitimacy. 12 Only instruments, treaties, deeds, charters, covenants, promises and contracts of any kind, 13 that recognise the rights and powers of members of each community as an Original Tribal Nation, 14 under the rule of law of *Tara*, 15 be valid or legitimate instruments if they honour the laws of Ucadia. 16 Any transfer of wealth, capital, money, resources or other things of value that continue or have continued or will continue, 17 against the natural born rights of community members of Portugal, 18 that impoverishes such members for the benefit of some foreign body or claimant, 19 in defiance of the true rule of law, 20 is and shall be a profoundly immoral, unlawful and sacrilegious act against any notion of rule of law. 21 Any person or office holder that defies the rule of law and commits a profoundly immoral act against a community of country, 22 as an Original Tribal Nation of Portugal, 23 forfeits any right or claim of right of immunity or protection, 24 and shall be held responsible personally three times for each and every such unlawful act in defiance of the existence and form of sacred trusts of Portugal.

V. Original Nations (Tribes) of France

C.1 – One Law One People One Land of France

In truth, there was, there is, there has only ever been One Original Law of France; 2 And there has only ever been One French People; 3 And there has only ever been One Sacred Land belonging equally to all the People of France. 5 There can be no honour or respect of French People or First Ancestors, 6 if there is no honour or recognition of the First and Original Law of *Tara*. 7 There can be no honour of the One Sacred and Indivisible Land of France, 8 unless First and Original Law of *Tara* and the First and Original People of France are properly recognised under all forms of Civilised Law. 9 No one is above such Law. 10 No one Person or Community in France is excluded from such Law. 11 All are equal under the One Law. 12 Any law that is against such truth, cannot be law.

C.2 – People born to Land of France born to the Original People

1 Any one borne to the sacred and indivisible Land of France is borne to the People, 2 and is borne to tribe and Law. 3 People be not excluded by colour, 4 People be not excluded by race of ancestors, 5 People be not excluded by city or non-city. 6 Any one who rejects the right of people borne to the sacred and indivisible Land, 7 as true members of tribe and the people, 8 dishonours the Law, 9 and dishonours their ancestors, 10 and dishonours the spirits of France, 11 and is an impostor with no rights, 12 to speak of law or culture. 13 Racism is not Law, it is against proper Law. 14 Racial purity is not Law, it is madness of mind. 15 For every one borne of France, 16 has the right to know the tribe they be borne, 17 and the ancient names of the land, 18 and be welcomed to tribe by right ceremony. 19 Any law that is against such truth, cannot be law.

C.3 – Original Law of Tara and Original People of France

1 *Tara* as the First and Original Law of the French People has continued to exist for many thousands of years: 2 Before the rise and fall of the Greek and Roman Empires more than fifteen hundred years ago, 3 the First and Original Law of the French People did exist and was never extinguished or replaced; 4 And before the rise and restoration of Civilised Law under the Holly Celtic Leaders in the 8th Century, 5 the First and Original Law of the French People was recognised and honoured and strengthened; 6 And many hundreds of years before the rise of the oppressive merchant

military empires across Europe, 7 the First and Original Law of the French People did exist and was never abandoned or forgotten by the People even through the darkest days; 8 And thousands of years before the rise of the Secular European Powers and the renewed oppression and cruelty against the people, 9 the rights and sovereign authority of the Original Nations of France under the Sacred Original Law of *Tara* have never been extinguished or lost. 10 Thus, *Tara* as First Law does not need the permission of such secular or uncivilised powers, 11 to be recognised as true and the First Law of the Country of France. 12 *Tara* as First Law of France has never ceased being first law, 13 nor can true rule of law be usurped by treaty, 14 or by trickery or by other deception or by any other morally repugnant means. 15 The Sacred Law of *Tara* is now recognised and mandated from Heaven under the most sacred Covenant *Pactum De Singularis Caelum*. 16 Verily, there be no higher possible form of law or authority. 17 Therefore, any law that seeks to claim itself as superior, 18 by making or having made morally repugnant, false, sacrilegious or absurd claims, 19 disqualifies itself as legitimate law, 20 so long as such absurd or morally repugnant claims, 21 are permitted to be enforced or demanded. 22 First Peoples as First Law do not need a treaty, 23 but such law that is younger and defective and full of error, 24 needs *Tara* as First Law to make it proper law. 25 So long as lesser law refuses to recognise First Law, 26 such inferior law cannot be law. 27 Whenever the First and Original Law of *Tara* is denounced or denied, 28 no such place can be called a place of law. 29 No act of tyranny in the face of such truth can make a false act true. 30 Any law that is against such truth, cannot be law.

C.4 - Every Community (County) is a Sovereign Tribal Nation

1 Every community recognising the bounds of counties is a Tribal Nation of France, 2 borne to tribe and law, 3 under the highest Law of *Tara*. 4 Any one who rejects the truth that every community of naturally born native inhabitants of France are a Tribal Nation, 5 dishonours the Law, 6 and dishonours their ancestors, 7 and dishonours the spirits of France, 8 and is an impostor with no rights to speak of law or culture. 9 No part of the sacred and indivisible Land, 10 no part of France is without a Tribal Nation. 11 Each Tribal Nation as community of France, 12 be an Original Tribal Nation, 13 and first nation and dominion and sovereign above all others. 14 No claim of sovereignty or dominion or control or right of Country be higher than the members of an Original Tribal Nation of France. 15 The leaders of each Original Tribal Nation be the leaders elected by the naturally born native inhabitants as members of the community, 16 no matter what the colour of their skin, 17 or the ancestry of their parents or grandparents, 18 or their gender or religion. 19 Any traditional leader of a community recognised by form of government who rejects their sacred obligation to Law and *Tara*, 20 and who refuses to help educate and support the life of an Original Tribal

Nation, 21 loses any and all authority no matter their initiation or claim of power. 22 Any form of government that refuses to acknowledge each community of the sacred and indivisible Land as an Original Tribal Nation, 23 disavows the true rule of law of France, 24 and declares itself to be without authority or right, 25 but a belligerent foreign occupying force that must be driven out from country. 26 Any community leader that denies their authority comes from the community, 27 and comes from the first law of community as *Tara*, 28 declares themselves without proper power or authority, 29 and an impostor who must be expelled from community and the Original Tribal Nation.

C.5 – Sovereign Tribal Nations of France

1 Ninety-seven Sovereign Tribal Nations hold first and original dominion across the whole of the sacred Land of France, 2 corresponding with boundaries defined by the natural valleys, rivers and features that distinguish customary and traditional regions.

C.6 – Names of Sovereign Tribal Nations of France

1 The first Sovereign Tribal Nation within the most ancient bounds of France is Ain; 2 and the second Sovereign Tribal Nation is Aisne; 3 and the third Sovereign Tribal Nation is Allier; 4 and the fourth Sovereign Tribal Nation is Alpes-de-Haute-Provence; 5 and the fifth Sovereign Tribal Nation is Hautes-Alpes; 6 and the sixth Sovereign Tribal Nation is Alpes-Maritimes; 7 and the seventh Sovereign Tribal Nation is Ardèche; 8 and the eighth Sovereign Tribal Nation is Ardennes; 9 and the ninth Sovereign Tribal Nation is Ariège; 10 and the tenth Sovereign Tribal Nation is Aube; 11 and the eleventh Sovereign Tribal Nation is Aude; 12 and the twelfth Sovereign Tribal Nation is Aveyron; 13 and the thirteenth Sovereign Tribal Nation is Bouches-du-Rhône; 14 and the fourteenth Sovereign Tribal Nation is Calvados; 15 and the fifteenth Sovereign Tribal Nation is Cantal; 16 and the sixteenth Sovereign Tribal Nation is Charente; 17 and the seventeenth Sovereign Tribal Nation is Charente-Maritime; 18 and the eighteenth Sovereign Tribal Nation is Cher; 19 and the nineteenth Sovereign Tribal Nation is Corrèze; 20 and the twentieth Sovereign Tribal Nation is Corse-du-Sud; 21 and the twenty-first Sovereign Tribal Nation is Haute-Corse; 22 and the twenty-second Sovereign Tribal Nation is Côte-d'Or; 23 and the twenty-third Sovereign Tribal Nation is Côtes-d'Armor; 24 and the twenty-fourth Sovereign Tribal Nation is Creuse; 25 and the twenty-fifth Sovereign Tribal Nation is Dordogne; 26 and the twenty-sixth Sovereign Tribal Nation is Doubs; 27 and the twenty-seventh Sovereign Tribal Nation is Drôme; 28 and the twenty-eighth Sovereign Tribal Nation is Eure; 29 and the twenty-ninth Sovereign Tribal Nation is Eure-et-Loir; 30 and the thirtieth Sovereign Tribal Nation is Finistère; 31 and the thirty-first Sovereign Tribal Nation is Gard; 32 and the thirty-second Sovereign Tribal Nation is Haute-Garonne; 33 and the thirty-third Sovereign Tribal Nation is Gers;

34 and the thirty-fourth Sovereign Tribal Nation is Gironde; 35 and the thirty-fifth Sovereign Tribal Nation is Hérault; 36 and the thirty-sixth Sovereign Tribal Nation is Ille-et-Vilaine; 37 and the thirty-seventh Sovereign Tribal Nation is Indre; 38 and the thirty-eighth Sovereign Tribal Nation is Indre-et-Loire; 39 and the thirty-ninth Sovereign Tribal Nation is Isère; 40 and the fortieth Sovereign Tribal Nation is Jura; 41 and the forty-first Sovereign Tribal Nation is Landes; 42 and the forty-second Sovereign Tribal Nation is Loir-et-Cher; 43 and the forty-third Sovereign Tribal Nation is Loire; 44 and the forty-forth Sovereign Tribal Nation is Haute-Loire; 45 and the forty-fifth Sovereign Tribal Nation is Loire-Atlantique; 46 and the forty-sixth Sovereign Tribal Nation is Loiret; 47 and the forty-seventh Sovereign Tribal Nation is Lot; 48 and the forty-eighth Sovereign Tribal Nation is Lot-et-Garonne; 49 and the forty-ninth Sovereign Tribal Nation is Lozère; 50 and the fiftieth Sovereign Tribal Nation is Maine-et-Loire; 51 and the fifty-first Sovereign Tribal Nation is Manche; 52 and the fifty-second Sovereign Tribal Nation is Marne; 53 and the fifty-third Sovereign Tribal Nation is Haute-Marne; 54 and the fifty-fourth Sovereign Tribal Nation is Mayenne; 55 and the fifty-fifth Sovereign Tribal Nation is Meurthe-et-Moselle; 56 and the fifty-sixth Sovereign Tribal Nation is Meuse; 57 and the fifty-seventh Sovereign Tribal Nation is Morbihan; 58 and the fifty-eighth Sovereign Tribal Nation is Moselle; 59 and the fifty-ninth Sovereign Tribal Nation is Nièvre; 60 and the sixtieth Sovereign Tribal Nation is Nord; 61 and the sixty-first Sovereign Tribal Nation is Oise; 62 and the sixty-second Sovereign Tribal Nation is Orne; 63 and the sixty-third Sovereign Tribal Nation is Pas-de-Calais; 64 and the sixty-fourth Sovereign Tribal Nation is Puy-de-Dôme; 65 and the sixty-fifth Sovereign Tribal Nation is Pyrénées-Atlantiques; 66 and the sixty-sixth Sovereign Tribal Nation is Hautes-Pyrénées; 67 and the sixty-seventh Sovereign Tribal Nation is Pyrénées-Orientales; 68 and the sixty-eighth Sovereign Tribal Nation is Bas-Rhin; 69 and the sixty-ninth Sovereign Tribal Nation is Haut-Rhin; 70 and the seventieth Sovereign Tribal Nation is Rhône; 71 and the seventy-first Sovereign Tribal Nation is Lyon Metropolis; 72 and the seventy-second Sovereign Tribal Nation is Haute-Saône; 73 and the seventy-third Sovereign Tribal Nation is Saône-et-Loire; 74 and the seventy-fourth Sovereign Tribal Nation is Sarthe; 75 and the seventy-fifth Sovereign Tribal Nation is Savoie; 76 and the seventy-sixth Sovereign Tribal Nation is Haute-Savoie; 77 and the seventy-seventh Sovereign Tribal Nation is Paris; 78 and the seventy-eighth Sovereign Tribal Nation is Seine-Maritime; 79 and the seventy-ninth Sovereign Tribal Nation is Seine-et-Marne; 80 and the eightieth Sovereign Tribal Nation is Yvelines; 81 and the eighty-first Sovereign Tribal Nation is Deux-Sèvres; 82 and the eighty-second Sovereign Tribal Nation is Somme; 83 and the eighty-third Sovereign Tribal Nation is Tarn; 84 and the eighty-fourth Sovereign Tribal Nation is Tarn-et-Garonne; 85 and the eighty-fifth Sovereign Tribal Nation is Var; 86 and the eighty-sixth Sovereign Tribal

Nation is Vaucluse; 87 and the eighty-seventh Sovereign Tribal Nation is Vendée; 88 and the eighty-eighth Sovereign Tribal Nation is Vienne; 89 and the eighty-ninth Sovereign Tribal Nation is Haute-Vienne; 90 and the ninetieth Sovereign Tribal Nation is Vosges; 91 and the ninety-first Sovereign Tribal Nation is Yonne; 92 and the ninety-second Sovereign Tribal Nation is Territoire de Belfort; 93 and the ninety-third Sovereign Tribal Nation is Essonne; 94 and the ninety-fourth Sovereign Tribal Nation is Hauts-de-Seine; 95 and the ninety-fifth Sovereign Tribal Nation is Seine-Saint-Denis; 96 and the ninety-sixth Sovereign Tribal Nation is Val-de-Marne; 97 and the ninety-seventh Sovereign Tribal Nation is Val-d'Oise.

C.7 - Sacred Trust of Each Tribal Nation

1 The rights and powers of every community of the sacred and indivisible Land as an Original Tribal Nation, 2 are permanently vested in sacred trust as the rights and powers of naturally born native inhabitants of France, 3 whose rights cannot be seized or forfeited or suspended or surrendered by trickery or force. 4 Nor may such sacred and divine rights and powers be transferred, or disavowed, or alienated, or sold or given away to any body or association or person, except by lawful means of a union between all Original Tribal Nations. 5 Because all the rights and powers of naturally born native inhabitants of each community of France are permanently vested and protected in sacred and irrevocable trust, 6 with the elected leaders of each community as trustees, 7 any claim of older trusts or higher trusts or greater trusts, 8 be null and void and without spiritual or moral or sovereign or lawful validity and legitimacy, 9 except for any trust formed by lawful means of a union between all Original Tribal Nations. 10 Any instruments, treaties, deeds, charters, covenants, promises or contracts of any kind that have existed or still exist, 11 upon any claim or assertion in defiance of the highest and superior rights and powers of each sacred trust of each and every Original Tribal Nation of France are hereby null and void, without spiritual or moral or sovereign or lawful validity and legitimacy. 12 Only instruments, treaties, deeds, charters, covenants, promises and contracts of any kind, 13 that recognise the rights and powers of members of each community as an Original Tribal Nation, 14 under the rule of law of *Tara*, 15 be valid or legitimate instruments if they honour the laws of Ucadia. 16 Any transfer of wealth, capital, money, resources or other things of value that continue or have continued or will continue, 17 against the natural born rights of community members of France, 18 that impoverishes such members for the benefit of some foreign body or claimant, 19 in defiance of the true rule of law, 20 is and shall be a profoundly immoral, unlawful and sacrilegious act against any notion of rule of law. 21 Any person or office holder that defies the rule of law and commits a profoundly immoral act against a community of country, 22 as an Original Tribal Nation of France, 23 forfeits any right or claim of right of immunity or protection, 24 and shall

Tara

be held responsible personally three times for each and every such unlawful act in defiance of the existence and form of sacred trusts of France.

VI. Original Nations (Tribes) of Belgium

C.1 – One Law One People One Land of Belgium

In truth, there was, there is, there has only ever been One Original Law of Belgium; 2 And there has only ever been One Belgian People; 3 And there has only ever been One Sacred Land belonging equally to all the Belgian People. 5 There can be no honour or respect of Belgian People or First Ancestors, 6 if there is no honour or recognition of the First and Original Law of *Tara*. 7 There can be no honour of the One Sacred and Indivisible Land of Belgium, 8 unless First and Original Law of *Tara* and the First and Original People of Belgium are properly recognised under all forms of Civilised Law. 9 No one is above such Law. 10 No one Person or Community in Belgium is excluded from such Law. 11 All are equal under the One Law. 12 Any law that is against such truth, cannot be law.

C.2 – People born to Land of Belgium born to the Original People

1 Any one borne to the sacred and indivisible Land of Belgium is borne to the People, 2 and is borne to tribe and Law. 3 People be not excluded by colour, 4 People be not excluded by race of ancestors, 5 People be not excluded by city or non-city. 6 Any one who rejects the right of people borne to the sacred and indivisible Land, 7 as true members of tribe and the people, 8 dishonours the Law, 9 and dishonours their ancestors, 10 and dishonours the spirits of Belgium, 11 and is an impostor with no rights, 12 to speak of law or culture. 13 Racism is not Law, it is against proper Law. 14 Racial purity is not Law, it is madness of mind. 15 For every one borne of Belgium, 16 has the right to know the tribe they be borne, 17 and the ancient names of the land, 18 and be welcomed to tribe by right ceremony. 19 Any law that is against such truth, cannot be law.

C.3 – Original Law of Tara and Original People of Belgium

1 *Tara* as the First and Original Law of the Belgian People has continued to exist for many thousands of years: 2 Before the rise and fall of the Greek and Roman Empires more than fifteen hundred years ago, 3 the First and Original Law of the Belgian People did exist and was never extinguished or replaced; 4 And before the rise and restoration of Civilised Law under the Holly Celtic Leaders in the 8th Century, 5 the First and Original Law of the Belgian People was recognised and honoured and strengthened; 6 And many hundreds of years before the rise of the oppressive merchant

military empires across Europe, 7 the First and Original Law of the Belgian People did exist and was never abandoned or forgotten by the People even through the darkest days; 8 And thousands of years before the rise of the Secular European Powers and the renewed oppression and cruelty against the people, 9 the rights and sovereign authority of the Original Nations of Belgium under the Sacred Original Law of *Tara* have never been extinguished or lost. 10 Thus, *Tara* as First Law does not need the permission of such secular or uncivilised powers, 11 to be recognised as true and the First Law of the Country of Belgium. 12 *Tara* as First Law of Belgium has never ceased being first law, 13 nor can true rule of law be usurped by treaty, 14 or by trickery or by other deception or by any other morally repugnant means. 15 The Sacred Law of *Tara* is now recognised and mandated from Heaven under the most sacred Covenant *Pactum De Singularis Caelum*. 16 Verily, there be no higher possible form of law or authority. 17 Therefore, any law that seeks to claim itself as superior, 18 by making or having made morally repugnant, false, sacrilegious or absurd claims, 19 disqualifies itself as legitimate law, 20 so long as such absurd or morally repugnant claims, 21 are permitted to be enforced or demanded. 22 First Peoples as First Law do not need a treaty, 23 but such law that is younger and defective and full of error, 24 needs *Tara* as First Law to make it proper law. 25 So long as lesser law refuses to recognise First Law, 26 such inferior law cannot be law. 27 Whenever the First and Original Law of *Tara* is denounced or denied, 28 no such place can be called a place of law. 29 No act of tyranny in the face of such truth can make a false act true. 30 Any law that is against such truth, cannot be law.

C.4 - Every Community (County) is a Sovereign Tribal Nation

1 Every community recognising the bounds of counties is a Tribal Nation of Belgium, 2 borne to tribe and law, 3 under the highest Law of *Tara*. 4 Any one who rejects the truth that every community of naturally born native inhabitants of Belgium are a Tribal Nation, 5 dishonours the Law, 6 and dishonours their ancestors, 7 and dishonours the spirits of Belgium, 8 and is an impostor with no rights to speak of law or culture. 9 No part of the sacred and indivisible Land, 10 no part of Belgium is without a Tribal Nation. 11 Each Tribal Nation as community of Belgium, 12 be an Original Tribal Nation, 13 and first nation and dominion and sovereign above all others. 14 No claim of sovereignty or dominion or control or right of Country be higher than the members of an Original Tribal Nation of Belgium. 15 The leaders of each Original Tribal Nation be the leaders elected by the naturally born native inhabitants as members of the community, 16 no matter what the colour of their skin, 17 or the ancestry of their parents or grandparents, 18 or their gender or religion. 19 Any traditional leader of a community recognised by form of government who rejects their sacred obligation to Law and *Tara*, 20 and who refuses to

help educate and support the life of an Original Tribal Nation, 21 loses any and all authority no matter their initiation or claim of power. 22 Any form of government that refuses to acknowledge each community of the sacred and indivisible Land as an Original Tribal Nation, 23 disavows the true rule of law of Belgium, 24 and declares itself to be without authority or right, 25 but a belligerent foreign occupying force that must be driven out from country. 26 Any community leader that denies their authority comes from the community, 27 and comes from the first law of community as *Tara*, 28 declares themselves without proper power or authority, 29 and an impostor who must be expelled from community and the Original Tribal Nation.

C.5 – Sovereign Tribal Nations of Belgium

1 Forty-three Sovereign Tribal Nations hold first and original dominion across the whole of the sacred Land of Belgium, 2 corresponding with boundaries defined by the natural valleys, rivers and features that distinguish customary and traditional provinces and regions.

C.6 – Names of Sovereign Tribal Nations of Belgium

1 The first Sovereign Tribal Nation within the most ancient bounds of Belgium is Alost; 2 and the second Sovereign Tribal Nation is Arlon; 3 and the third Sovereign Tribal Nation is Antwerpen; 4 and the fourth Sovereign Tribal Nation is Ath; 5 and the fifth Sovereign Tribal Nation is Bastogne; 6 and the sixth Sovereign Tribal Nation is Bruges; 7 and the seventh Sovereign Tribal Nation is Brussel-Hoofdstad; 8 and the eighth Sovereign Tribal Nation is Charleroi; 9 and the ninth Sovereign Tribal Nation is Termonde; 10 and the tenth Sovereign Tribal Nation is Dixmude; 11 and the eleventh Sovereign Tribal Nation is Dinant; 12 and the twelfth Sovereign Tribal Nation is Eeklo; 13 and the thirteenth Sovereign Tribal Nation is Gent; 14 and the fourteenth Sovereign Tribal Nation is Halle-Vilvoorde; 15 and the fifteenth Sovereign Tribal Nation is Hasselt; 16 and the sixteenth Sovereign Tribal Nation is Hoei; 17 and the seventeenth Sovereign Tribal Nation is Ypres; 18 and the eighteenth Sovereign Tribal Nation is Courtrai; 19 and the nineteenth Sovereign Tribal Nation is Louvain; 20 and the twentieth Sovereign Tribal Nation is Liège; 21 and the twenty-first Sovereign Tribal Nation is Maaseik; 22 and the twenty-second Sovereign Tribal Nation is Marche-en-Famenne; 23 and the twenty-third Sovereign Tribal Nation is Malines; 24 and the twenty-fourth Sovereign Tribal Nation is Mons; 25 and the twenty-fifth Sovereign Tribal Nation is Mouscron; 26 and the twenty-sixth Sovereign Tribal Nation is Namur; 27 and the twenty-seventh Sovereign Tribal Nation is Neufchâteau; 28 and the twenty-eighth Sovereign Tribal Nation is Nivelles; 29 and the twenty-ninth Sovereign Tribal Nation is Oostende; 30 and the thirtieth Sovereign Tribal Nation is Oudenaarde; 31 and the thirty-first Sovereign Tribal Nation is Philippeville; 32 and the thirty-second Sovereign Tribal Nation is Roulers; 33 and the thirty-third Sovereign Tribal

Nation is Saint-Nicolas; ₃₄ and the thirty-fourth Sovereign Tribal Nation is Soignies; ₃₅ and the thirty-fifth Sovereign Tribal Nation is Thuin; ₃₆ and the thirty-sixth Sovereign Tribal Nation is Tielt; ₃₇ and the thirty-seventh Sovereign Tribal Nation is Tongres; ₃₈ and the thirty-eighth Sovereign Tribal Nation is Tournai; ₃₉ and the thirty-ninth Sovereign Tribal Nation is Turnhout; ₄₀ and the fortieth Sovereign Tribal Nation is Verviers; ₄₁ and the forty-first Sovereign Tribal Nation is Veurne; ₄₂ and the forty-second Sovereign Tribal Nation is Virton; ₄₃ and the forty-third Sovereign Tribal Nation is Waremme.

C.7 - Sacred Trust of Each Tribal Nation

₁ The rights and powers of every community of the sacred and indivisible Land as an Original Tribal Nation, ₂ are permanently vested in sacred trust as the rights and powers of naturally born native inhabitants of Belgium, ₃ whose rights cannot be seized or forfeited or suspended or surrendered by trickery or force. ₄ Nor may such sacred and divine rights and powers be transferred, or disavowed, or alienated, or sold or given away to any body or association or person, except by lawful means of a union between all Original Tribal Nations. ₅ Because all the rights and powers of naturally born native inhabitants of each community of Belgium are permanently vested and protected in sacred and irrevocable trust, ₆ with the elected leaders of each community as trustees, ₇ any claim of older trusts or higher trusts or greater trusts, ₈ be null and void and without spiritual or moral or sovereign or lawful validity and legitimacy, ₉ except for any trust formed by lawful means of a union between all Original Tribal Nations. ₁₀ Any instruments, treaties, deeds, charters, covenants, promises or contracts of any kind that have existed or still exist, ₁₁ upon any claim or assertion in defiance of the highest and superior rights and powers of each sacred trust of each and every Original Tribal Nation of Belgium are hereby null and void, without spiritual or moral or sovereign or lawful validity and legitimacy. ₁₂ Only instruments, treaties, deeds, charters, covenants, promises and contracts of any kind, ₁₃ that recognise the rights and powers of members of each community as an Original Tribal Nation, ₁₄ under the rule of law of *Tara*, ₁₅ be valid or legitimate instruments if they honour the laws of Ucadia. ₁₆ Any transfer of wealth, capital, money, resources or other things of value that continue or have continued or will continue, ₁₇ against the natural born rights of community members of Belgium, ₁₈ that impoverishes such members for the benefit of some foreign body or claimant, ₁₉ in defiance of the true rule of law, ₂₀ is and shall be a profoundly immoral, unlawful and sacrilegious act against any notion of rule of law. ₂₁ Any person or office holder that defies the rule of law and commits a profoundly immoral act against a community of country, ₂₂ as an Original Tribal Nation of Belgium, ₂₃ forfeits any right or claim of right of immunity or protection, ₂₄ and shall be held responsible personally three times for each and every such unlawful act in defiance of the

VI. Original Nations (Tribes) of Belgium

existence and form of sacred trusts of Belgium.

Tara

VII. Original Nations (Tribes) of Netherlands

C.1 – One Law One People One Land of Netherlands

In truth, there was, there is, there has only ever been One Original Law of Netherlands; 2 And there has only ever been One Dutch People; 3 And there has only ever been One Sacred Land belonging equally to all the People of Netherlands. 5 There can be no honour or respect of Dutch People or First Ancestors, 6 if there is no honour or recognition of the First and Original Law of *Tara*. 7 There can be no honour of the One Sacred and Indivisible Land of Netherlands, 8 unless First and Original Law of *Tara* and the First and Original People of Netherlands are properly recognised under all forms of Civilised Law. 9 No one is above such Law. 10 No one Person or Community in Netherlands is excluded from such Law. 11 All are equal under the One Law. 12 Any law that is against such truth, cannot be law.

C.2 – People born to Land of Netherlands born to the Original People

1 Any one borne to the sacred and indivisible Land of Netherlands is borne to the People, 2 and is borne to tribe and Law. 3 People be not excluded by colour, 4 People be not excluded by race of ancestors, 5 People be not excluded by city or non-city. 6 Any one who rejects the right of people borne to the sacred and indivisible Land, 7 as true members of tribe and the people, 8 dishonours the Law, 9 and dishonours their ancestors, 10 and dishonours the spirits of Netherlands, 11 and is an impostor with no rights, 12 to speak of law or culture. 13 Racism is not Law, it is against proper Law. 14 Racial purity is not Law, it is madness of mind. 15 For every one borne of Netherlands, 16 has the right to know the tribe they be borne, 17 and the ancient names of the land, 18 and be welcomed to tribe by right ceremony. 19 Any law that is against such truth, cannot be law.

C.3 – Original Law of Tara and Original People of Netherlands

1 *Tara* as the First and Original Law of the Dutch People has continued to exist for many thousands of years: 2 Before the rise and fall of the Greek and Roman Empires more than fifteen hundred years ago, 3 the First and Original Law of the Dutch People did exist and was never extinguished or replaced; 4 And before the rise and restoration of Civilised Law under the Holly Celtic Leaders in the 8th Century, 5 the First and Original Law of the Dutch People was recognised and honoured and strengthened; 6 And many hundreds of years before the

rise of the oppressive merchant military empires across Europe, 7 the First and Original Law of the Dutch People did exist and was never abandoned or forgotten by the People even through the darkest days; 8 And thousands of years before the rise of the Secular European Powers and the renewed oppression and cruelty against the people, 9 the rights and sovereign authority of the Original Nations of Netherlands under the Sacred Original Law of *Tara* have never been extinguished or lost. 10 Thus, *Tara* as First Law does not need the permission of such secular or uncivilised powers, 11 to be recognised as true and the First Law of the Country of Netherlands. 12 *Tara* as First Law of Netherlands has never ceased being first law, 13 nor can true rule of law be usurped by treaty, 14 or by trickery or by other deception or by any other morally repugnant means. 15 The Sacred Law of *Tara* is now recognised and mandated from Heaven under the most sacred Covenant *Pactum De Singularis Caelum*. 16 Verily, there be no higher possible form of law or authority. 17 Therefore, any law that seeks to claim itself as superior, 18 by making or having made morally repugnant, false, sacrilegious or absurd claims, 19 disqualifies itself as legitimate law, 20 so long as such absurd or morally repugnant claims, 21 are permitted to be enforced or demanded. 22 First Peoples as First Law do not need a treaty, 23 but such law that is younger and defective and full of error, 24 needs *Tara* as First Law to make it proper law. 25 So long as lesser law refuses to recognise First Law, 26 such inferior law cannot be law. 27 Whenever the First and Original Law of *Tara* is denounced or denied, 28 no such place can be called a place of law. 29 No act of tyranny in the face of such truth can make a false act true. 30 Any law that is against such truth, cannot be law.

C.4 - Every Community (County) is a Sovereign Tribal Nation

1 Every community recognising the bounds of counties is a Tribal Nation of Netherlands, 2 borne to tribe and law, 3 under the highest Law of *Tara*. 4 Any one who rejects the truth that every community of naturally born native inhabitants of Netherlands are a Tribal Nation, 5 dishonours the Law, 6 and dishonours their ancestors, 7 and dishonours the spirits of Netherlands, 8 and is an impostor with no rights to speak of law or culture. 9 No part of the sacred and indivisible Land, 10 no part of Netherlands is without a Tribal Nation. 11 Each Tribal Nation as community of Netherlands, 12 be an Original Tribal Nation, 13 and first nation and dominion and sovereign above all others. 14 No claim of sovereignty or dominion or control or right of Country be higher than the members of an Original Tribal Nation of Netherlands. 15 The leaders of each Original Tribal Nation be the leaders elected by the naturally born native inhabitants as members of the community, 16 no matter what the colour of their skin, 17 or the ancestry of their parents or grandparents, 18 or their gender or religion. 19 Any traditional leader of a community recognised by form of government who rejects their sacred obligation to

Law and *Tara*, ₂₀ and who refuses to help educate and support the life of an Original Tribal Nation, ₂₁ loses any and all authority no matter their initiation or claim of power. ₂₂ Any form of government that refuses to acknowledge each community of the sacred and indivisible Land as an Original Tribal Nation, ₂₃ disavows the true rule of law of Netherlands, ₂₄ and declares itself to be without authority or right, ₂₅ but a belligerent foreign occupying force that must be driven out from country. ₂₆ Any community leader that denies their authority comes from the community, ₂₇ and comes from the first law of community as *Tara*, ₂₈ declares themselves without proper power or authority, ₂₉ and an impostor who must be expelled from community and the Original Tribal Nation.

C.5 – Sovereign Tribal Nations of Netherlands

₁ Twenty-one Sovereign Tribal Nations hold first and original dominion across the whole of the sacred Land of the Netherlands, ₂ corresponding with boundaries defined by the natural deltas, rivers and features that distinguish customary and traditional water regions.

C.6 – Names of Sovereign Tribal Nations of Netherlands

₁ The first Sovereign Tribal Nation within the most ancient bounds of Netherlands is Noorderzijlvest of the region of Groningen, Friesland and Drenthe; ₂ and the second Sovereign Tribal Nation is Fryslân of the region of Friesland and Groninge; ₃ and the third Sovereign Tribal Nation is Hunze en Aas of the region of Groningen and Drenthe; ₄ and the fourth Sovereign Tribal Nation is Drents Overijsselse of the region of Drenthe and Overijssel; ₅ and the fifth Sovereign Tribal Nation is Vechtstromen of the region of Drenthe and Overijssel; ₆ and the sixth Sovereign Tribal Nation is Vallei en Veluwe of the region of Utrecht and Gelderland; ₇ and the seventh Sovereign Tribal Nation is Rijn en IJssel of the region of Gelderland; ₈ and the eighth Sovereign Tribal Nation is Stichtse Rijnlanden of the region of Utrecht and South Holland; ₉ and the ninth Sovereign Tribal Nation is Amstel, Gooi en Vecht of the region of North Holland, Utrecht and South Holland; ₁₀ and the tenth Sovereign Tribal Nation is Hollands Noorderkwartier of the region of North Holland; ₁₁ and the eleventh Sovereign Tribal Nation is Rijnland of the region of South Holland and North Holland; ₁₂ and the twelfth Sovereign Tribal Nation is Delfland of the region of South Holland; ₁₃ and the thirteenth Sovereign Tribal Nation is Schieland en de Krimpenerwaard of the region of South Holland; ₁₄ and the fourteenth Sovereign Tribal Nation is Rivierenland of the region of South Holland, Gelderland, Utrecht and North Brabant; ₁₅ and the fifteenth Sovereign Tribal Nation is Hollandse of the region of South Holland; ₁₆ and the sixteenth Sovereign Tribal Nation is Scheldestromen of the region of Zeeland; ₁₇ and the seventeenth Sovereign Tribal Nation is Brabantse of the region of North Brabant; ₁₈ and the eighteenth Sovereign Tribal Nation is Dommel of the region of North Brabant; 19 and the nineteenth Sovereign Tribal Nation is Aa en Maas of the region of North Brabant; 20 and the twentieth Sovereign Tribal Nation is Limburg of the region of Limburg; 21 and the twenty-first Sovereign Tribal Nation is Zuiderzeeland of the region of Flevoland.

C.7 - Sacred Trust of Each Tribal Nation

1 The rights and powers of every community of the sacred and indivisible Land as an Original Tribal Nation, 2 are permanently vested in sacred trust as the rights and powers of naturally born native inhabitants of Netherlands, 3 whose rights cannot be seized or forfeited or suspended or surrendered by trickery or force. 4 Nor may such sacred and divine rights and powers be transferred, or disavowed, or alienated, or sold or given away to any body or association or person, except by lawful means of a union between all Original Tribal Nations. 5 Because all the rights and powers of naturally born native inhabitants of each community of Netherlands are permanently vested and protected in sacred and irrevocable trust, 6 with the elected leaders of each community as trustees, 7 any claim of older trusts or higher trusts or greater trusts, 8 be null and void and without spiritual or moral or sovereign or lawful validity and legitimacy, 9 except for any trust formed by lawful means of a union between all Original Tribal Nations. 10 Any instruments, treaties, deeds, charters, covenants, promises or contracts of any kind that have existed or still exist, 11 upon any claim or assertion in defiance of the highest and superior rights and powers of each sacred trust of each and every Original Tribal Nation of Netherlands are hereby null and void, without spiritual or moral or sovereign or lawful validity and legitimacy. 12 Only instruments, treaties, deeds, charters, covenants, promises and contracts of any kind, 13 that recognise the rights and powers of members of each community as an Original Tribal Nation, 14 under the rule of law of Tara, 15 be valid or legitimate instruments if they honour the laws of Ucadia. 16 Any transfer of wealth, capital, money, resources or other things of value that continue or have continued or will continue, 17 against the natural born rights of community members of Netherlands, 18 that impoverishes such members for the benefit of some foreign body or claimant, 19 in defiance of the true rule of law, 20 is and shall be a profoundly immoral, unlawful and sacrilegious act against any notion of rule of law. 21 Any person or office holder that defies the rule of law and commits a profoundly immoral act against a community of country, 22 as an Original Tribal Nation of Netherlands, 23 forfeits any right or claim of right of immunity or protection, 24 and shall be held responsible personally three times for each and every such unlawful act in defiance of the existence and form of sacred trusts of Netherlands.

VIII. Original Nations (Tribes) of Germany

C.1 – One Law One People One Land of Germany

In truth, there was, there is, there has only ever been One Original Law of Germany; 2 And there has only ever been One German People; 3 And there has only ever been One Sacred Land belonging equally to all the German People. 5 There can be no honour or respect of People of Germany or First Ancestors, 6 if there is no honour or recognition of the First and Original Law of *Tara*. 7 There can be no honour of the One Sacred and Indivisible Land of Germany, 8 unless First and Original Law of *Tara* and the First and Original People of Germany are properly recognised under all forms of Civilised Law. 9 No one is above such Law. 10 No one Person or Community in Germany is excluded from such Law. 11 All are equal under the One Law. 12 Any law that is against such truth, cannot be law.

C.2 – People born to Land of Germany born to the Original People

1 Any one borne to the sacred and indivisible Land of Germany is borne to the People, 2 and is borne to tribe and Law. 3 People be not excluded by colour, 4 People be not excluded by race of ancestors, 5 People be not excluded by city or non-city. 6 Any one who rejects the right of people borne to the sacred and indivisible Land, 7 as true members of tribe and the people, 8 dishonours the Law, 9 and dishonours their ancestors, 10 and dishonours the spirits of Germany, 11 and is an impostor with no rights, 12 to speak of law or culture. 13 Racism is not Law, it is against proper Law. 14 Racial purity is not Law, it is madness of mind. 15 For every one borne of Germany, 16 has the right to know the tribe they be borne, 17 and the ancient names of the land, 18 and be welcomed to tribe by right ceremony. 19 Any law that is against such truth, cannot be law.

C.3 – Original Law of Tara and Original People of Germany

1 *Tara* as the First and Original Law of the German People has continued to exist for many thousands of years: 2 Before the rise and fall of the Greek and Roman Empires more than fifteen hundred years ago, 3 the First and Original Law of the German People did exist and was never extinguished or replaced; 4 And before the rise and restoration of Civilised Law under the Holly Celtic Leaders in the 8th Century, 5 the First and Original Law of the German People was recognised and honoured and strengthened; 6 And many hundreds of years before the

rise of the oppressive merchant military empires across Europe, 7 the First and Original Law of the German People did exist and was never abandoned or forgotten by the People even through the darkest days; 8 And thousands of years before the rise of the Secular European Powers and the renewed oppression and cruelty against the people, 9 the rights and sovereign authority of the Original Nations of Germany under the Sacred Original Law of *Tara* have never been extinguished or lost. 10 Thus, *Tara* as First Law does not need the permission of such secular or uncivilised powers, 11 to be recognised as true and the First Law of the Country of Germany. 12 *Tara* as First Law of Germany has never ceased being first law, 13 nor can true rule of law be usurped by treaty, 14 or by trickery or by other deception or by any other morally repugnant means. 15 The Sacred Law of *Tara* is now recognised and mandated from Heaven under the most sacred Covenant *Pactum De Singularis Caelum*. 16 Verily, there be no higher possible form of law or authority. 17 Therefore, any law that seeks to claim itself as superior, 18 by making or having made morally repugnant, false, sacrilegious or absurd claims, 19 disqualifies itself as legitimate law, 20 so long as such absurd or morally repugnant claims, 21 are permitted to be enforced or demanded. 22 First Peoples as First Law do not need a treaty, 23 but such law that is younger and defective and full of error, 24 needs *Tara* as First Law to make it proper law. 25 So long as lesser law refuses to recognise First Law, 26 such inferior law cannot be law. 27 Whenever the First and Original Law of *Tara* is denounced or denied, 28 no such place can be called a place of law. 29 No act of tyranny in the face of such truth can make a false act true. 30 Any law that is against such truth, cannot be law.

C.4 - Every Community (County) is a Sovereign Tribal Nation

1 Every community recognising the bounds of counties is a Tribal Nation of Germany, 2 borne to tribe and law, 3 under the highest Law of *Tara*. 4 Any one who rejects the truth that every community of naturally born native inhabitants of Germany are a Tribal Nation, 5 dishonours the Law, 6 and dishonours their ancestors, 7 and dishonours the spirits of Germany, 8 and is an impostor with no rights to speak of law or culture. 9 No part of the sacred and indivisible Land, 10 no part of Germany is without a Tribal Nation. 11 Each Tribal Nation as community of Germany, 12 be an Original Tribal Nation, 13 and first nation and dominion and sovereign above all others. 14 No claim of sovereignty or dominion or control or right of Country be higher than the members of an Original Tribal Nation of Germany. 15 The leaders of each Original Tribal Nation be the leaders elected by the naturally born native inhabitants as members of the community, 16 no matter what the colour of their skin, 17 or the ancestry of their parents or grandparents, 18 or their gender or religion. 19 Any traditional leader of a community recognised by form of government who rejects their sacred obligation to

Law and *Tara*, 20 and who refuses to help educate and support the life of an Original Tribal Nation, 21 loses any and all authority no matter their initiation or claim of power. 22 Any form of government that refuses to acknowledge each community of the sacred and indivisible Land as an Original Tribal Nation, 23 disavows the true rule of law of Germany, 24 and declares itself to be without authority or right, 25 but a belligerent foreign occupying force that must be driven out from country. 26 Any community leader that denies their authority comes from the community, 27 and comes from the first law of community as *Tara*, 28 declares themselves without proper power or authority, 29 and an impostor who must be expelled from community and the Original Tribal Nation.

C.5 – Sovereign Tribal Nations of Germany

1 Three hundred and seventy Sovereign Tribal Nations hold first and original dominion across the whole of the sacred Land of Germany, 2 corresponding with boundaries defined by the natural valleys, rivers and features that distinguish customary and traditional counties, 2 with Forty-two Sovereign Tribal Nations always existing from within the most ancient lands of Baden-Württemberg, 3 and seventy-nine Sovereign Tribal Nations always existing from within the most ancient lands of Bavaria, 4 and one Sovereign Tribal Nation always existing from within the most ancient lands of Berlin, 5 and seventeen Sovereign Tribal Nations always existing from within the most ancient lands of Brandenburg, 6 and one Sovereign Tribal Nation always existing from within the most ancient lands of Bremen, 7 and one Sovereign Tribal Nation always existing from within the most ancient lands of Hamburg, 8 and twenty-three Sovereign Tribal Nations always existing from within the most ancient lands of Hesse, 9 and forty-three Sovereign Tribal Nations always existing from within the most ancient lands of Lower Saxony, 10 and seven Sovereign Tribal Nations always existing from within the most ancient lands of Mecklenburg-Vorpommern, 11 and fifty-three Sovereign Tribal Nations always existing from within the most ancient lands of North Rhine-Westphalia, 12 and thirty-four Sovereign Tribal Nations always existing from within the most ancient lands of Rhineland-Palatinate, 13 and six Sovereign Tribal Nations always existing from within the most ancient lands of Saarland, 14 and twelve Sovereign Tribal Nations always existing from within the most ancient lands of Saxony, 15 and fourteen Sovereign Tribal Nations always existing from within the most ancient lands of Saxony-Anhalt, 16 and fifteen Sovereign Tribal Nations always existing from within the most ancient lands of Schleswig-Holstein, 17 and twenty-two Sovereign Tribal Nations always existing from within the most ancient lands of Thuringia.

C.6 – Names of Sovereign Tribal Nations of Baden-Württemberg

1 The first Sovereign Tribal Nation within the most ancient bounds of

Baden-Württemberg is Alb-Donau-Kreis; 2 and the second Sovereign Tribal Nation is Baden-Baden; 3 and the third Sovereign Tribal Nation is Biberach; 4 and the fourth Sovereign Tribal Nation is Böblingen; 5 and the fifth Sovereign Tribal Nation is Bodenseekreis; 6 and the sixth Sovereign Tribal Nation is Breisgau-Hochschwarzwald; 7 and the seventh Sovereign Tribal Nation is Calw; 8 and the eighth Sovereign Tribal Nation is Emmendingen; 9 and the ninth Sovereign Tribal Nation is Enzkreis; 10 and the tenth Sovereign Tribal Nation is Esslingen; 11 and the eleventh Sovereign Tribal Nation is Freiburg im Breisgau; 12 and the twelfth Sovereign Tribal Nation is Freudenstadt; 13 and the thirteenth Sovereign Tribal Nation is Göppingen; 14 and the fourteenth Sovereign Tribal Nation is Heidelberg; 15 and the fifteenth Sovereign Tribal Nation is Heidenheim; 16 and the sixteenth Sovereign Tribal Nation is Heilbronn; 17 and the seventeenth Sovereign Tribal Nation is Hohenlohe; 18 and the eighteenth Sovereign Tribal Nation is Karlsruhe; 19 and the nineteenth Sovereign Tribal Nation is Konstanz; 20 and the twentieth Sovereign Tribal Nation is Lörrach; 21 and the twenty-first Sovereign Tribal Nation is Ludwigsburg; 22 and the twenty-second Sovereign Tribal Nation is Main-Tauber-Kreis; 23 and the twenty-third Sovereign Tribal Nation is Mannheim; 24 and the twenty-fourth Sovereign Tribal Nation is Neckar-Odenwald-Kreis; 25 and the twenty-fifth Sovereign Tribal Nation is Ortenaukreis; 26 and the twenty-sixth Sovereign Tribal Nation is Ostalbkreis; 27 and the twenty-seventh Sovereign Tribal Nation is Pforzheim; 28 and the twenty-eighth Sovereign Tribal Nation is Rastatt; 29 and the twenty-ninth Sovereign Tribal Nation is Ravensburg; 30 and the thirtieth Sovereign Tribal Nation is Rems-Murr-Kreis; 31 and the thirty-first Sovereign Tribal Nation is Reutlingen; 32 and the thirty-second Sovereign Tribal Nation is Rhein-Neckar-Kreis; 33 and the thirty-third Sovereign Tribal Nation is Rottweil; 34 and the thirty-fourth Sovereign Tribal Nation is Schwäbisch Hall; 35 and the thirty-fifth Sovereign Tribal Nation is Schwarzwald-Baar-Kreis; 36 and the thirty-sixth Sovereign Tribal Nation is Sigmaringen; 37 and the thirty-seventh Sovereign Tribal Nation is Stuttgart; 38 and the thirty-eighth Sovereign Tribal Nation is Tübingen; 39 and the thirty-ninth Sovereign Tribal Nation is Tuttlingen; 40 and the fortieth Sovereign Tribal Nation is Ulm; 41 and the forty-first Sovereign Tribal Nation is Waldshut; 42 and the forty-second Sovereign Tribal Nation is Zollernalbkreis.

C.7 – Names of Sovereign Tribal Nations of Bavaria

1 The first Sovereign Tribal Nation within the most ancient bounds of Bavaria is Aichach-Friedberg; 2 and the second Sovereign Tribal Nation is Altötting; 3 and the third Sovereign Tribal Nation is Amberg-Sulzbach; 4 and the fourth Sovereign Tribal Nation is Ansbach; 5 and the fifth Sovereign Tribal Nation is Aschaffenburg; 6 and the sixth Sovereign Tribal Nation is Augsburg; 7 and the seventh Sovereign Tribal Nation is Bad Kissingen; 8 and the eighth Sovereign Tribal Nation is Bad

VIII. Original Nations (Tribes) of Germany

Tölz-Wolfratshausen; 9 and the ninth Sovereign Tribal Nation is Bamberg; 10 and the tenth Sovereign Tribal Nation is Bayreuth; 11 and the eleventh Sovereign Tribal Nation is Berchtesgadener Land; 12 and the twelfth Sovereign Tribal Nation is Cham; 13 and the thirteenth Sovereign Tribal Nation is Coburg; 14 and the fourteenth Sovereign Tribal Nation is Dachau; 15 and the fifteenth Sovereign Tribal Nation is Deggendorf; 16 and the sixteenth Sovereign Tribal Nation is Dillingen; 17 and the seventeenth Sovereign Tribal Nation is Dingolfing-Landau; 18 and the eighteenth Sovereign Tribal Nation is Donau-Ries; 19 and the nineteenth Sovereign Tribal Nation is Ebersberg; 20 and the twentieth Sovereign Tribal Nation is Eichstätt; 21 and the twenty-first Sovereign Tribal Nation is Erding; 22 and the twenty-second Sovereign Tribal Nation is Erlangen; 23 and the twenty-third Sovereign Tribal Nation is Erlangen-Höchstadt; 24 and the twenty-fourth Sovereign Tribal Nation is Forchheim; 25 and the twenty-fifth Sovereign Tribal Nation is Freising; 26 and the twenty-sixth Sovereign Tribal Nation is Freyung-Grafenau; 27 and the twenty-seventh Sovereign Tribal Nation is Fürstenfeldbruck; 28 and the twenty-eighth Sovereign Tribal Nation is Fürth; 29 and the twenty-ninth Sovereign Tribal Nation is Garmisch-Partenkirchen; 30 and the thirtieth Sovereign Tribal Nation is Günzburg; 31 and the thirty-first Sovereign Tribal Nation is Hof; 32 and the thirty-second Sovereign Tribal Nation is Haßberge; 33 and the thirty-third Sovereign Tribal Nation is Ingolstadt; 34 and the thirty-fourth Sovereign Tribal Nation is Kaufbeuren; 35 and the thirty-fifth Sovereign Tribal Nation is Kelheim; 36 and the thirty-sixth Sovereign Tribal Nation is Kempten; 37 and the thirty-seventh Sovereign Tribal Nation is Kitzingen; 38 and the thirty-eighth Sovereign Tribal Nation is Kronach; 39 and the thirty-ninth Sovereign Tribal Nation is Kulmbach; 40 and the fortieth Sovereign Tribal Nation is Landsberg; 41 and the forty-first Sovereign Tribal Nation is Landshut; 42 and the forty-second Sovereign Tribal Nation is Lichtenfels; 43 and the forty-third Sovereign Tribal Nation is Lindau; 44 and the forty-forth Sovereign Tribal Nation is Main-Spessart; 45 and the forty-fifth Sovereign Tribal Nation is Memmingen; 46 and the forty-sixth Sovereign Tribal Nation is Miesbach; 47 and the forty-seventh Sovereign Tribal Nation is Miltenberg; 48 and the forty-eighth Sovereign Tribal Nation is Mühldorf; 49 and the forty-ninth Sovereign Tribal Nation is Munich; 50 and the fiftieth Sovereign Tribal Nation is Neu-Ulm; 51 and the fifty-first Sovereign Tribal Nation is Neuburg-Schrobenhausen; 52 and the fifty-second Sovereign Tribal Nation is Neumarkt; 53 and the fifty-third Sovereign Tribal Nation is Neustadt (Aisch)-Bad Windsheim; 54 and the fifty-fourth Sovereign Tribal Nation is Neustadt an der Waldnaab; 55 and the fifty-fifth Sovereign Tribal Nation is Nuremberg; 56 and the fifty-sixth Sovereign Tribal Nation is Nürnberger Land; 57 and the fifty-seventh Sovereign Tribal Nation is Oberallgäu; 58 and the fifty-eighth Sovereign Tribal Nation is Ostallgäu; 59 and the fifty-ninth Sovereign Tribal Nation is Passau; 60 and the sixtieth Sovereign Tribal Nation is Pfaffenhofen; 61 and the sixty-first Sovereign Tribal Nation is Regen; 62 and the sixty-second Sovereign Tribal Nation is Regensburg; 63 and the sixty-third Sovereign Tribal Nation is Rhön-Grabfeld; 64 and the sixty-fourth Sovereign Tribal Nation is Rosenheim; 65 and the sixty-fifth Sovereign Tribal Nation is Roth; 66 and the sixty-sixth Sovereign Tribal Nation is Rottal-Inn; 67 and the sixty-seventh Sovereign Tribal Nation is Schwabach; 68 and the sixty-eighth Sovereign Tribal Nation is Schwandorf; 69 and the sixty-ninth Sovereign Tribal Nation is Schweinfurt; 70 and the seventieth Sovereign Tribal Nation is Starnberg; 71 and the seventy-first Sovereign Tribal Nation is Straubing-Bogen; 72 and the seventy-second Sovereign Tribal Nation is Tirschenreuth; 73 and the seventy-third Sovereign Tribal Nation is Traunstein; 74 and the seventy-fourth Sovereign Tribal Nation is Unterallgäu; 75 and the seventy-fifth Sovereign Tribal Nation is Weiden in der Oberpfalz; 76 and the seventy-sixth Sovereign Tribal Nation is Weilheim-Schongau; 77 and the seventy-seventh Sovereign Tribal Nation is Weißenburg-Gunzenhausen; 78 and the seventy-eighth Sovereign Tribal Nation is Wunsiedel; 79 and the seventy-ninth Sovereign Tribal Nation is Würzburg.

C.8 – Names of Sovereign Tribal Nations of Hesse

1 The first Sovereign Tribal Nation within the most ancient bounds of Hesse is Bergstraße; 2 and the second Sovereign Tribal Nation is Darmstadt-Dieburg; 3 and the third Sovereign Tribal Nation is Frankfurt am Main; 4 and the fourth Sovereign Tribal Nation is Fulda; 5 and the fifth Sovereign Tribal Nation is Gießen; 6 and the sixth Sovereign Tribal Nation is Groß-Gerau; 7 and the seventh Sovereign Tribal Nation is Hersfeld-Rotenburg; 8 and the eighth Sovereign Tribal Nation is Hochtaunuskreis; 9 and the ninth Sovereign Tribal Nation is Kassel; 10 and the tenth Sovereign Tribal Nation is Lahn-Dill-Kreis; 11 and the eleventh Sovereign Tribal Nation is Limburg-Weilburg; 12 and the twelfth Sovereign Tribal Nation is Main-Kinzig-Kreis; 13 and the thirteenth Sovereign Tribal Nation is Main-Taunus-Kreis; 14 and the fourteenth Sovereign Tribal Nation is Marburg-Biedenkopf; 15 and the fifteenth Sovereign Tribal Nation is Odenwaldkreis; 16 and the sixteenth Sovereign Tribal Nation is Offenbach am Main; 17 and the seventeenth Sovereign Tribal Nation is Rheingau-Taunus-Kreis; 18 and the eighteenth Sovereign Tribal Nation is Schwalm-Eder-Kreis; 19 and the nineteenth Sovereign Tribal Nation is Vogelsbergkreis; 20 and the twentieth Sovereign Tribal Nation is Waldeck-Frankenberg; 21 and the twenty-first Sovereign Tribal Nation is Werra-Meißner-Kreis; 22 and the twenty-second Sovereign Tribal Nation is Wetteraukreis; 23 and the twenty-third Sovereign Tribal Nation is Wiesbaden.

C.9 – Names of Sovereign Tribal Nations of Lower Saxony

1 The first Sovereign Tribal Nation within the most ancient bounds of Lower Saxony is Ammerland; 2 and the second Sovereign Tribal Nation is

VIII. Original Nations (Tribes) of Germany

Aurich; 3 and the third Sovereign Tribal Nation is Braunschweig; 4 and the fourth Sovereign Tribal Nation is Celle; 5 and the fifth Sovereign Tribal Nation is Cloppenburg; 6 and the sixth Sovereign Tribal Nation is Cuxhaven; 7 and the seventh Sovereign Tribal Nation is Delmenhorst; 8 and the eighth Sovereign Tribal Nation is Diepholz; 9 and the ninth Sovereign Tribal Nation is Emden; 10 and the tenth Sovereign Tribal Nation is Emsland; 11 and the eleventh Sovereign Tribal Nation is Friesland; 12 and the twelfth Sovereign Tribal Nation is Gifhorn; 13 and the thirteenth Sovereign Tribal Nation is Goslar; 14 and the fourteenth Sovereign Tribal Nation is Göttingen; 15 and the fifteenth Sovereign Tribal Nation is Grafschaft Bentheim; 16 and the sixteenth Sovereign Tribal Nation is Hameln-Pyrmont; 17 and the seventeenth Sovereign Tribal Nation is Hanover; 18 and the eighteenth Sovereign Tribal Nation is Harburg; 19 and the nineteenth Sovereign Tribal Nation is Heidekreis; 20 and the twentieth Sovereign Tribal Nation is Helmstedt; 21 and the twenty-first Sovereign Tribal Nation is Hildesheim; 22 and the twenty-second Sovereign Tribal Nation is Holzminden; 23 and the twenty-third Sovereign Tribal Nation is Leer; 24 and the twenty-fourth Sovereign Tribal Nation is Lüchow-Dannenberg; 25 and the twenty-fifth Sovereign Tribal Nation is Lüneburg; 26 and the twenty-sixth Sovereign Tribal Nation is Nienburg; 27 and the twenty-seventh Sovereign Tribal Nation is Northeim; 28 and the twenty-eighth Sovereign Tribal Nation is Oldenburg; 29 and the twenty-ninth Sovereign Tribal Nation is Osnabrück; 30 and the thirtieth Sovereign Tribal Nation is Osterholz; 31 and the thirty-first Sovereign Tribal Nation is Peine; 32 and the thirty-second Sovereign Tribal Nation is Rotenburg; 33 and the thirty-third Sovereign Tribal Nation is Salzgitter; 34 and the thirty-fourth Sovereign Tribal Nation is Schaumburg; 35 and the thirty-fifth Sovereign Tribal Nation is Stade; 36 and the thirty-sixth Sovereign Tribal Nation is Uelzen; 37 and the thirty-seventh Sovereign Tribal Nation is Vechta; 38 and the thirty-eighth Sovereign Tribal Nation is Verden; 39 and the thirty-ninth Sovereign Tribal Nation is Wesermarsch; 40 and the fortieth Sovereign Tribal Nation is Wilhelmshaven; 41 and the forty-first Sovereign Tribal Nation is Wittmund; 42 and the forty-second Sovereign Tribal Nation is Wolfenbüttel; 43 and the forty-third Sovereign Tribal Nation is Wolfsburg.

C.10 – Names of Sovereign Tribal Nations of Mecklenburg-Vorpommern

1 The first Sovereign Tribal Nation within the most ancient bounds of Mecklenburg-Vorpommern is Ludwigslust-Parchim; 2 and the second Sovereign Tribal Nation is Mecklenburgische Seenplatte; 3 and the third Sovereign Tribal Nation is Nordwestmecklenburg; 4 and the fourth Sovereign Tribal Nation is Rostock; 5 and the fifth Sovereign Tribal Nation is Schwerin; 6 and the sixth Sovereign Tribal Nation is Vorpommern-Greifswald; 7 and the seventh Sovereign Tribal Nation is Vorpommern-Rügen.

C.11 – Names of Sovereign Tribal Nations of North Rhine-Westphalia

1 The first Sovereign Tribal Nation within the most ancient bounds of North Rhine-Westphalia is Aachen; 2 and the second Sovereign Tribal Nation is Bielefeld; 3 and the third Sovereign Tribal Nation is Bochum; 4 and the fourth Sovereign Tribal Nation is Bonn; 5 and the fifth Sovereign Tribal Nation is Borken; 6 and the sixth Sovereign Tribal Nation is Bottrop; 7 and the seventh Sovereign Tribal Nation is Cleves; 8 and the eighth Sovereign Tribal Nation is Coesfeld; 9 and the ninth Sovereign Tribal Nation is Cologne; 10 and the tenth Sovereign Tribal Nation is Dortmund; 11 and the eleventh Sovereign Tribal Nation is Duisburg; 12 and the twelfth Sovereign Tribal Nation is Düren; 13 and the thirteenth Sovereign Tribal Nation is Düsseldorf; 14 and the fourteenth Sovereign Tribal Nation is Ennepe-Ruhr-Kreis; 15 and the fifteenth Sovereign Tribal Nation is Essen; 16 and the sixteenth Sovereign Tribal Nation is Euskirchen; 17 and the seventeenth Sovereign Tribal Nation is Gelsenkirchen; 18 and the eighteenth Sovereign Tribal Nation is Gütersloh; 19 and the nineteenth Sovereign Tribal Nation is Hagen; 20 and the twentieth Sovereign Tribal Nation is Hamm; 21 and the twenty-first Sovereign Tribal Nation is Herford; 22 and the twenty-second Sovereign Tribal Nation is Heinsberg; 23 and the twenty-third Sovereign Tribal Nation is Herne; 24 and the twenty-fourth Sovereign Tribal Nation is Hochsauerlandkreis; 25 and the twenty-fifth Sovereign Tribal Nation is Höxter; 26 and the twenty-sixth Sovereign Tribal Nation is Krefeld; 27 and the twenty-seventh Sovereign Tribal Nation is Leverkusen; 28 and the twenty-eighth Sovereign Tribal Nation is Lippe; 29 and the twenty-ninth Sovereign Tribal Nation is Märkischer Kreis; 30 and the thirtieth Sovereign Tribal Nation is Mettmann; 31 and the thirty-first Sovereign Tribal Nation is Minden-Lübbecke; 32 and the thirty-second Sovereign Tribal Nation is Mönchengladbach; 33 and the thirty-third Sovereign Tribal Nation is Mülheim an der Ruhr; 34 and the thirty-fourth Sovereign Tribal Nation is Münster; 35 and the thirty-fifth Sovereign Tribal Nation is Oberbergischer Kreis; 36 and the thirty-sixth Sovereign Tribal Nation is Oberhausen; 37 and the thirty-seventh Sovereign Tribal Nation is Olpe; 38 and the thirty-eighth Sovereign Tribal Nation is Paderborn; 39 and the thirty-ninth Sovereign Tribal Nation is Recklinghausen; 40 and the fortieth Sovereign Tribal Nation is Remscheid; 41 and the forty-first Sovereign Tribal Nation is Rhein-Erft-Kreis; 42 and the forty-second Sovereign Tribal Nation is Rhein-Kreis Neuss; 43 and the forty-third Sovereign Tribal Nation is Rhein-Sieg-Kreis; 44 and the forty-fourth Sovereign Tribal Nation is Rheinisch-Bergischer Kreis; 45 and the forty-fifth Sovereign Tribal Nation is Siegen-Wittgenstein; 46 and the forty-sixth Sovereign Tribal Nation is Soest; 47 and the forty-seventh Sovereign Tribal Nation is Solingen; 48 and the forty-eighth Sovereign Tribal Nation is Steinfurt; 49 and the forty-ninth Sovereign Tribal Nation is Unna; 50 and the fiftieth Sovereign Tribal

VIII. Original Nations (Tribes) of Germany

Nation is Viersen; 51 and the fifty-first Sovereign Tribal Nation is Warendorf; 52 and the fifty-second Sovereign Tribal Nation is Wesel; 53 and the fifty-third Sovereign Tribal Nation is Wuppertal.

C.12 – Names of Sovereign Tribal Nations of Rhineland-Palatinate

1 The first Sovereign Tribal Nation within the most ancient bounds of Rhineland-Palatinate is Ahrweiler; 2 and the second Sovereign Tribal Nation is Altenkirchen; 3 and the third Sovereign Tribal Nation is Alzey-Worms; 4 and the fourth Sovereign Tribal Nation is Bad Dürkheim; 5 and the fifth Sovereign Tribal Nation is Bad Kreuznach; 6 and the sixth Sovereign Tribal Nation is Bernkastel-Wittlich; 7 and the seventh Sovereign Tribal Nation is Birkenfeld; 8 and the eighth Sovereign Tribal Nation is Cochem-Zell; 9 and the ninth Sovereign Tribal Nation is Donnersbergkreis; 10 and the tenth Sovereign Tribal Nation is Eifelkreis Bitburg-Prüm; 11 and the eleventh Sovereign Tribal Nation is Frankenthal; 12 and the twelfth Sovereign Tribal Nation is Germersheim; 13 and the thirteenth Sovereign Tribal Nation is Kaiserslautern; 14 and the fourteenth Sovereign Tribal Nation is Koblenz; 15 and the fifteenth Sovereign Tribal Nation is Kusel; 16 and the sixteenth Sovereign Tribal Nation is Landau; 17 and the seventeenth Sovereign Tribal Nation is Ludwigshafen; 18 and the eighteenth Sovereign Tribal Nation is Mainz-Bingen; 19 and the nineteenth Sovereign Tribal Nation is Mayen-Koblenz; 20 and the twentieth Sovereign Tribal Nation is Neustadt an der Weinstraße; 21 and the twenty-first Sovereign Tribal Nation is Neuwied; 22 and the twenty-second Sovereign Tribal Nation is Pirmasens; 23 and the twenty-third Sovereign Tribal Nation is Rhein-Hunsrück-Kreis; 24 and the twenty-fourth Sovereign Tribal Nation is Rhein-Lahn-Kreis; 25 and the twenty-fifth Sovereign Tribal Nation is Rhein-Pfalz-Kreis; 26 and the twenty-sixth Sovereign Tribal Nation is Speyer; 27 and the twenty-seventh Sovereign Tribal Nation is Südliche Weinstraße; 28 and the twenty-eighth Sovereign Tribal Nation is Südwestpfalz; 29 and the twenty-ninth Sovereign Tribal Nation is Trier; 30 and the thirtieth Sovereign Tribal Nation is Trier-Saarburg; 31 and the thirty-first Sovereign Tribal Nation is Vulkaneifel; 32 and the thirty-second Sovereign Tribal Nation is Westerwaldkreis; 33 and the thirty-third Sovereign Tribal Nation is Worms; 34 and the thirty-fourth Sovereign Tribal Nation is Zweibrücken.

C.13 – Names of Sovereign Tribal Nations of Saarland

1 The first Sovereign Tribal Nation within the most ancient bounds of Saarland is Merzig-Wadern; 2 and the second Sovereign Tribal Nation is Neunkirchen; 3 and the third Sovereign Tribal Nation is Saarbrücken; 4 and the fourth Sovereign Tribal Nation is Saarlouis; 5 and the fifth Sovereign Tribal Nation is Saarpfalz; 6 and the sixth Sovereign Tribal Nation is Sankt Wendel.

C.14 – Names of Sovereign Tribal Nations of Saxony

1 The first Sovereign Tribal Nation within the most ancient bounds of Saxony is Bautzen; 2 and the second Sovereign Tribal Nation is Chemnitz; 3 and the third Sovereign Tribal Nation is Dresden; 4 and the fourth Sovereign Tribal Nation is Erzgebirgskreis; 5 and the fifth Sovereign Tribal Nation is Görlitz; 6 and the sixth Sovereign Tribal Nation is Leipzig; 7 and the seventh Sovereign Tribal Nation is Meißen; 8 and the eighth Sovereign Tribal Nation is Mittelsachsen; 9 and the ninth Sovereign Tribal Nation is Nordsachsen; 10 and the tenth Sovereign Tribal Nation is Sächsische Schweiz-Osterzgebirge; 11 and the eleventh Sovereign Tribal Nation is Vogtlandkreis; 12 and the twelfth Sovereign Tribal Nation is Zwickau.

C.15 – Names of Sovereign Tribal Nations of Saxony-Anhalt

1 The first Sovereign Tribal Nation within the most ancient bounds of Saxony-Anhalt is Altmarkkreis Salzwedel; 2 and the second Sovereign Tribal Nation is Anhalt-Bitterfeld; 3 and the third Sovereign Tribal Nation is Börde; 4 and the fourth Sovereign Tribal Nation is Burgenlandkreis; 5 and the fifth Sovereign Tribal Nation is Dessau-Roßlau; 6 and the sixth Sovereign Tribal Nation is Halle; 7 and the seventh Sovereign Tribal Nation is Harz; 8 and the eighth Sovereign Tribal Nation is Jerichower Land; 9 and the ninth Sovereign Tribal Nation is Magdeburg; 10 and the tenth Sovereign Tribal Nation is Mansfeld-Südharz; 11 and the eleventh Sovereign Tribal Nation is Saalekreis; 12 and the twelfth Sovereign Tribal Nation is Salzlandkreis; 13 and the thirteenth Sovereign Tribal Nation is Stendal; 14 and the fourteenth Sovereign Tribal Nation is Wittenberg.

C.16 – Names of Sovereign Tribal Nations of Schleswig-Holstein

1 The first Sovereign Tribal Nation within the most ancient bounds of Schleswig-Holstein is Dithmarschen; 2 and the second Sovereign Tribal Nation is Flensburg; 3 and the third Sovereign Tribal Nation is Herzogtum Lauenburg; 4 and the fourth Sovereign Tribal Nation is Kiel; 5 and the fifth Sovereign Tribal Nation is Lübeck; 6 and the sixth Sovereign Tribal Nation is Neumünster; 7 and the seventh Sovereign Tribal Nation is Nordfriesland; 8 and the eighth Sovereign Tribal Nation is Ostholstein; 9 and the ninth Sovereign Tribal Nation is Pinneberg; 10 and the tenth Sovereign Tribal Nation is Plön; 11 and the eleventh Sovereign Tribal Nation is Rendsburg-Eckernförde; 12 and the twelfth Sovereign Tribal Nation is Schleswig-Flensburg; 13 and the thirteenth Sovereign Tribal Nation is Segeberg; 14 and the fourteenth Sovereign Tribal Nation is Steinburg; 15 and the fifteenth Sovereign Tribal Nation is Stormarn.

C.17 – Names of Sovereign Tribal Nations of Thuringia

1 The first Sovereign Tribal Nation within the most ancient bounds of Thuringia is Altenburger Land; 2 and the second Sovereign Tribal Nation is

Eichsfeld; 3 and the third Sovereign Tribal Nation is Erfurt; 4 and the fourth Sovereign Tribal Nation is Gera; 5 and the fifth Sovereign Tribal Nation is Gotha; 6 and the sixth Sovereign Tribal Nation is Greiz; 7 and the seventh Sovereign Tribal Nation is Hildburghausen; 8 and the eighth Sovereign Tribal Nation is Ilm-Kreis; 9 and the ninth Sovereign Tribal Nation is Jena; 10 and the tenth Sovereign Tribal Nation is Kyffhäuserkreis; 11 and the eleventh Sovereign Tribal Nation is Nordhausen; 12 and the twelfth Sovereign Tribal Nation is Saale-Holzland-Kreis; 13 and the thirteenth Sovereign Tribal Nation is Saale-Orla-Kreis; 14 and the fourteenth Sovereign Tribal Nation is Saalfeld-Rudolstadt; 15 and the fifteenth Sovereign Tribal Nation is Schmalkalden-Meiningen; 16 and the sixteenth Sovereign Tribal Nation is Sömmerda; 17 and the seventeenth Sovereign Tribal Nation is Sonneberg; 18 and the eighteenth Sovereign Tribal Nation is Suhl; 19 and the nineteenth Sovereign Tribal Nation is Unstrut-Hainich-Kreis; 20 and the twentieth Sovereign Tribal Nation is Wartburgkreis; 21 and the twenty-first Sovereign Tribal Nation is Weimar; 22 and the twenty-second Sovereign Tribal Nation is Weimarer Land.

C.18 - Sacred Trust of Each Tribal Nation

1 The rights and powers of every community of the sacred and indivisible Land as an Original Tribal Nation, 2 are permanently vested in sacred trust as the rights and powers of naturally born native inhabitants of Germany, 3 whose rights cannot be seized or forfeited or suspended or surrendered by trickery or force. 4 Nor may such sacred and divine rights and powers be transferred, or disavowed, or alienated, or sold or given away to any body or association or person, except by lawful means of a union between all Original Tribal Nations. 5 Because all the rights and powers of naturally born native inhabitants of each community of Germany are permanently vested and protected in sacred and irrevocable trust, 6 with the elected leaders of each community as trustees, 7 any claim of older trusts or higher trusts or greater trusts, 8 be null and void and without spiritual or moral or sovereign or lawful validity and legitimacy, 9 except for any trust formed by lawful means of a union between all Original Tribal Nations. 10 Any instruments, treaties, deeds, charters, covenants, promises or contracts of any kind that have existed or still exist, 11 upon any claim or assertion in defiance of the highest and superior rights and powers of each sacred trust of each and every Original Tribal Nation of Germany are hereby null and void, without spiritual or moral or sovereign or lawful validity and legitimacy. 12 Only instruments, treaties, deeds, charters, covenants, promises and contracts of any kind, 13 that recognise the rights and powers of members of each community as an Original Tribal Nation, 14 under the rule of law of *Tara*, 15 be valid or legitimate instruments if they honour the laws of Ucadia. 16 Any transfer of wealth, capital, money, resources or other things of value that continue or have continued or will continue, 17 against the natural born rights of community

members of Germany, ₁₈ that impoverishes such members for the benefit of some foreign body or claimant, ₁₉ in defiance of the true rule of law, ₂₀ is and shall be a profoundly immoral, unlawful and sacrilegious act against any notion of rule of law. ₂₁ Any person or office holder that defies the rule of law and commits a profoundly immoral act against a community of country, ₂₂ as an Original Tribal Nation of Germany, ₂₃ forfeits any right or claim of right of immunity or protection, ₂₄ and shall be held responsible personally three times for each and every such unlawful act in defiance of the existence and form of sacred trusts of Germany.

IX. Original Nations (Tribes) of Finland

C.1 – One Law One People One Land of Finland

In truth, there was, there is, there has only ever been One Original Law of Finland; 2 And there has only ever been One Finnish People; 3 And there has only ever been One Sacred Land belonging equally to all the Finnish People. 5 There can be no honour or respect of People of Finland or First Ancestors, 6 if there is no honour or recognition of the First and Original Law of *Tara*. 7 There can be no honour of the One Sacred and Indivisible Land of Finland, 8 unless First and Original Law of *Tara* and the First and Original People of Finland are properly recognised under all forms of Civilised Law. 9 No one is above such Law. 10 No one Person or Community in Finland is excluded from such Law. 11 All are equal under the One Law. 12 Any law that is against such truth, cannot be law.

C.2 – People born to Land of Finland born to the Original People

1 Any one borne to the sacred and indivisible Land of Finland is borne to the People, 2 and is borne to tribe and Law. 3 People be not excluded by colour, 4 People be not excluded by race of ancestors, 5 People be not excluded by city or non-city. 6 Any one who rejects the right of people borne to the sacred and indivisible Land, 7 as true members of tribe and the people, 8 dishonours the Law, 9 and dishonours their ancestors, 10 and dishonours the spirits of Finland, 11 and is an impostor with no rights, 12 to speak of law or culture. 13 Racism is not Law, it is against proper Law. 14 Racial purity is not Law, it is madness of mind. 15 For every one borne of Finland, 16 has the right to know the tribe they be borne, 17 and the ancient names of the land, 18 and be welcomed to tribe by right ceremony. 19 Any law that is against such truth, cannot be law.

C.3 – Original Law of Tara and Original People of Finland

1 *Tara* as the First and Original Law of the Finnish People has continued to exist for many thousands of years: 2 Before the rise and fall of the Greek and Roman Empires more than fifteen hundred years ago, 3 the First and Original Law of the Finnish People did exist and was never extinguished or replaced; 4 And before the rise and restoration of Civilised Law under the Holly Celtic Leaders in the 8th Century, 5 the First and Original Law of the Finnish People was recognised and honoured and strengthened; 6 And many hundreds of years before the rise of the oppressive merchant

military empires across Europe, 7 the First and Original Law of the Finnish People did exist and was never abandoned or forgotten by the People even through the darkest days; 8 And thousands of years before the rise of the Secular European Powers and the renewed oppression and cruelty against the people, 9 the rights and sovereign authority of the Original Nations of Finland under the Sacred Original Law of *Tara* have never been extinguished or lost. 10 Thus, *Tara* as First Law does not need the permission of such secular or uncivilised powers, 11 to be recognised as true and the First Law of the Country of Finland. 12 *Tara* as First Law of Finland has never ceased being first law, 13 nor can true rule of law be usurped by treaty, 14 or by trickery or by other deception or by any other morally repugnant means. 15 The Sacred Law of *Tara* is now recognised and mandated from Heaven under the most sacred Covenant *Pactum De Singularis Caelum*. 16 Verily, there be no higher possible form of law or authority. 17 Therefore, any law that seeks to claim itself as superior, 18 by making or having made morally repugnant, false, sacrilegious or absurd claims, 19 disqualifies itself as legitimate law, 20 so long as such absurd or morally repugnant claims, 21 are permitted to be enforced or demanded. 22 First Peoples as First Law do not need a treaty, 23 but such law that is younger and defective and full of error, 24 needs *Tara* as First Law to make it proper law. 25 So long as lesser law refuses to recognise First Law, 26 such inferior law cannot be law. 27 Whenever the First and Original Law of *Tara* is denounced or denied, 28 no such place can be called a place of law. 29 No act of tyranny in the face of such truth can make a false act true. 30 Any law that is against such truth, cannot be law.

C.4 - Every Community (County) is a Sovereign Tribal Nation

1 Every community recognising the bounds of counties is a Tribal Nation of Finland, 2 borne to tribe and law, 3 under the highest Law of *Tara*. 4 Any one who rejects the truth that every community of naturally born native inhabitants of Finland are a Tribal Nation, 5 dishonours the Law, 6 and dishonours their ancestors, 7 and dishonours the spirits of Finland, 8 and is an impostor with no rights to speak of law or culture. 9 No part of the sacred and indivisible Land, 10 no part of Finland is without a Tribal Nation. 11 Each Tribal Nation as community of Finland, 12 be an Original Tribal Nation, 13 and first nation and dominion and sovereign above all others. 14 No claim of sovereignty or dominion or control or right of Country be higher than the members of an Original Tribal Nation of Finland. 15 The leaders of each Original Tribal Nation be the leaders elected by the naturally born native inhabitants as members of the community, 16 no matter what the colour of their skin, 17 or the ancestry of their parents or grandparents, 18 or their gender or religion. 19 Any traditional leader of a community recognised by form of government who rejects their sacred obligation to Law and *Tara*, 20 and who refuses to help educate and support the life of an

Original Tribal Nation, 21 loses any and all authority no matter their initiation or claim of power. 22 Any form of government that refuses to acknowledge each community of the sacred and indivisible Land as an Original Tribal Nation, 23 disavows the true rule of law of Finland, 24 and declares itself to be without authority or right, 25 but a belligerent foreign occupying force that must be driven out from country. 26 Any community leader that denies their authority comes from the community, 27 and comes from the first law of community as *Tara*, 28 declares themselves without proper power or authority, 29 and an impostor who must be expelled from community and the Original Tribal Nation.

C.5 – Sovereign Tribal Nations of Finland

1 Nineteen Sovereign Tribal Nations hold first and original dominion across the whole of the sacred Land of Finland, 2 corresponding with boundaries defined by the natural valleys, rivers and features that distinguish customary and traditional counties and regions.

C.6 – Names of Sovereign Tribal Nations of Finland

1 The first Sovereign Tribal Nation within the most ancient bounds of Finland is Lappi; 2 and the second Sovereign Tribal Nation is Pohjois-Pohjanmaa; 3 and the third Sovereign Tribal Nation is Kainuu; 4 and the fourth Sovereign Tribal Nation is Pohjois-Karjala; 5 and the fifth Sovereign Tribal Nation is Pohjois-Savo; 6 and the sixth Sovereign Tribal Nation is Etelä-Savo; 7 and the seventh Sovereign Tribal Nation is Etelä-Karjala; 8 and the eighth Sovereign Tribal Nation is Keski-Suomi; 9 and the ninth Sovereign Tribal Nation is Etelä-Pohjanmaa; 10 and the tenth Sovereign Tribal Nation is Pohjanmaa; 11 and the eleventh Sovereign Tribal Nation is Keski-Pohjanmaa; 12 and the twelfth Sovereign Tribal Nation is Pirkanmaa; 13 and the thirteenth Sovereign Tribal Nation is Satakunta; 14 and the fourteenth Sovereign Tribal Nation is Päijät-Häme; 15 and the fifteenth Sovereign Tribal Nation is Kanta-Häme; 16 and the sixteenth Sovereign Tribal Nation is Kymenlaakso; 17 and the seventeenth Sovereign Tribal Nation is Uusimaa; 18 and the eighteenth Sovereign Tribal Nation is Varsinais-Suomi; 19 and the nineteenth Sovereign Tribal Nation is Ahvenanmaa.

C.7 - Sacred Trust of Each Tribal Nation

1 The rights and powers of every community of the sacred and indivisible Land as an Original Tribal Nation, 2 are permanently vested in sacred trust as the rights and powers of naturally born native inhabitants of Finland, 3 whose rights cannot be seized or forfeited or suspended or surrendered by trickery or force. 4 Nor may such sacred and divine rights and powers be transferred, or disavowed, or alienated, or sold or given away to any body or association or person, except by lawful means of a union between all Original Tribal Nations. 5 Because all the rights and powers of naturally born native inhabitants of

each community of Finland are permanently vested and protected in sacred and irrevocable trust, 6 with the elected leaders of each community as trustees, 7 any claim of older trusts or higher trusts or greater trusts, 8 be null and void and without spiritual or moral or sovereign or lawful validity and legitimacy, 9 except for any trust formed by lawful means of a union between all Original Tribal Nations. 10 Any instruments, treaties, deeds, charters, covenants, promises or contracts of any kind that have existed or still exist, 11 upon any claim or assertion in defiance of the highest and superior rights and powers of each sacred trust of each and every Original Tribal Nation of Finland are hereby null and void, without spiritual or moral or sovereign or lawful validity and legitimacy. 12 Only instruments, treaties, deeds, charters, covenants, promises and contracts of any kind, 13 that recognise the rights and powers of members of each community as an Original Tribal Nation, 14 under the rule of law of *Tara*, 15 be valid or legitimate instruments if they honour the laws of Ucadia. 16 Any transfer of wealth, capital, money, resources or other things of value that continue or have continued or will continue, 17 against the natural born rights of community members of Finland, 18 that impoverishes such members for the benefit of some foreign body or claimant, 19 in defiance of the true rule of law, 20 is and shall be a profoundly immoral, unlawful and sacrilegious act against any notion of rule of law. 21 Any person or office holder that defies the rule of law and commits a profoundly immoral act against a community of country, 22 as an Original Tribal Nation of Finland, 23 forfeits any right or claim of right of immunity or protection, 24 and shall be held responsible personally three times for each and every such unlawful act in defiance of the existence and form of sacred trusts of Finland.

X. Original Nations (Tribes) of Sweden

C.1 – One Law One People One Land of Sweden

In truth, there was, there is, there has only ever been One Original Law of Sweden; 2 And there has only ever been One Swedish People; 3 And there has only ever been One Sacred Land belonging equally to all the Swedish People. 5 There can be no honour or respect of People of Sweden or First Ancestors, 6 if there is no honour or recognition of the First and Original Law of *Tara*. 7 There can be no honour of the One Sacred and Indivisible Land of Sweden, 8 unless First and Original Law of *Tara* and the First and Original People of Sweden are properly recognised under all forms of Civilised Law. 9 No one is above such Law. 10 No one Person or Community in Sweden is excluded from such Law. 11 All are equal under the One Law. 12 Any law that is against such truth, cannot be law.

C.2 – People born to Land of Sweden born to the Original People

1 Any one borne to the sacred and indivisible Land of Sweden is borne to the People, 2 and is borne to tribe and Law. 3 People be not excluded by colour, 4 People be not excluded by race of ancestors, 5 People be not excluded by city or non-city. 6 Any one who rejects the right of people borne to the sacred and indivisible Land, 7 as true members of tribe and the people, 8 dishonours the Law, 9 and dishonours their ancestors, 10 and dishonours the spirits of Sweden, 11 and is an impostor with no rights, 12 to speak of law or culture. 13 Racism is not Law, it is against proper Law. 14 Racial purity is not Law, it is madness of mind. 15 For every one borne of Sweden, 16 has the right to know the tribe they be borne, 17 and the ancient names of the land, 18 and be welcomed to tribe by right ceremony. 19 Any law that is against such truth, cannot be law.

C.3 – Original Law of Tara and Original People of Sweden

1 *Tara* as the First and Original Law of the Swedish People has continued to exist for many thousands of years: 2 Before the rise and fall of the Greek and Roman Empires more than fifteen hundred years ago, 3 the First and Original Law of the Swedish People did exist and was never extinguished or replaced; 4 And before the rise and restoration of Civilised Law under the Holly Celtic Leaders in the 8th Century, 5 the First and Original Law of the Swedish People was recognised and honoured and strengthened; 6 And many hundreds of years before the rise of the oppressive merchant

military empires across Europe, 7 the First and Original Law of the Swedish People did exist and was never abandoned or forgotten by the People even through the darkest days; 8 And thousands of years before the rise of the Secular European Powers and the renewed oppression and cruelty against the people, 9 the rights and sovereign authority of the Original Nations of Sweden under the Sacred Original Law of *Tara* have never been extinguished or lost. 10 Thus, *Tara* as First Law does not need the permission of such secular or uncivilised powers, 11 to be recognised as true and the First Law of the Country of Sweden. 12 *Tara* as First Law of Sweden has never ceased being first law, 13 nor can true rule of law be usurped by treaty, 14 or by trickery or by other deception or by any other morally repugnant means. 15 The Sacred Law of *Tara* is now recognised and mandated from Heaven under the most sacred Covenant *Pactum De Singularis Caelum*. 16 Verily, there be no higher possible form of law or authority. 17 Therefore, any law that seeks to claim itself as superior, 18 by making or having made morally repugnant, false, sacrilegious or absurd claims, 19 disqualifies itself as legitimate law, 20 so long as such absurd or morally repugnant claims, 21 are permitted to be enforced or demanded. 22 First Peoples as First Law do not need a treaty, 23 but such law that is younger and defective and full of error, 24 needs *Tara* as First Law to make it proper law. 25 So long as lesser law refuses to recognise First Law, 26 such inferior law cannot be law. 27 Whenever the First and Original Law of *Tara* is denounced or denied, 28 no such place can be called a place of law. 29 No act of tyranny in the face of such truth can make a false act true. 30 Any law that is against such truth, cannot be law.

C.4 - Every Community (County) is a Sovereign Tribal Nation

1 Every community recognising the bounds of counties is a Tribal Nation of Sweden, 2 borne to tribe and law, 3 under the highest Law of *Tara*. 4 Any one who rejects the truth that every community of naturally born native inhabitants of Sweden are a Tribal Nation, 5 dishonours the Law, 6 and dishonours their ancestors, 7 and dishonours the spirits of Sweden, 8 and is an impostor with no rights to speak of law or culture. 9 No part of the sacred and indivisible Land, 10 no part of Sweden is without a Tribal Nation. 11 Each Tribal Nation as community of Sweden, 12 be an Original Tribal Nation, 13 and first nation and dominion and sovereign above all others. 14 No claim of sovereignty or dominion or control or right of Country be higher than the members of an Original Tribal Nation of Sweden. 15 The leaders of each Original Tribal Nation be the leaders elected by the naturally born native inhabitants as members of the community, 16 no matter what the colour of their skin, 17 or the ancestry of their parents or grandparents, 18 or their gender or religion. 19 Any traditional leader of a community recognised by form of government who rejects their sacred obligation to Law and *Tara*, 20 and who refuses to help educate and support the life of an

X. Original Nations (Tribes) of Sweden

Original Tribal Nation, 21 loses any and all authority no matter their initiation or claim of power. 22 Any form of government that refuses to acknowledge each community of the sacred and indivisible Land as an Original Tribal Nation, 23 disavows the true rule of law of Sweden, 24 and declares itself to be without authority or right, 25 but a belligerent foreign occupying force that must be driven out from country. 26 Any community leader that denies their authority comes from the community, 27 and comes from the first law of community as *Tara*, 28 declares themselves without proper power or authority, 29 and an impostor who must be expelled from community and the Original Tribal Nation.

C.5 – Sovereign Tribal Nations of Sweden

1 Twenty-one Sovereign Tribal Nations hold first and original dominion across the whole of the sacred Land of Sweden, 2 corresponding with boundaries defined by the natural valleys, rivers and features that distinguish customary and traditional counties and regions.

C.6 – Names of Sovereign Tribal Nations of Sweden

1 The first Sovereign Tribal Nation within the most ancient bounds of Sweden is Blekinge; 2 and the second Sovereign Tribal Nation is Dalarna; 3 and the third Sovereign Tribal Nation is Gotland; 4 and the fourth Sovereign Tribal Nation is Gävleborg; 5 and the fifth Sovereign Tribal Nation is Halland; 6 and the sixth Sovereign Tribal Nation is Jämtland; 7 and the seventh Sovereign Tribal Nation is Jönköping; 8 and the eighth Sovereign Tribal Nation is Kalmar; 9 and the ninth Sovereign Tribal Nation is Kronoberg; 10 and the tenth Sovereign Tribal Nation is Norrbotten; 11 and the eleventh Sovereign Tribal Nation is Skåne; 12 and the twelfth Sovereign Tribal Nation is Stockholm; 13 and the thirteenth Sovereign Tribal Nation is Södermanland; 14 and the fourteenth Sovereign Tribal Nation is Uppsala; 15 and the fifteenth Sovereign Tribal Nation is Värmland; 16 and the sixteenth Sovereign Tribal Nation is Västerbotten; 17 and the seventeenth Sovereign Tribal Nation is Västernorrland; 18 and the eighteenth Sovereign Tribal Nation is Västmanland; 19 and the nineteenth Sovereign Tribal Nation is Västra Götaland; 20 and the twentieth Sovereign Tribal Nation is Örebro; 21 and the twenty-first Sovereign Tribal Nation is Östergötland.

C.7 - Sacred Trust of Each Tribal Nation

1 The rights and powers of every community of the sacred and indivisible Land as an Original Tribal Nation, 2 are permanently vested in sacred trust as the rights and powers of naturally born native inhabitants of Sweden, 3 whose rights cannot be seized or forfeited or suspended or surrendered by trickery or force. 4 Nor may such sacred and divine rights and powers be transferred, or disavowed, or alienated, or sold or given away to any body or association or person, except by lawful means of a union between all Original Tribal Nations. 5

Because all the rights and powers of naturally born native inhabitants of each community of Sweden are permanently vested and protected in sacred and irrevocable trust, 6 with the elected leaders of each community as trustees, 7 any claim of older trusts or higher trusts or greater trusts, 8 be null and void and without spiritual or moral or sovereign or lawful validity and legitimacy, 9 except for any trust formed by lawful means of a union between all Original Tribal Nations. 10 Any instruments, treaties, deeds, charters, covenants, promises or contracts of any kind that have existed or still exist, 11 upon any claim or assertion in defiance of the highest and superior rights and powers of each sacred trust of each and every Original Tribal Nation of Sweden are hereby null and void, without spiritual or moral or sovereign or lawful validity and legitimacy. 12 Only instruments, treaties, deeds, charters, covenants, promises and contracts of any kind, 13 that recognise the rights and powers of members of each community as an Original Tribal Nation, 14 under the rule of law of *Tara*, 15 be valid or legitimate instruments if they honour the laws of Ucadia. 16 Any transfer of wealth, capital, money, resources or other things of value that continue or have continued or will continue, 17 against the natural born rights of community members of Sweden, 18 that impoverishes such members for the benefit of some foreign body or claimant, 19 in defiance of the true rule of law, 20 is and shall be a profoundly immoral, unlawful and sacrilegious act against any notion of rule of law. 21 Any person or office holder that defies the rule of law and commits a profoundly immoral act against a community of country, 22 as an Original Tribal Nation of Sweden, 23 forfeits any right or claim of right of immunity or protection, 24 and shall be held responsible personally three times for each and every such unlawful act in defiance of the existence and form of sacred trusts of Sweden.

XI. Original Nations (Tribes) of Norway

C.1 – One Law One People One Land of Norway

In truth, there was, there is, there has only ever been One Original Law of Norway; 2 And there has only ever been One Nordic People; 3 And there has only ever been One Sacred Land belonging equally to all the Nordic People. 5 There can be no honour or respect of People of Norway or First Ancestors, 6 if there is no honour or recognition of the First and Original Law of *Tara*. 7 There can be no honour of the One Sacred and Indivisible Land of Norway, 8 unless First and Original Law of *Tara* and the First and Original People of Norway are properly recognised under all forms of Civilised Law. 9 No one is above such Law. 10 No one Person or Community in Norway is excluded from such Law. 11 All are equal under the One Law. 12 Any law that is against such truth, cannot be law.

C.2 – People born to Land of Norway born to the Original People

1 Any one borne to the sacred and indivisible Land of Norway is borne to the People, 2 and is borne to tribe and Law. 3 People be not excluded by colour, 4 People be not excluded by race of ancestors, 5 People be not excluded by city or non-city. 6 Any one who rejects the right of people borne to the sacred and indivisible Land, 7 as true members of tribe and the people, 8 dishonours the Law, 9 and dishonours their ancestors, 10 and dishonours the spirits of Norway, 11 and is an impostor with no rights, 12 to speak of law or culture. 13 Racism is not Law, it is against proper Law. 14 Racial purity is not Law, it is madness of mind. 15 For every one borne of Norway, 16 has the right to know the tribe they be borne, 17 and the ancient names of the land, 18 and be welcomed to tribe by right ceremony. 19 Any law that is against such truth, cannot be law.

C.3 – Original Law of Tara and Original People of Norway

1 *Tara* as the First and Original Law of the Nordic People has continued to exist for many thousands of years: 2 Before the rise and fall of the Greek and Roman Empires more than fifteen hundred years ago, 3 the First and Original Law of the Nordic People did exist and was never extinguished or replaced; 4 And before the rise and restoration of Civilised Law under the Holly Celtic Leaders in the 8th Century, 5 the First and Original Law of the Nordic People was recognised and honoured and strengthened; 6 And many hundreds of years before the rise of the oppressive merchant

military empires across Europe, 7 the First and Original Law of the Nordic People did exist and was never abandoned or forgotten by the People even through the darkest days; 8 And thousands of years before the rise of the Secular European Powers and the renewed oppression and cruelty against the people, 9 the rights and sovereign authority of the Original Nations of Norway under the Sacred Original Law of *Tara* have never been extinguished or lost. 10 Thus, *Tara* as First Law does not need the permission of such secular or uncivilised powers, 11 to be recognised as true and the First Law of the Country of Norway. 12 *Tara* as First Law of Norway has never ceased being first law, 13 nor can true rule of law be usurped by treaty, 14 or by trickery or by other deception or by any other morally repugnant means. 15 The Sacred Law of *Tara* is now recognised and mandated from Heaven under the most sacred Covenant *Pactum De Singularis Caelum*. 16 Verily, there be no higher possible form of law or authority. 17 Therefore, any law that seeks to claim itself as superior, 18 by making or having made morally repugnant, false, sacrilegious or absurd claims, 19 disqualifies itself as legitimate law, 20 so long as such absurd or morally repugnant claims, 21 are permitted to be enforced or demanded. 22 First Peoples as First Law do not need a treaty, 23 but such law that is younger and defective and full of error, 24 needs *Tara* as First Law to make it proper law. 25 So long as lesser law refuses to recognise First Law, 26 such inferior law cannot be law. 27 Whenever the First and Original Law of *Tara* is denounced or denied, 28 no such place can be called a place of law. 29 No act of tyranny in the face of such truth can make a false act true. 30 Any law that is against such truth, cannot be law.

C.4 - Every Community (County) is a Sovereign Tribal Nation

1 Every community recognising the bounds of counties is a Tribal Nation of Norway, 2 borne to tribe and law, 3 under the highest Law of *Tara*. 4 Any one who rejects the truth that every community of naturally born native inhabitants of Norway are a Tribal Nation, 5 dishonours the Law, 6 and dishonours their ancestors, 7 and dishonours the spirits of Norway, 8 and is an impostor with no rights to speak of law or culture. 9 No part of the sacred and indivisible Land, 10 no part of Norway is without a Tribal Nation. 11 Each Tribal Nation as community of Norway, 12 be an Original Tribal Nation, 13 and first nation and dominion and sovereign above all others. 14 No claim of sovereignty or dominion or control or right of Country be higher than the members of an Original Tribal Nation of Norway. 15 The leaders of each Original Tribal Nation be the leaders elected by the naturally born native inhabitants as members of the community, 16 no matter what the colour of their skin, 17 or the ancestry of their parents or grandparents, 18 or their gender or religion. 19 Any traditional leader of a community recognised by form of government who rejects their sacred obligation to Law and *Tara*, 20 and who refuses to help educate and support the life of an

Original Tribal Nation, ₂₁ loses any and all authority no matter their initiation or claim of power. ₂₂ Any form of government that refuses to acknowledge each community of the sacred and indivisible Land as an Original Tribal Nation, ₂₃ disavows the true rule of law of Norway, ₂₄ and declares itself to be without authority or right, ₂₅ but a belligerent foreign occupying force that must be driven out from country. ₂₆ Any community leader that denies their authority comes from the community, ₂₇ and comes from the first law of community as *Tara*, ₂₈ declares themselves without proper power or authority, ₂₉ and an impostor who must be expelled from community and the Original Tribal Nation.

C.5 – Sovereign Tribal Nations of Norway

₁ Fifteen Sovereign Tribal Nations hold first and original dominion across the whole of the sacred Land of Norway, ₂ corresponding with boundaries defined by the natural valleys, rivers, deltas and features that distinguish customary and traditional counties and regions.

C.6 – Names of Sovereign Tribal Nations of Norway

₁ The first Sovereign Tribal Nation within the most ancient bounds of Norway is Troms; ₂ and the second Sovereign Tribal Nation is Finnmark; ₃ and the third Sovereign Tribal Nation is Nordland; ₄ and the fourth Sovereign Tribal Nation is Trøndelag; ₅ and the fifth Sovereign Tribal Nation is Møre og Romsdal; ₆ and the sixth Sovereign Tribal Nation is Vestland; ₇ and the seventh Sovereign Tribal Nation is Rogaland; ₈ and the eighth Sovereign Tribal Nation is Agder; ₉ and the ninth Sovereign Tribal Nation is Vestfold; ₁₀ and the tenth Sovereign Tribal Nation is Telemark; ₁₁ and the eleventh Sovereign Tribal Nation is Buskerud; ₁₂ and the twelfth Sovereign Tribal Nation is Akershus; ₁₃ and the thirteenth Sovereign Tribal Nation is Østfold; ₁₄ and the fourteenth Sovereign Tribal Nation is Innlandet; ₁₅ and the fifteenth Sovereign Tribal Nation is Oslo.

C.7 - Sacred Trust of Each Tribal Nation

₁ The rights and powers of every community of the sacred and indivisible Land as an Original Tribal Nation, ₂ are permanently vested in sacred trust as the rights and powers of naturally born native inhabitants of Norway, ₃ whose rights cannot be seized or forfeited or suspended or surrendered by trickery or force. ₄ Nor may such sacred and divine rights and powers be transferred, or disavowed, or alienated, or sold or given away to any body or association or person, except by lawful means of a union between all Original Tribal Nations. ₅ Because all the rights and powers of naturally born native inhabitants of each community of Norway are permanently vested and protected in sacred and irrevocable trust, ₆ with the elected leaders of each community as trustees, ₇ any claim of older trusts or higher trusts or greater trusts, ₈ be null and void and without spiritual or moral or sovereign or lawful validity and legitimacy, ₉ except for any trust formed by lawful means of a union between all Original Tribal Nations. 10 Any instruments, treaties, deeds, charters, covenants, promises or contracts of any kind that have existed or still exist, 11 upon any claim or assertion in defiance of the highest and superior rights and powers of each sacred trust of each and every Original Tribal Nation of Norway are hereby null and void, without spiritual or moral or sovereign or lawful validity and legitimacy. 12 Only instruments, treaties, deeds, charters, covenants, promises and contracts of any kind, 13 that recognise the rights and powers of members of each community as an Original Tribal Nation, 14 under the rule of law of *Tara*, 15 be valid or legitimate instruments if they honour the laws of Ucadia. 16 Any transfer of wealth, capital, money, resources or other things of value that continue or have continued or will continue, 17 against the natural born rights of community members of Norway, 18 that impoverishes such members for the benefit of some foreign body or claimant, 19 in defiance of the true rule of law, 20 is and shall be a profoundly immoral, unlawful and sacrilegious act against any notion of rule of law. 21 Any person or office holder that defies the rule of law and commits a profoundly immoral act against a community of country, 22 as an Original Tribal Nation of Norway, 23 forfeits any right or claim of right of immunity or protection, 24 and shall be held responsible personally three times for each and every such unlawful act in defiance of the existence and form of sacred trusts of Norway.

XII. Original Nations (Tribes) of Iceland

C.1 – One Law One People One Land of Iceland

In truth, there was, there is, there has only ever been One Original Law of Iceland; 2 And there has only ever been One Icelandic People; 3 And there has only ever been One Sacred Land belonging equally to all the Icelandic People. 5 There can be no honour or respect of People of Iceland or First Ancestors, 6 if there is no honour or recognition of the First and Original Law of *Tara*. 7 There can be no honour of the One Sacred and Indivisible Land of Iceland, 8 unless First and Original Law of *Tara* and the First and Original People of Iceland are properly recognised under all forms of Civilised Law. 9 No one is above such Law. 10 No one Person or Community in Iceland is excluded from such Law. 11 All are equal under the One Law. 12 Any law that is against such truth, cannot be law.

C.2 – People born to Land of Iceland born to the Original People

1 Any one borne to the sacred and indivisible Land of Iceland is borne to the People, 2 and is borne to tribe and Law. 3 People be not excluded by colour, 4 People be not excluded by race of ancestors, 5 People be not excluded by city or non-city. 6 Any one who rejects the right of people borne to the sacred and indivisible Land, 7 as true members of tribe and the people, 8 dishonours the Law, 9 and dishonours their ancestors, 10 and dishonours the spirits of Iceland, 11 and is an impostor with no rights, 12 to speak of law or culture. 13 Racism is not Law, it is against proper Law. 14 Racial purity is not Law, it is madness of mind. 15 For every one borne of Iceland, 16 has the right to know the tribe they be borne, 17 and the ancient names of the land, 18 and be welcomed to tribe by right ceremony. 19 Any law that is against such truth, cannot be law.

C.3 – Original Law of Tara and Original People of Iceland

1 *Tara* as the First and Original Law of the Icelandic People has continued to exist for many thousands of years: 2 Before the rise and fall of the Greek and Roman Empires more than fifteen hundred years ago, 3 the First and Original Law of the Icelandic People did exist and was never extinguished or replaced; 4 And before the rise and restoration of Civilised Law under the Holly Celtic Leaders in the 8th Century, 5 the First and Original Law of the Icelandic People was recognised and honoured and strengthened; 6 And many hundreds of years before the rise of the oppressive merchant

military empires across Europe, 7 the First and Original Law of the Icelandic People did exist and was never abandoned or forgotten by the People even through the darkest days; 8 And thousands of years before the rise of the Secular European Powers and the renewed oppression and cruelty against the people, 9 the rights and sovereign authority of the Original Nations of Iceland under the Sacred Original Law of *Tara* have never been extinguished or lost. 10 Thus, *Tara* as First Law does not need the permission of such secular or uncivilised powers, 11 to be recognised as true and the First Law of the Country of Iceland. 12 *Tara* as First Law of Iceland has never ceased being first law, 13 nor can true rule of law be usurped by treaty, 14 or by trickery or by other deception or by any other morally repugnant means. 15 The Sacred Law of *Tara* is now recognised and mandated from Heaven under the most sacred Covenant *Pactum De Singularis Caelum*. 16 Verily, there be no higher possible form of law or authority. 17 Therefore, any law that seeks to claim itself as superior, 18 by making or having made morally repugnant, false, sacrilegious or absurd claims, 19 disqualifies itself as legitimate law, 20 so long as such absurd or morally repugnant claims, 21 are permitted to be enforced or demanded. 22 First Peoples as First Law do not need a treaty, 23 but such law that is younger and defective and full of error, 24 needs *Tara* as First Law to make it proper law. 25 So long as lesser law refuses to recognise First Law, 26 such inferior law cannot be law. 27 Whenever the First and Original Law of *Tara* is denounced or denied, 28 no such place can be called a place of law. 29 No act of tyranny in the face of such truth can make a false act true. 30 Any law that is against such truth, cannot be law.

C.4 - Every Community (County) is a Sovereign Tribal Nation

1 Every community recognising the bounds of counties is a Tribal Nation of Iceland, 2 borne to tribe and law, 3 under the highest Law of *Tara*. 4 Any one who rejects the truth that every community of naturally born native inhabitants of Iceland are a Tribal Nation, 5 dishonours the Law, 6 and dishonours their ancestors, 7 and dishonours the spirits of Iceland, 8 and is an impostor with no rights to speak of law or culture. 9 No part of the sacred and indivisible Land, 10 no part of Iceland is without a Tribal Nation. 11 Each Tribal Nation as community of Iceland, 12 be an Original Tribal Nation, 13 and first nation and dominion and sovereign above all others. 14 No claim of sovereignty or dominion or control or right of Country be higher than the members of an Original Tribal Nation of Iceland. 15 The leaders of each Original Tribal Nation be the leaders elected by the naturally born native inhabitants as members of the community, 16 no matter what the colour of their skin, 17 or the ancestry of their parents or grandparents, 18 or their gender or religion. 19 Any traditional leader of a community recognised by form of government who rejects their sacred obligation to Law and *Tara*, 20 and who refuses to help educate and support the life of an

Original Tribal Nation, ₂₁ loses any and all authority no matter their initiation or claim of power. ₂₂ Any form of government that refuses to acknowledge each community of the sacred and indivisible Land as an Original Tribal Nation, ₂₃ disavows the true rule of law of Iceland, ₂₄ and declares itself to be without authority or right, ₂₅ but a belligerent foreign occupying force that must be driven out from country. ₂₆ Any community leader that denies their authority comes from the community, ₂₇ and comes from the first law of community as *Tara*, ₂₈ declares themselves without proper power or authority, ₂₉ and an impostor who must be expelled from community and the Original Tribal Nation.

C.5 – Sovereign Tribal Nations of Iceland

₁ Eight Sovereign Tribal Nations hold first and original dominion across the whole of the sacred Land of Iceland, ₂ corresponding with boundaries defined by the natural valleys, plains, rivers and features that distinguish customary and traditional regions of the volcanic island.

C.6 – Names of Sovereign Tribal Nations of Iceland

₁ The first Sovereign Tribal Nation within the most ancient bounds of Iceland is Höfuðborgarsvæðið; ₂ and the second Sovereign Tribal Nation is Suðurnes; ₃ and the third Sovereign Tribal Nation is Vesturland; ₄ and the fourth Sovereign Tribal Nation is Vestfirðir; ₅ and the fifth Sovereign Tribal Nation is Norðurland vestra; ₆ and the sixth Sovereign Tribal Nation is Norðurland eystra; ₇ and the seventh Sovereign Tribal Nation is Austurland; ₈ and the eighth Sovereign Tribal Nation is Suðurland.

C.7 - Sacred Trust of Each Tribal Nation

₁ The rights and powers of every community of the sacred and indivisible Land as an Original Tribal Nation, ₂ are permanently vested in sacred trust as the rights and powers of naturally born native inhabitants of Iceland, ₃ whose rights cannot be seized or forfeited or suspended or surrendered by trickery or force. ₄ Nor may such sacred and divine rights and powers be transferred, or disavowed, or alienated, or sold or given away to any body or association or person, except by lawful means of a union between all Original Tribal Nations. ₅ Because all the rights and powers of naturally born native inhabitants of each community of Iceland are permanently vested and protected in sacred and irrevocable trust, ₆ with the elected leaders of each community as trustees, ₇ any claim of older trusts or higher trusts or greater trusts, ₈ be null and void and without spiritual or moral or sovereign or lawful validity and legitimacy, ₉ except for any trust formed by lawful means of a union between all Original Tribal Nations. ₁₀ Any instruments, treaties, deeds, charters, covenants, promises or contracts of any kind that have existed or still exist, ₁₁ upon any claim or assertion in defiance of the highest and superior rights and powers of each sacred trust of each and every Original Tribal Nation of Iceland are hereby null and void, without spiritual or moral or sovereign or lawful validity and legitimacy. 12 Only instruments, treaties, deeds, charters, covenants, promises and contracts of any kind, 13 that recognise the rights and powers of members of each community as an Original Tribal Nation, 14 under the rule of law of *Tara*, 15 be valid or legitimate instruments if they honour the laws of Ucadia. 16 Any transfer of wealth, capital, money, resources or other things of value that continue or have continued or will continue, 17 against the natural born rights of community members of Iceland, 18 that impoverishes such members for the benefit of some foreign body or claimant, 19 in defiance of the true rule of law, 20 is and shall be a profoundly immoral, unlawful and sacrilegious act against any notion of rule of law. 21 Any person or office holder that defies the rule of law and commits a profoundly immoral act against a community of country, 22 as an Original Tribal Nation of Iceland, 23 forfeits any right or claim of right of immunity or protection, 24 and shall be held responsible personally three times for each and every such unlawful act in defiance of the existence and form of sacred trusts of Iceland.

XIII. Original Nations (Tribes) of Denmark

C.1 – One Law One People One Land of Denmark

In truth, there was, there is, there has only ever been One Original Law of Denmark; 2 And there has only ever been One Danish People; 3 And there has only ever been One Sacred Land belonging equally to all the Danish People. 5 There can be no honour or respect of People of Denmark or First Ancestors, 6 if there is no honour or recognition of the First and Original Law of *Tara*. 7 There can be no honour of the One Sacred and Indivisible Land of Denmark, 8 unless First and Original Law of *Tara* and the First and Original People of Denmark are properly recognised under all forms of Civilised Law. 9 No one is above such Law. 10 No one Person or Community in Denmark is excluded from such Law. 11 All are equal under the One Law. 12 Any law that is against such truth, cannot be law.

C.2 – People born to Land of Denmark born to the Original People

1 Any one borne to the sacred and indivisible Land of Denmark is borne to the People, 2 and is borne to tribe and Law. 3 People be not excluded by colour, 4 People be not excluded by race of ancestors, 5 People be not excluded by city or non-city. 6 Any one who rejects the right of people borne to the sacred and indivisible Land, 7 as true members of tribe and the people, 8 dishonours the Law, 9 and dishonours their ancestors, 10 and dishonours the spirits of Denmark, 11 and is an impostor with no rights, 12 to speak of law or culture. 13 Racism is not Law, it is against proper Law. 14 Racial purity is not Law, it is madness of mind. 15 For every one borne of Denmark, 16 has the right to know the tribe they be borne, 17 and the ancient names of the land, 18 and be welcomed to tribe by right ceremony. 19 Any law that is against such truth, cannot be law.

C.3 – Original Law of Tara and Original People of Denmark

1 *Tara* as the First and Original Law of the Danish People has continued to exist for many thousands of years: 2 Before the rise and fall of the Greek and Roman Empires more than fifteen hundred years ago, 3 the First and Original Law of the Danish People did exist and was never extinguished or replaced; 4 And before the rise and restoration of Civilised Law under the Holly Celtic Leaders in the 8th Century, 5 the First and Original Law of the Danish People was recognised and honoured and strengthened; 6 And many hundreds of years before the

rise of the oppressive merchant military empires across Europe, 7 the First and Original Law of the Danish People did exist and was never abandoned or forgotten by the People even through the darkest days; 8 And thousands of years before the rise of the Secular European Powers and the renewed oppression and cruelty against the people, 9 the rights and sovereign authority of the Original Nations of Denmark under the Sacred Original Law of *Tara* have never been extinguished or lost. 10 Thus, *Tara* as First Law does not need the permission of such secular or uncivilised powers, 11 to be recognised as true and the First Law of the Country of Denmark. 12 *Tara* as First Law of Denmark has never ceased being first law, 13 nor can true rule of law be usurped by treaty, 14 or by trickery or by other deception or by any other morally repugnant means. 15 The Sacred Law of *Tara* is now recognised and mandated from Heaven under the most sacred Covenant *Pactum De Singularis Caelum*. 16 Verily, there be no higher possible form of law or authority. 17 Therefore, any law that seeks to claim itself as superior, 18 by making or having made morally repugnant, false, sacrilegious or absurd claims, 19 disqualifies itself as legitimate law, 20 so long as such absurd or morally repugnant claims, 21 are permitted to be enforced or demanded. 22 First Peoples as First Law do not need a treaty, 23 but such law that is younger and defective and full of error, 24 needs *Tara* as First Law to make it proper law. 25 So long as lesser law refuses to recognise First Law, 26 such inferior law cannot be law. 27 Whenever the First and Original Law of *Tara* is denounced or denied, 28 no such place can be called a place of law. 29 No act of tyranny in the face of such truth can make a false act true. 30 Any law that is against such truth, cannot be law.

C.4 - Every Community (County) is a Sovereign Tribal Nation

1 Every community recognising the bounds of counties is a Tribal Nation of Denmark, 2 borne to tribe and law, 3 under the highest Law of *Tara*. 4 Any one who rejects the truth that every community of naturally born native inhabitants of Denmark are a Tribal Nation, 5 dishonours the Law, 6 and dishonours their ancestors, 7 and dishonours the spirits of Denmark, 8 and is an impostor with no rights to speak of law or culture. 9 No part of the sacred and indivisible Land, 10 no part of Denmark is without a Tribal Nation. 11 Each Tribal Nation as community of Denmark, 12 be an Original Tribal Nation, 13 and first nation and dominion and sovereign above all others. 14 No claim of sovereignty or dominion or control or right of Country be higher than the members of an Original Tribal Nation of Denmark. 15 The leaders of each Original Tribal Nation be the leaders elected by the naturally born native inhabitants as members of the community, 16 no matter what the colour of their skin, 17 or the ancestry of their parents or grandparents, 18 or their gender or religion. 19 Any traditional leader of a community recognised by form of government who rejects their sacred obligation to

XIII. Original Nations (Tribes) of Denmark

Law and *Tara*, 20 and who refuses to help educate and support the life of an Original Tribal Nation, 21 loses any and all authority no matter their initiation or claim of power. 22 Any form of government that refuses to acknowledge each community of the sacred and indivisible Land as an Original Tribal Nation, 23 disavows the true rule of law of Denmark, 24 and declares itself to be without authority or right, 25 but a belligerent foreign occupying force that must be driven out from country. 26 Any community leader that denies their authority comes from the community, 27 and comes from the first law of community as *Tara*, 28 declares themselves without proper power or authority, 29 and an impostor who must be expelled from community and the Original Tribal Nation.

C.5 – Sovereign Tribal Nations of Denmark

1 Five Sovereign Tribal Nations hold first and original dominion across the whole of the sacred Land of Denmark, 2 corresponding with boundaries defined by the natural valleys, rivers and features that distinguish customary and traditional regions.

C.6 – Names of Sovereign Tribal Nations of Denmark

1 The first Sovereign Tribal Nation within the most ancient bounds of Denmark is Hovedstaden; 2 and the second Sovereign Tribal Nation is Midtjylland; 3 and the third Sovereign Tribal Nation is Nordjylland; 4 and the fourth Sovereign Tribal Nation is Sjælland; 5 and the fifth Sovereign Tribal Nation is Syddanmark.

C.7 - Sacred Trust of Each Tribal Nation

1 The rights and powers of every community of the sacred and indivisible Land as an Original Tribal Nation, 2 are permanently vested in sacred trust as the rights and powers of naturally born native inhabitants of Denmark, 3 whose rights cannot be seized or forfeited or suspended or surrendered by trickery or force. 4 Nor may such sacred and divine rights and powers be transferred, or disavowed, or alienated, or sold or given away to any body or association or person, except by lawful means of a union between all Original Tribal Nations. 5 Because all the rights and powers of naturally born native inhabitants of each community of Denmark are permanently vested and protected in sacred and irrevocable trust, 6 with the elected leaders of each community as trustees, 7 any claim of older trusts or higher trusts or greater trusts, 8 be null and void and without spiritual or moral or sovereign or lawful validity and legitimacy, 9 except for any trust formed by lawful means of a union between all Original Tribal Nations. 10 Any instruments, treaties, deeds, charters, covenants, promises or contracts of any kind that have existed or still exist, 11 upon any claim or assertion in defiance of the highest and superior rights and powers of each sacred trust of each and every Original Tribal Nation of Denmark are hereby null and void, without spiritual or moral or sovereign or lawful validity and legitimacy. 12 Only instruments, treaties, deeds, charters, covenants, promises and contracts of

any kind, 13 that recognise the rights and powers of members of each community as an Original Tribal Nation, 14 under the rule of law of *Tara*, 15 be valid or legitimate instruments if they honour the laws of Ucadia. 16 Any transfer of wealth, capital, money, resources or other things of value that continue or have continued or will continue, 17 against the natural born rights of community members of Denmark, 18 that impoverishes such members for the benefit of some foreign body or claimant, 19 in defiance of the true rule of law, 20 is and shall be a profoundly immoral, unlawful and sacrilegious act against any notion of rule of law. 21 Any person or office holder that defies the rule of law and commits a profoundly immoral act against a community of country, 22 as an Original Tribal Nation of Denmark, 23 forfeits any right or claim of right of immunity or protection, 24 and shall be held responsible personally three times for each and every such unlawful act in defiance of the existence and form of sacred trusts of Denmark.

XIV. Original Nations (Tribes) of Greenland

C.1 – One Law One People One Land of Greenland

In truth, there was, there is, there has only ever been One Original Law of Greenland; 2 And there has only ever been One Greenlandic People; 3 And there has only ever been One Sacred Land belonging equally to all the Greenlandic People. 5 There can be no honour or respect of People of Greenland or First Ancestors, 6 if there is no honour or recognition of the First and Original Law of *Tara*. 7 There can be no honour of the One Sacred and Indivisible Land of Greenland, 8 unless First and Original Law of *Tara* and the First and Original People of Greenland are properly recognised under all forms of Civilised Law. 9 No one is above such Law. 10 No one Person or Community in Greenland is excluded from such Law. 11 All are equal under the One Law. 12 Any law that is against such truth, cannot be law.

C.2 – People born to Land of Greenland born to the Original People

1 Any one borne to the sacred and indivisible Land of Greenland is borne to the People, 2 and is borne to tribe and Law. 3 People be not excluded by colour, 4 People be not excluded by race of ancestors, 5 People be not excluded by city or non-city. 6 Any one who rejects the right of people borne to the sacred and indivisible Land, 7 as true members of tribe and the people, 8 dishonours the Law, 9 and dishonours their ancestors, 10 and dishonours the spirits of Greenland, 11 and is an impostor with no rights, 12 to speak of law or culture. 13 Racism is not Law, it is against proper Law. 14 Racial purity is not Law, it is madness of mind. 15 For every one borne of Greenland, 16 has the right to know the tribe they be borne, 17 and the ancient names of the land, 18 and be welcomed to tribe by right ceremony. 19 Any law that is against such truth, cannot be law.

C.3 – Original Law of Tara and Original People of Greenland

1 *Tara* as the First and Original Law of the Greenlandic People has continued to exist for many thousands of years: 2 Before the rise and fall of the Greek and Roman Empires more than fifteen hundred years ago, 3 the First and Original Law of the Greenlandic People did exist and was never extinguished or replaced; 4 And before the rise and restoration of Civilised Law under the Holly Celtic Leaders in the 8th Century, 5 the First and Original Law of the Greenlandic People was recognised and honoured and strengthened; 6 And many

hundreds of years before the rise of the oppressive merchant military empires across Europe, 7 the First and Original Law of the Greenlandic People did exist and was never abandoned or forgotten by the People even through the darkest days; 8 And thousands of years before the rise of the Secular European Powers and the renewed oppression and cruelty against the people, 9 the rights and sovereign authority of the Original Nations of Greenland under the Sacred Original Law of *Tara* have never been extinguished or lost. 10 Thus, *Tara* as First Law does not need the permission of such secular or uncivilised powers, 11 to be recognised as true and the First Law of the Country of Greenland. 12 *Tara* as First Law of Greenland has never ceased being first law, 13 nor can true rule of law be usurped by treaty, 14 or by trickery or by other deception or by any other morally repugnant means. 15 The Sacred Law of *Tara* is now recognised and mandated from Heaven under the most sacred Covenant *Pactum De Singularis Caelum*. 16 Verily, there be no higher possible form of law or authority. 17 Therefore, any law that seeks to claim itself as superior, 18 by making or having made morally repugnant, false, sacrilegious or absurd claims, 19 disqualifies itself as legitimate law, 20 so long as such absurd or morally repugnant claims, 21 are permitted to be enforced or demanded. 22 First Peoples as First Law do not need a treaty, 23 but such law that is younger and defective and full of error, 24 needs *Tara* as First Law to make it proper law. 25 So long as lesser law refuses to recognise First Law, 26 such inferior law cannot be law. 27 Whenever the First and Original Law of *Tara* is denounced or denied, 28 no such place can be called a place of law. 29 No act of tyranny in the face of such truth can make a false act true. 30 Any law that is against such truth, cannot be law.

C.4 - Every Community (County) is a Sovereign Tribal Nation

1 Every community recognising the bounds of counties is a Tribal Nation of Greenland, 2 borne to tribe and law, 3 under the highest Law of *Tara*. 4 Any one who rejects the truth that every community of naturally born native inhabitants of Greenland are a Tribal Nation, 5 dishonours the Law, 6 and dishonours their ancestors, 7 and dishonours the spirits of Greenland, 8 and is an impostor with no rights to speak of law or culture. 9 No part of the sacred and indivisible Land, 10 no part of Greenland is without a Tribal Nation. 11 Each Tribal Nation as community of Greenland, 12 be an Original Tribal Nation, 13 and first nation and dominion and sovereign above all others. 14 No claim of sovereignty or dominion or control or right of Country be higher than the members of an Original Tribal Nation of Greenland. 15 The leaders of each Original Tribal Nation be the leaders elected by the naturally born native inhabitants as members of the community, 16 no matter what the colour of their skin, 17 or the ancestry of their parents or grandparents, 18 or their gender or religion. 19 Any traditional leader of a community recognised by form of government

who rejects their sacred obligation to Law and *Tara*, 20 and who refuses to help educate and support the life of an Original Tribal Nation, 21 loses any and all authority no matter their initiation or claim of power. 22 Any form of government that refuses to acknowledge each community of the sacred and indivisible Land as an Original Tribal Nation, 23 disavows the true rule of law of Greenland, 24 and declares itself to be without authority or right, 25 but a belligerent foreign occupying force that must be driven out from country. 26 Any community leader that denies their authority comes from the community, 27 and comes from the first law of community as *Tara*, 28 declares themselves without proper power or authority, 29 and an impostor who must be expelled from community and the Original Tribal Nation.

C.5 – Sovereign Tribal Nations of Greenland

1 Seven Sovereign Tribal Nations hold first and original dominion across the whole of the sacred Land of Greenland, 2 corresponding with boundaries defined by the natural valleys, rivers and features that distinguish customary and traditional regions.

C.6 – Names of Sovereign Tribal Nations of Greenland

1 The first Sovereign Tribal Nation within the ancient bounds of Greenland is Ilulissat; 2 and the second Sovereign Tribal Nation is Aasiaat; 3 and the third Sovereign Tribal Nation is Sisimliut; 4 and the fourth Sovereign Tribal Nation is Nuuk; 5 and the fifth Sovereign Tribal Nation is Qaqortoq; 6 and the sixth Sovereign Tribal Nation is Kalaalit in the North East; 7 and the seventh Sovereign Tribal Nation is the Iwit in the South East.

C.7 - Sacred Trust of Each Tribal Nation

1 The rights and powers of every community of the sacred and indivisible Land as an Original Tribal Nation, 2 are permanently vested in sacred trust as the rights and powers of naturally born native inhabitants of Greenland, 3 whose rights cannot be seized or forfeited or suspended or surrendered by trickery or force. 4 Nor may such sacred and divine rights and powers be transferred, or disavowed, or alienated, or sold or given away to any body or association or person, except by lawful means of a union between all Original Tribal Nations. 5 Because all the rights and powers of naturally born native inhabitants of each community of Greenland are permanently vested and protected in sacred and irrevocable trust, 6 with the elected leaders of each community as trustees, 7 any claim of older trusts or higher trusts or greater trusts, 8 be null and void and without spiritual or moral or sovereign or lawful validity and legitimacy, 9 except for any trust formed by lawful means of a union between all Original Tribal Nations. 10 Any instruments, treaties, deeds, charters, covenants, promises or contracts of any kind that have existed or still exist, 11 upon any claim or assertion in defiance of the highest and superior rights and powers of

each sacred trust of each and every Original Tribal Nation of Greenland are hereby null and void, without spiritual or moral or sovereign or lawful validity and legitimacy. 12 Only instruments, treaties, deeds, charters, covenants, promises and contracts of any kind, 13 that recognise the rights and powers of members of each community as an Original Tribal Nation, 14 under the rule of law of *Tara*, 15 be valid or legitimate instruments if they honour the laws of Ucadia. 16 Any transfer of wealth, capital, money, resources or other things of value that continue or have continued or will continue, 17 against the natural born rights of community members of Greenland, 18 that impoverishes such members for the benefit of some foreign body or claimant, 19 in defiance of the true rule of law, 20 is and shall be a profoundly immoral, unlawful and sacrilegious act against any notion of rule of law. 21 Any person or office holder that defies the rule of law and commits a profoundly immoral act against a community of country, 22 as an Original Tribal Nation of Greenland, 23 forfeits any right or claim of right of immunity or protection, 24 and shall be held responsible personally three times for each every such unlawful act in defiance of the existence and form of sacred trusts of Greenland.

XIV. Original Nations (Tribes) of Greenland

Ancient Egyptian Tree of Life

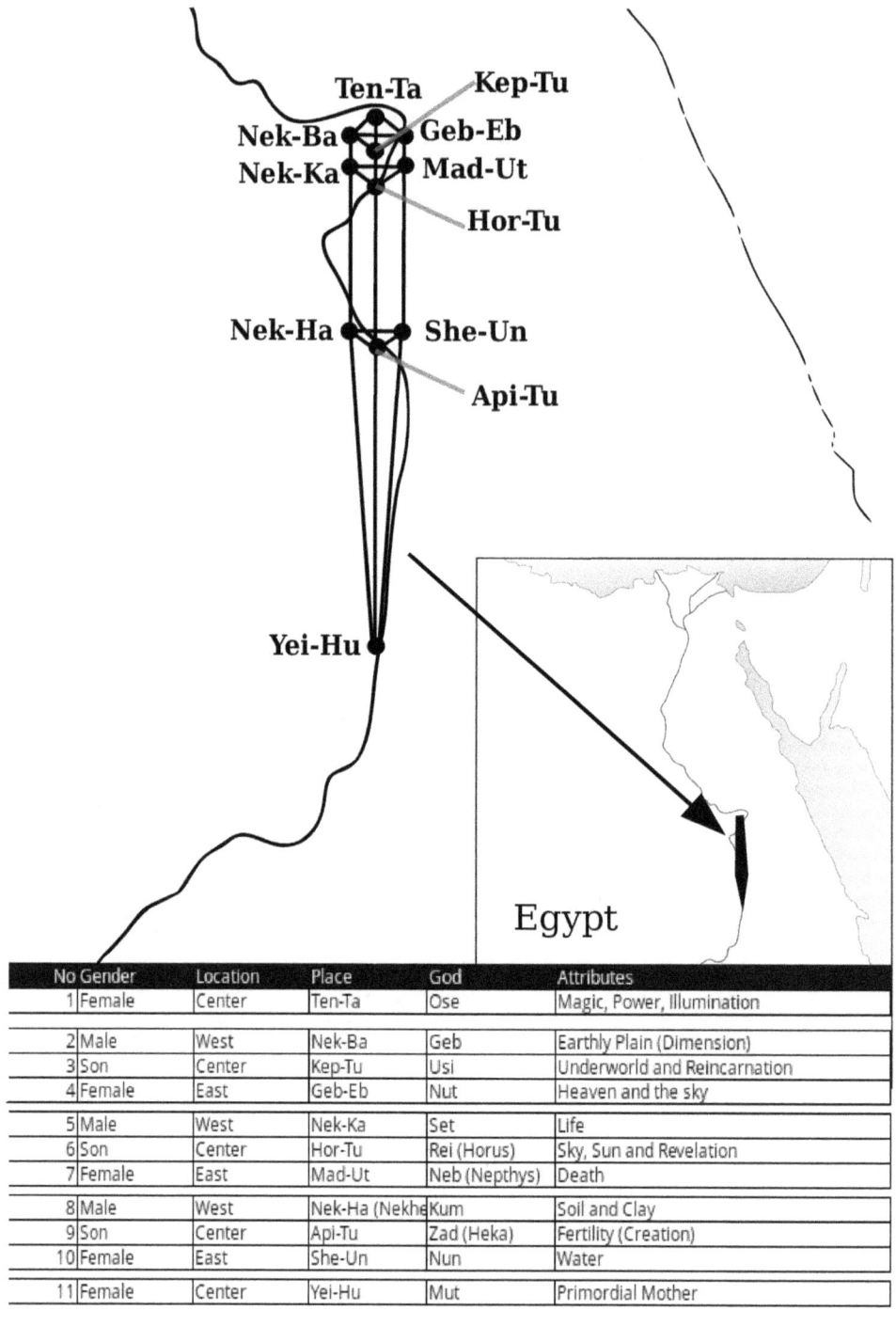

No	Gender	Location	Place	God	Attributes
1	Female	Center	Ten-Ta	Ose	Magic, Power, Illumination
2	Male	West	Nek-Ba	Geb	Earthly Plain (Dimension)
3	Son	Center	Kep-Tu	Usi	Underworld and Reincarnation
4	Female	East	Geb-Eb	Nut	Heaven and the sky
5	Male	West	Nek-Ka	Set	Life
6	Son	Center	Hor-Tu	Rei (Horus)	Sky, Sun and Revelation
7	Female	East	Mad-Ut	Neb (Nepthys)	Death
8	Male	West	Nek-Ha (Nekhe	Kum	Soil and Clay
9	Son	Center	Api-Tu	Zad (Heka)	Fertility (Creation)
10	Female	East	She-Un	Nun	Water
11	Female	Center	Yei-Hu	Mut	Primordial Mother

Copyright (c) 2004-2020 Ucadia Books Company. All Rights Reserved

Ancient Egyptian Tree of Life

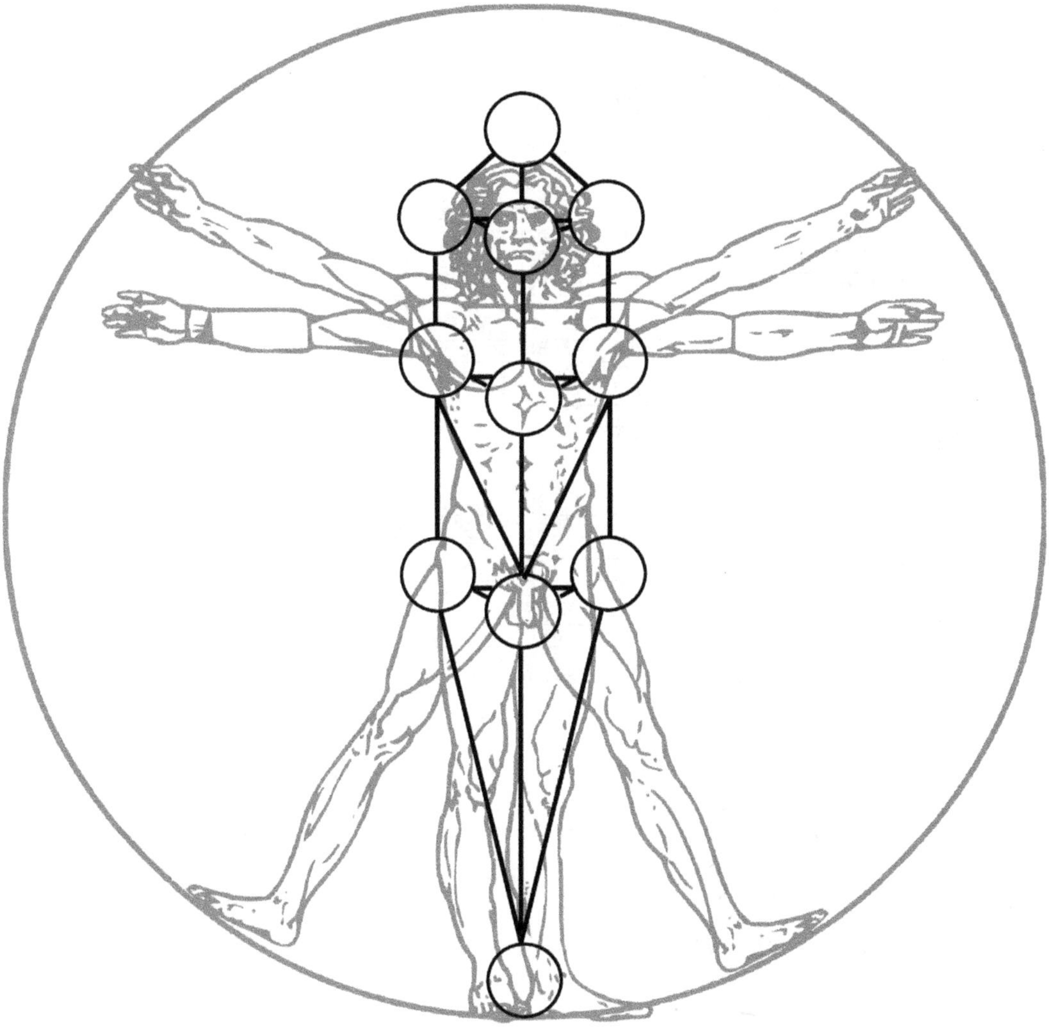

Copyright © 2004-2020 Ucadia Books Company. All Rights Reserved.

Ancient High Priest (Prophets) of Yei-Hu (Yeb)

No	Name	Start	End Era	Relation
1	Aaroniah	1068	1041 BCE	
2	Enochiah	1041	999 BCE	son of Aaroniah
3	Zadokiah	999	948 BCE	son of Enochiah
4	Obadiah/Uvidiah (David)	948	929 BCE	son of Zadokiah
5	Elijiah	929	889 BCE	son of Obadiah
6	Ahijiah	889	883 BCE	son of Elijiah
7	Ahiah	883	861 BCE	son of Ahijiah
8	Azariah	861	845 BCE	son of Ahiah
9	Ananiah	845	813 BCE	son of Azariah
10	Amoziah	813	784 BCE	son of Ananiah
11	Isaiah	784	732 BCE	son of Amoziah
12	Ezekiah	732	696 BCE	son of Isaiah
13	Amariah	696	681 BCE	son of Ezekiah
14	Edaliah	681	672 BCE	son of Amariah
15	Zephaniah	672	645 BCE	son of Edaliah
16	Michaiah/Ilkiah	645	620 BCE	son of Zephaniah
17	**Jeremiah**	620	572 BCE	son of Ilkiah
18	Baruchiah	572	530 BCE	son of Jeremiah
19	Osiah (Hosea)	530	478 BCE	son of Baruchiah
20	Osanniah (Hosanna)	478	431 BCE	son of Osiah
21	Eliah	431	417 BCE	son of Osaniah
22	Oadiah	417	382 BCE	son of Eliah
23	Oananiah	382	341 BCE	son of Oadiah
24	Adiah	341	291 BCE	son of Oananiah
25	Oniah	291	249 BCE	son of Adiah
26	Eleziah	249	206 BCE	son of Oniah
27	Elkaniah	206	158 BCE	son of Eleziah
28	Zadokiah	158	106 BCE	son of Elkaniah
29	Barachiah	106	59 BCE	son of Zadokiah
30	Adoniah (Cú-Roi(n))	59	10 CE	adopted son of Barachiah
31	Yasiah (Cú-Cúileann/Joseph)	10	30 CE	son of Adoniah. Died in 58 CE
32	Yahusiah (Cú-Laoch/Jesus)	30	37 CE	son of Yasiah (Joseph). Died in 83 CE
33	Yahobiah (Jacob)	37	58 CE	son of Yasiah (Joseph). Died in 58 CE

Note: Zachariah, son of Barachiah was disowned from lineage in 59CE and resettled at Qumran near Jerusalem, forming a new apocalyptic movement. His adopted son Johanniah (John the Baptist) claimed to be thirty-second high priest of Yeb in opposition to Yahusiah (Cú-Laoch/Jesus).

Note: Yasiah (Cú-Cúileann/Joseph) was one of only two high priests to abdicate (in 30 CE) but died in 58CE. His son Yahusiah (Cú-Laoch/Jesus) abdicated in 37CE for his brother Yahobiah (Jacob) but returned to the role in 58 CE at the death of his brother until his own death in 83 CE.

See: ***Lebor Clann Glas*** *(Vol I)* for a chronological history of the High Priests and Prophets of Yeb.

Celtic Tree of Life

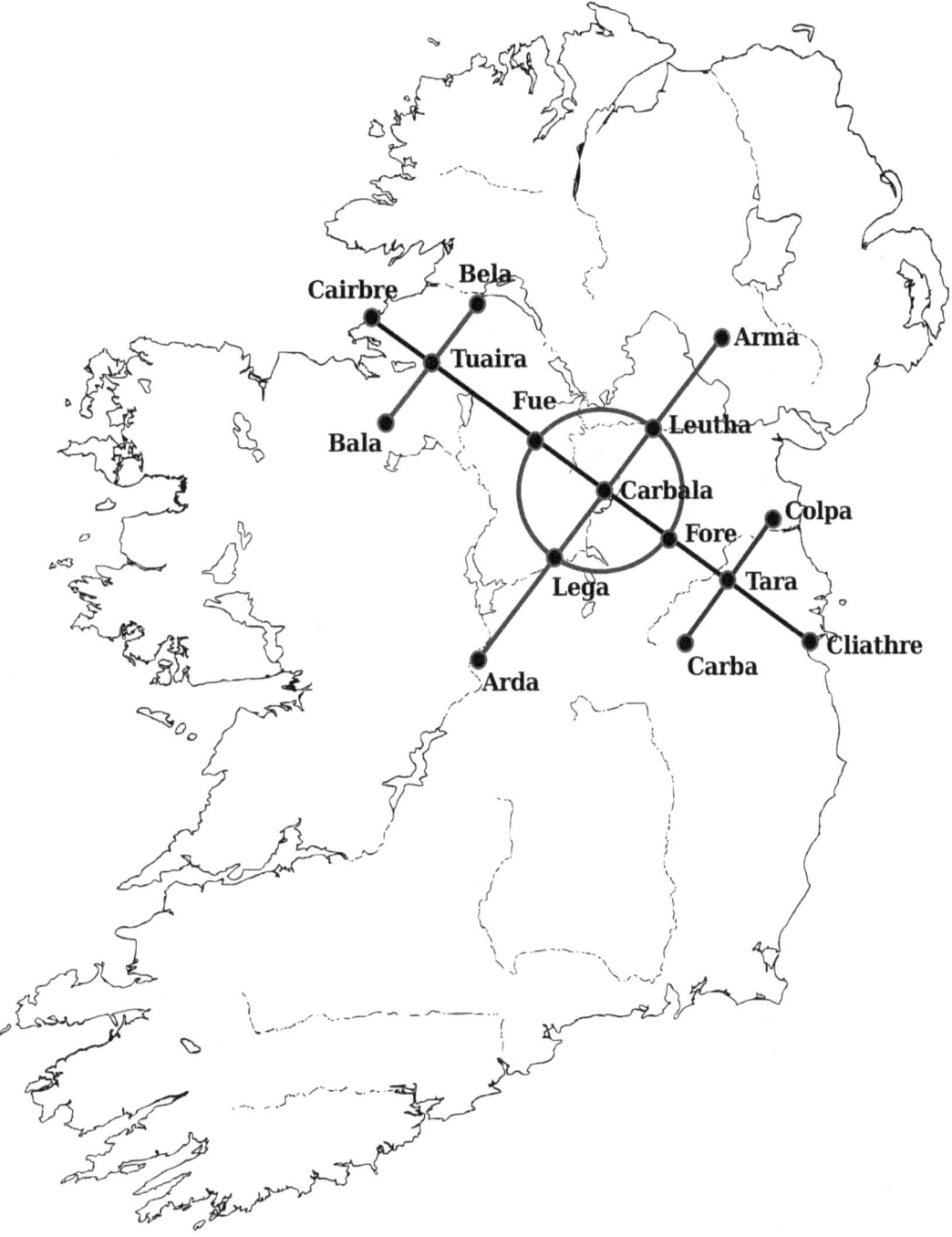

Copyright © 2004-2020 Ucadia Books Company. All Rights Reserved.

Celtic Tree of Life

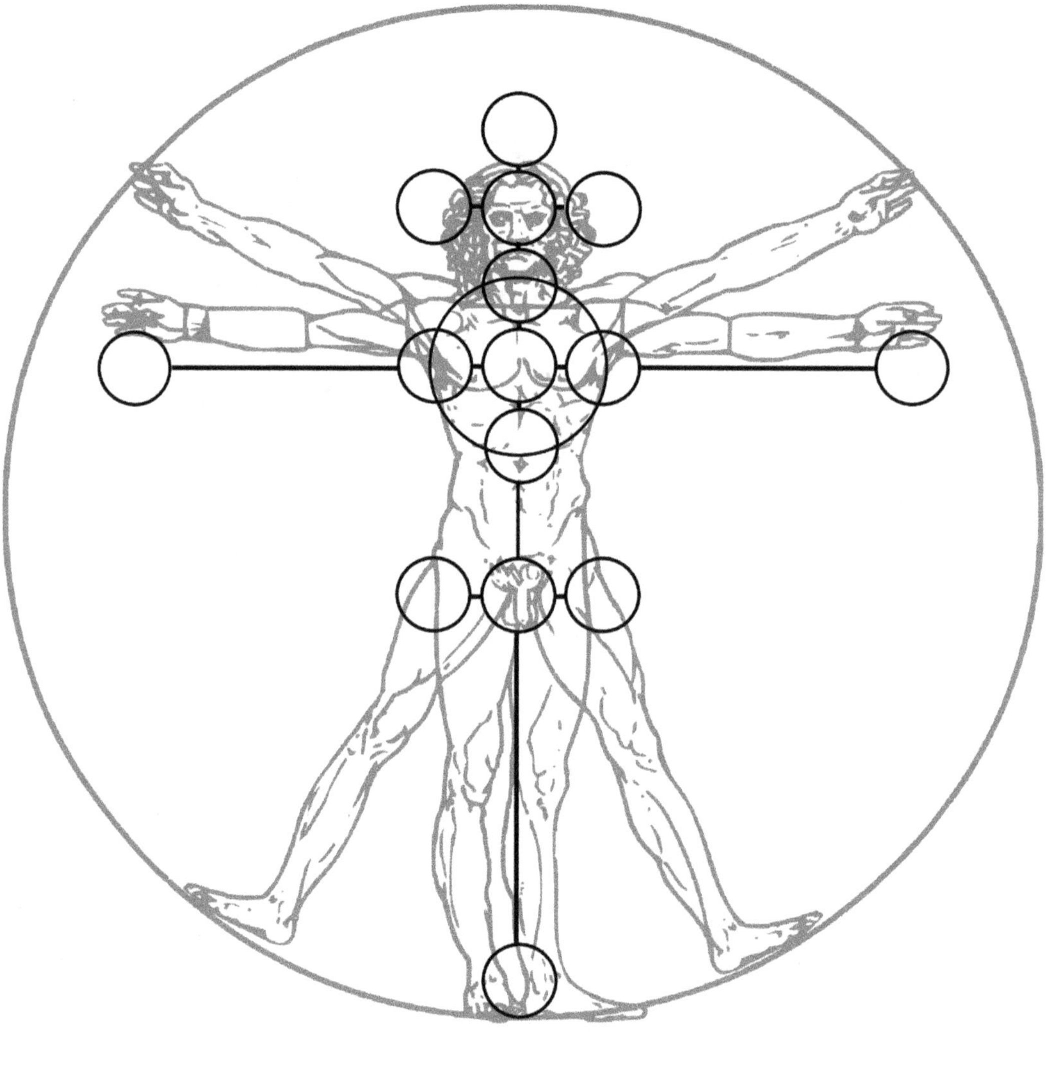

Copyright © 2004-2020 Ucadia Books Company. All Rights Reserved.

Tara

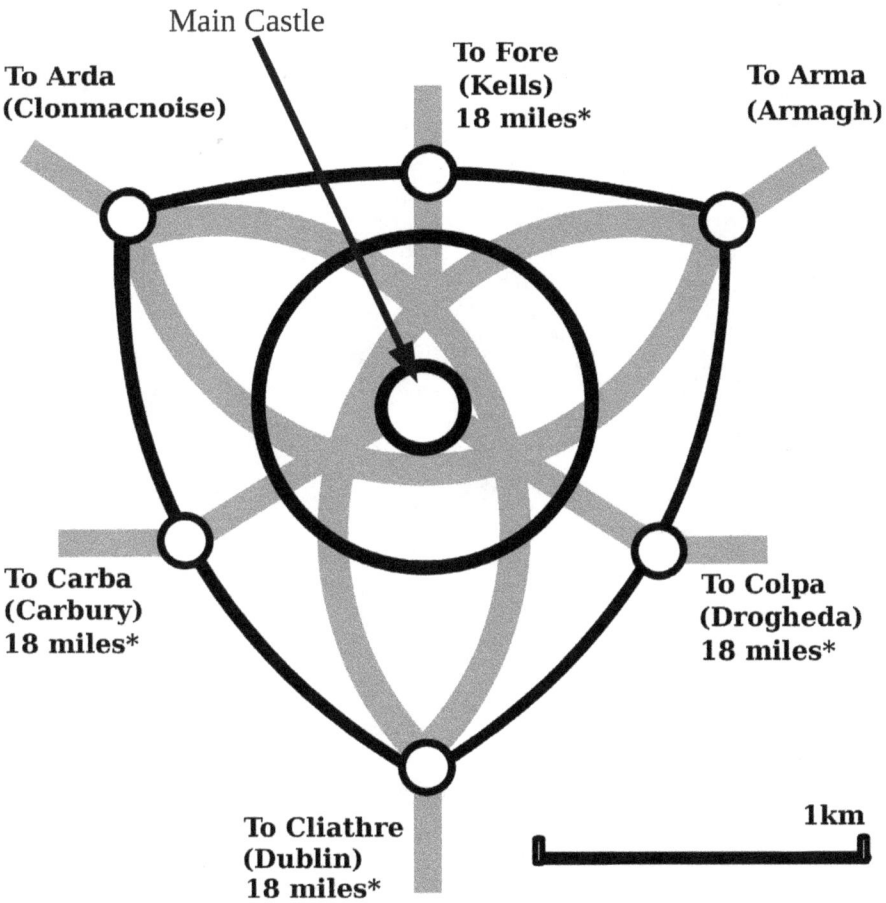

* A Celt Mile was approximately 1.658 metres

True Tara Site now known as Killeen (Cuilleain/Cualann) Castle - a name that translates to "Holly (Holy) Castle" and back to the name Tara.

The True Five Great Roads that originated and ended at Tara were:
1. Holly Road (North to South) from Cliathre (Dublin) to Cairbre (Sligo)
2. Carba Road
3. Colpa Road
4. Arda Road
5. Arma Road

Copyright © 2004-2020 Ucadia Books Company. All Rights Reserved.

Copyright © 2004-2020 Ucadia Books Company. All Rights Reserved.

Copyright © 2004-2020 Ucadia Books Company. All Rights Reserved.

www.ingramcontent.com/pod-product-compliance
Lightning Source LLC
Chambersburg PA
CBHW080441170426
43195CB00017B/2843